Mia

AQA BUSINESS STUDIES *for* GCSE

15
Ellie fields

D1376326

NEIL DENBY

DAVID HAMMAN

DYNAMIC LEARNING

HODDER EDUCATION
AN HACHETTE UK COMPANY

Orders: please contact Bookpoint Ltd, 130 Milton Park, Abingdon, Oxon OX14 4SB. Telephone: (44) 01235 827720. Fax: (44) 01235 400454. Lines are open 9.00–5.00, Monday to Saturday, with a 24-hour message answering service. You can also order through our website www.hoddereducation.co.uk.

British Library Cataloguing in Publication Data

A catalogue record for this title is available from the British Library

ISBN: 978 0340 987384

First Published 2009

Impression number 10 9 8 7 6 5 4 3 2 1

Year   2012 2011 2010 2009

Cover photo © Murat Giray/Kaya/iStockphoto.com

Typeset by Phoenix Photosetting, Chatham, Kent.

Illustrations by Oxford Designers and Illustrators.

Printed in Italy for Hodder Education, an Hachette UK Company, 338 Euston Road, London NW1 3BH

Contents

How to use this book

This book provides information, exercises and materials to cover the learning required for the new AQA GCSE Business Studies Full and Short courses.

The new qualification has several routes, but all begin with 'Setting Up a Business'. This unit is an introduction to setting up and running a business, and looks at the factors that might help the business to succeed, or cause it to fail. It also shows that businesses operate within societies and communities, and that they must therefore take a number of people and their views into account when operating. This is covered in the first part of this book (from Chapter 1 to Chapter 30).

From this starting point, you may go on to take one of the following routes.

- Take the **Full GCSE** by studying how businesses grow and completing a coursework-style assignment called a Controlled Assessment. The Controlled Assessment is explained on page 320 of this book. The unit on business growth is covered in the second half of this book (from Chapter 31 onwards).

- Take the **Short Course GCSE** by completing a coursework-style assignment called a Controlled Assessment. The Controlled Assessment is explained on page 320 of this book.

- Take the **GCSE Applied Business (Double Award)** by completing the unit 'Setting up a Business', plus sitting an exam on Business Finance and completing two more Controlled Assessments on two of the following topics:
  ○ People in Business
  ○ Marketing and Customer Needs
  ○ Enterprise.
  These additional topics are covered in another book, *AQA Business for GCSE: Applied Options*.

NB This book covers the National Criteria for Business, on which all business GCSE courses are based, so it will be equally useful for GCSE courses other than AQA.

Getting the most out of this book

The book is divided into two parts, each of six sections. Section 1 provides key information about businesses, markets and the nature of enterprise. Sections 2 to 5 then reflect the AQA GCSE specification requirements: Starting a Business, Marketing, Finance, People in Businesses and Operations Management. You don't have to study the course in this order: that's up to you and your teacher. In the second part, each topic is approached in a more advanced way, with the focus on business growth and therefore larger businesses.

Each chapter is designed to be approached in the same way:

- **Read** the 'In the News' section so that you have put the ideas into context, and can think about how they apply to the real world.

- **Read** the text explaining the ideas.

- **Read** 'Core Knowledge' and 'And More' which give the basic information and then further knowledge about the ideas in the chapter.

- **'Have a Go'** at the exercises and activities to see how well you have understood the material. You can come back to the activities at any time if you need to revise the topic for tests or examinations, or you need to refresh your memory for Controlled Assessments.

IN THE NEWS

Each chapter starts with a short news piece, based on recent events or a situation that puts the ideas discussed in the chapter into a real-world context.

This is followed by links to current websites and e-learning materials, so that the story can be followed up or investigated further, or so that additional information can be found.

After the news piece, the key information needed for the chapter is explained.

Summary

- This set of bullet points summarises the most important information contained in the chapter. You could think of this as the absolute minimum that you should learn from the chapter.

Core knowledge

The Core Knowledge then gives the basic knowledge that all students will need regarding this topic.

And more

Following on from the Core Knowledge, And More provides higher level or more in-depth knowledge for students who are aiming at higher grades or just want to improve their knowledge of a particular area.

Did you know...

These boxes are scattered throughout the book. They contain extra information that is either useful or interesting, and which can often help to put the topic into a real-world context.

Have a go!

This section contains a set of activities and exercises that can be carried out in class or at home in study time. Some are designed to be carried out on your own, others with friends or by using web resources.

Group activity

The group activity is designed to be used with the group that you work with in school or college. It is not usually possible for this activity to be carried out by a single person, though sometimes a pair of people might complete the exercise. Often it is a way to gather a wider sample of opinions or skills than you have on your own, or to test your opinions against those of others.

Discussion

The discussion may follow on directly from the group activity, perhaps so that you can explore why you did or did not agree, had different views, or had different experiences to share. It will make you think more deeply about the area that you are studying!

Web-based activity

This activity requires access to a computer and an internet connection. It may take you to a specific site or sites, perhaps to see how an idea or knowledge has been put into practice in the real world, or it may ask you to use a search engine to find out more information. There is then a short activity based on what you have found.

Quickfire questions

These questions appear in every chapter. They will test your knowledge of the ideas and information in the chapter. Your teacher might use them to start or end a lesson, as a quiz with the class, or may ask you to complete them on your own. They are usually simple questions with simple answers, designed to check basic knowledge so, for instance, they might ask for definitions and brief explanations.

Hit the spot

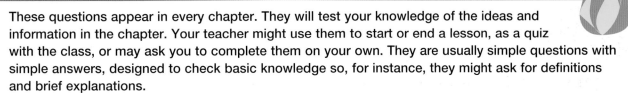

> These questions require longer answers, where you can demonstrate your understanding of ideas and information in greater depth.

>> The chevrons (>) show the difficulty levels of the questions. One chevron is used for easier questions, that everyone should be able to do; two chevrons indicate harder questions, where some explanation of the answer is needed. The hardest questions, which may require you to state and justify an opinion, or to weigh up two sides of an argument, have three chevrons.

Cracking the code

Some words in the text are highlighted. These terms are explained under the 'Cracking the Code' heading. In business studies many words have a particular meaning, and it may even be different to how you use the word in normal speech. Cracking the Code will help you to use these words and terms in the correct way.

The AQA GCSE Business specification

The AQA GCSE Business specification is based on the 'story' of a small business enterprise which can then successfully expand. Unit 1 is called Setting up a Business and looks at the business concepts and ideas that are needed to establish a small business – and at how that business might measure its success. Unit 2, Growing as a Business, shows how the business could grow, and the changes that it would have to make along the way as it developed. Unit 3, Investigating Small Businesses, follows this through by asking you to apply your knowledge to a business that you are asked to study. Many businesses do not grow beyond their small beginnings so, if you are taking the short course, you will only study Setting up a Business and Investigating Small Businesses.

Unit 1 is intended to provide you with enough information to understand the basics of running a small business. After all, many young people study the subject because they feel they might want to run their own business at some stage in the future.

Unit 1 is covered in Sections 1–6 of this book.

● It covers how the idea for a business might be created, how a gap in the market could be found (or made) and how an entrepreneur might go about filling that gap.

● It looks at the reasons why people want to go into business – not always just to make money, but for independence, or to carry out an ambition.

● You will study how a business sets its targets, how it plans and locates, and the way in which it must handle its legal paperwork.

● Of course, a business is unlikely to sell anything unless it lets people know what it is selling, where, when and at what price. You will therefore study the nature of markets and how a business markets its products.

● It is important to know how a small business raises and records its finance, and the tools that it can use to help it to manage its accounts.

● In addition, you will look at how a business recruits its people, makes them want to work hard and keeps the best of them.

● How are the operations of the business carried out? This is the final section in Unit 1.

Many of the topics that you will meet in Unit 2 have similar titles to those in Unit 1. Don't think that you will be covering the same work, however. What Unit 2 does is:

● Extend your understanding of the topics by considering how they apply to larger businesses

● Look in more detail at the topics, so you have a firmer understanding of them and are able to use them in different circumstances.

Most large businesses started life as small organisations, but have developed into much more powerful concerns. These companies tend to have many of the same problems as those experienced by a small business, but at a much bigger scale. The way that they go about dealing with these challenges is covered in Unit 2. It shows how the business could grow, and the changes that it would have to make along the way. It might need a different legal structure, for example, or its growth might cause problems amongst its stakeholders. As it grows, it is likely to change its targets: personal success or independence may no longer be enough; the business might want to become the biggest in its market, or even to expand overseas. Much will change as the business grows – the marketing mix will be different, larger businesses are financed differently and, with larger and more complex organisational structures, might need to be organised more formally. In Unit 2, you will also be developing your understanding of those business terms and ideas that apply more to larger companies.

Finally, in Unit 3, you will use all that you have learned to investigate a real business and present those investigations in a professional – businesslike – manner.

The specification is designed to encourage you, through your study, to think about the practical aspects of business and how the concepts and ideas that you learn can be applied in the real world. If you take the full GCSE, by the end of your course you should have a complete overview of business studies. The specification also provides a good route to higher qualifications such as AS and A level and the Advanced Diploma in Business, Administration and Finance.

The examination papers

The GCSE course will be assessed by a combination of controlled assessments (see page 320) and exams.

The Unit 1 and Unit 2 exam papers have been purposely designed to have a similar feel, even though Unit 1 looks at small businesses and Unit 2 large businesses. Each paper will consist of about three separate questions, based on their own short case study. Each of the questions will have three or four parts or sub-questions. These get more challenging as you work through them, so be prepared for that. The number of marks for each sub-question tends to increase as you work down the list, indicating that more depth needs to be included in your answers to gain these marks.

Early questions are mainly descriptive, assessing your knowledge of business ideas and terms. The later questions assess your ability to apply that knowledge, or in other words to use it in different situations. These questions are also designed to get you to explore your own thoughts on the case study and consider alternative solutions to any problems that have been identified. These skills are called analysis and evaluation.

You will be asked to read the case study and then answer the questions that follow. The case study could contain clues to help you with your answers, but its main purpose is to set the scene for the questions. The nature of business studies means that there are often different interpretations and solutions to problems. The people who mark your scripts (completed exam papers) are aware of this and will reward you for answers that have been considered and are realistic. So be creative and try to find your own way through the questions. Just make sure you support everything you say with solid business ideas.

Both papers have up to 60 marks available. Individual sub-questions can be worth as little as 2, and as many as 10 marks. Use the number of marks available to help guide you on how much detail is needed in your answer. The amount of available space on the question paper is another important clue.

Make sure that you are familiar with the 'command words' in the questions. These are the instructions, such as state, give, describe, explain, advise, and comment. These words are the biggest clues as to what skills (knowledge, understanding, application, analysis and evaluation) the examiner is looking for in your answers.

Finally, remember that, as with other GCSEs, your examiner will look at the standard of your written English and the presentation of your work. The answers to certain questions will be used to assess your writing skills, and marks will be awarded: check the front cover of the exam paper to see which questions will be used.

Acknowledgements

Every effort has been made to trace the copyright holders of quoted material. The publishers apologise if any sources remain unacknowledged and will be glad to make the necessary arrangements at the earliest opportunity. The authors and publishers would like to thank the following for permission to reproduce copyright photos:

Title page, istockphoto.com; p.1 © Patryk Galka/iStockphoto.com; p.2 BP; p.7 PlayPumps International; p.14 courtesy of Fraser Doherty; p.17 Photodisc; p.20 Colin Underhill/Alamy; p.23 The Franchise Magazine; p.26 Mike Webster/Rex Features; p.27 mediablitzimages (uk) Limited/ Alamy; p.33 © Boris Ryaposov/iStockphoto.com; p.34 Coffee Nation; p.38 Photodisc; p.40 Somos Images/Photolibrary Group; p.49 The Prince's Trust; p.50 (top) Innocent Drinks, (bottom) Barking Dog Art; p.55 Natasha Japp/ iStockphoto.com; p.61 © mipan – Fotolia.com; p.62 Wayne Linden/Alamy; p.68 Robert Stainforth/Alamy; p.73 © BBC; p.79 Nick Randall/Rex Features; p.85 Action Press/Rex Features; p.91 © malcolm romain/iStockphoto .com; p.92 Christopher Furlong/Getty Images; p.98 Clark's Pet Couriers; p.104 Business Active; p.110 aberystwyth/Alamy; p.116 Adrian Sherratt/Alamy; p.123 © Chad Anderson/ iStockphoto.com; p.124 Ian Shaw/Alamy; p.129 © Andrew Winning/Reuters/Corbis; p.134 Sonny Meddle/Rex Features; pp.135, 139, 140 (left) Photodisc; p.144 Colin Palmer Photography/ Alamy; p.149 Photodisc; p.150 funkyfood London – Paul Williams/Alamy; p.155 Banana Stock/ Photolibrary Group; p.160 Nick Hanna/Alamy; p.165 Imagesource/Photolibrary Group; p.169 Alan Curtis/Alamy; p.175 © cogal/iStockphoto. com; p.179 Rob Cousins/Alamy; p.180 © Arcaid/Corbis; p.185 Kumar Sriskandan/Alamy; p.187 MAURICIO LIMA/AFP/Getty Images; p.191 © Michał Kram/iStockphoto.com; p.193 © Bakaleev Aleksey/iStockphoto.com; p.196 Edward Moss/Alamy; p.197 © Photodisc/Getty Images; p.198 david pearson/Alamy; p.203 © Marcela Barsse/iStockphoto.com; p.204 © Gino Santa Maria/iStockphoto.com; p.206 ©Photodisc/Getty Images; p.207 © Sergey Lavrentev/iStockphoto .com; p.210 © Quavondo Nguyen/ iStockphoto.com; p.213 Oleksiy Maksymenko/ Alamy; p.214 Hugh Threlfall/Alamy; p.216 INTERFOTO Pressebildagentur/Alamy; p.218 David Cannon/Getty Images for Dubai Sports City; p.219 John Peters/Manchester United via Getty Images; p.224 Michael Ochs Archives/Getty Images; p.226 © Tony Tremblay/iStockphoto.com; p.228 © iStockphoto.com; p.231 ©endrille/ iStockphoto.com; p.232 ©Ralf Siemieniec/ iStockphoto.com; p.235 David Beauchamp/Rex Features; p.237 © mark yuill – Fotolia.com; p.238 Peter Lawson/Rex Features; p.241 Luca Ghidoni/ Getty Images; p.248 PAUL ELLIS/AFP/Getty Images; p.249 © Rafal Zdeb/iStockphoto.com; p.255 Mario Tama/Getty Images; p.258 © Design Pics Inc./Alamy; p.263 ©Pavel Losevsky/ iStockphoto.com; p.265 fStop/Alamy; p.266 © Don Bayley/iStockphoto.com; p.272 Jim Wileman/Alamy; p.273 © www.fotoie.com/ iStockphoto.com; p.276 Greg Balfour Evans/ Alamy; p.279 David J. Green – work themes/ Alamy; p.281 © Lisa F. Young/iStockphoto.com; p.285 © Dean Mitchell/iStockphoto.com; p.289 © David H. Lewis/iStockphoto.com; p.293 © N_design/iStockphoto.com; p.295 © Bulent Ince/ iStockphoto.com; p.297 Kevin Foy/Alamy; p.299 © Jorgen Udvang/iStockphoto.com; p.300 © ricardo azoury/iStockphoto.com; p.303 Jonathan Player/ Rex Features; p.304 Barking Dog Art; p.305 AFP/ Getty Images; p.309 Christopher Furlong/Getty Images; p.310 Leon Neal/AFP/Getty Images; p.315 © The British Standards Institution 2009; p.318 (left) © Brasil2/iStockphoto.com, (right) © Alexander Raths/iStockphoto.com.

The photo on p.2 is printed with kind permission of BP. The photo on p.98 is printed with kind permission of Clark's Pet Couriers.

SECTION 1

DEFINING BUSINESS AND ENTERPRISE

Chapter 1
What is business?

IN THE NEWS

Without business, you would not be reading this book, or living in a house, travelling by bus or car, listening to music or wearing fashion. You would not be warm, or fed, or clothed. Business provides all of these goods and services and ranges from the tiniest, one person business, to huge multinationals with greater wealth than many countries.

In March 2008, the Duke and Duchess of York both appeared in the newspapers, both working with businesses. The Duke of York, in his role as a 'business ambassador' for the UK government, was visiting Indonesia to inspect BP's new natural gas plant in Bintuni Bay. The Duchess of York was involved in a reality TV show, trying to show people on low incomes how to eat more healthily. The Duke was visiting BP, a global oil and fuels company. The Duchess was encouraging people to buy from local producers, markets and stalls.

BP has operations and bases in about 100 countries, in every continent, from Austria, Algeria and Australia to Venezuela, Vietnam and Zambia. Its turnover approaches $300,000,000,000 a year and its profit almost $30,000,000,000. A typical fruit and vegetable market stall is tiny, with no employees, operating in one spot in one town. It may take £1000 a week, giving it a turnover of about £50,000, with profits of £15,000.

So what do they both share that makes them a business? Each provides something, and it is willing to sell to someone, who is willing to buy. Each provides either a good or service, or a combination of goods and services, to consumers in a market. Each tries to provide the good or service at a profit – in other words, they try to make more out of the sale of a product than it costs them to buy or make it. Businesses are involved in supplying goods and services to a market. BP supplies oil, gas and energy services to a market that is global in scope. A fruit and vegetable stall supplies food to a group of local customers. Each has costs that it must try to meet, and revenue from sales with which it must try to meet them. Each is at risk of failure if its business model does not work. (Big businesses have the chance of failing, just as much as small businesses, it's just more visible when they do!)

BP's new natural gas plant in Bintuni Bay

@ BP's background is at:
**www.bp.com/extendedsectiongeneric
article.do?categoryId=5&contentId=
70144157**
The Duchess of York's show is at:
**http://entertainment.timesonline.
co.uk/tol/arts_and_entertainment/
tv_and_radio/article3492502.ece**
Statistics on small businesses may be found at:
**www.statistics.gov.uk/cci/
nugget.asp?id=11**

Why do businesses exist?

A long time ago people saw to their own needs by providing for themselves. They recognised the sort of things that they needed – food, shelter, clothing, protection from the weather – they then provided these for themselves in order to survive. They collected water from streams and lakes. They grew or hunted their own food, and prepared it themselves. They made clothes from animal skins. They built their own shelters or lived in natural shelter.

Early societies provided for their own needs

Barter

At some point, people realised that certain people were better at some jobs than others. They decided that it would be better to let them do the jobs at which they were more efficient. So those who hunted best, hunted; those who were good at farming, looked after fields and animals, those who could build good shelters specialised in this. What this meant was that people were able to meet their needs more efficiently, and trade skills to make their lives better. This is called specialisation. At first, they just swapped the goods that they produced, or exchanged skills – a system known as barter. Later, when a way to measure value was invented (called 'money') they were able to carry out complicated transactions. Anyone who produced more of something than they needed was able to trade it for something they needed but did not have. This more efficient system also meant that people could trade for things that they did not need, but wanted. So production was not limited to food, clothes and shelter, but expanded not just to different types of clothes and different types of food but also to areas such as entertainment and leisure.

Profit

Businesses add value in order to make a product. They take a set of inputs (such as raw materials, say wheat) add value through a process (such as milling and baking) and produce an output (such as flour or bread). They add up the costs of all the inputs, then try to set a price that covers the costs and rewards them for their efforts. The money they receive from sales is called revenue. If revenue is greater than cost, this is called profit.

Business and production

There are two main classes of products. One is goods – these are things that we can touch and hold. The other is services. In olden times, these were things like milling wheat, shoeing horses, being defended from enemies. Nowadays they include banking, insurance and communication. Production is the process that a good or service goes through in order to be made and sold.

- **Primary** production is the first stage, when raw materials are farmed, quarried or extracted. It includes industries like mining, farming, fishing and companies like BP.

- **Secondary** production is when the raw materials are turned into finished products or component parts of products. Businesses in this sector are called manufacturing or

processing businesses. BP also operates in this sector, refining oil.

- **Tertiary** businesses provide services so that other businesses can operate efficiently. In this sector you will find insurance, transport, distribution (getting the goods to shops and customers), advertising, marketing, banking and finance. BP distributes and sells petrol, and advertises and markets itself, so it operates here as well. The market stall operates a service, so is in this sector.

Changes

The most important sectors to the UK economy are manufacturing and service, in particular the service sector. One in every five jobs in the UK is now in the financial and business sector, more than twice as many as ten years ago (see link). At the same time manufacturing businesses have been in decline over the past 20 years, as competition from overseas has been able to make goods more efficiently.

Primary, secondary and tertiary businesses

Did you know...

Britain's labour force has seen many changes over the past 20 years. A major change is the increase in the number and types of jobs carried out by women. In 1981, there were 3.2 million more men in work than women. Now the numbers are almost equal, with men performing 12.8 million jobs and women 12.7 million.

Summary

- People have to satisfy their needs
- If they can do this efficiently, they can move on to wants
- Business provides goods and services that people need and want
- Businesses operate in markets
- Markets are where buyers and seller together agree a price for a quantity of goods or services
- Many businesses are in business to make a profit

Core knowledge

Most people would say that the reason businesses are in business is to make a profit and they would be right. But although profit may be at the heart of much business activity, it is not the only reason for businesses to exist. Before a small business can decide what is, or is not, profit, it needs to add in the hours that the owners have put in. Many small businesses fail to do this and look profitable, whereas owners might be better off working for someone else.

Businesses have a number of different aims, as you will see in Chapter 5, some of which are linked to profit and some to wider or different targets. Before a small business can decide what is, or is not, profit, it needs to add in the hours that the owners have worked. Many small businesses fail to do this, which makes them look profitable, when in reality the owners might be better off working for someone else. Someone might set up a business because they want to provide a certain service, they might want the independence of working for themselves, they might just like the thrill of taking a risk and may not be too bothered about the consequences.

Some enterprises use a business model in order to provide benefits to society, or parts of society. These are called social enterprises, and include charities and cooperatives. Social enterprise is defined by the government as having 'social objectives, whose surpluses are … reinvested for that purpose in the business or the community, rather than being driven by the need to maximise profit'. What this means is that 'profit' is not for owners, but for the good of the community or to help the business grow so that it can do more good. There are around 55,000 social enterprises, with an annual turnover between them of almost £30 billion. There are some well-known names that are social enterprises ranging from *The Big Issue* and Jamie Oliver's Fifteen to the Co-operative Group, Café direct, Glas Cymru (Welsh Water) and The Eden Project.

And more

Businesses find out what people want and need – this is called demand – and then supply the goods and services to meet this demand. 'Needs' are the basic things required for survival, such as food, water and shelter; anything beyond this is a 'want'. Businesses have to make sure that goods and services are available at the right time, in the right place and at a price that people – consumers – are willing to pay. Goods and services are both 'products'. All that this means is that they are the result of a production process. This means that certain 'inputs' have been combined in a 'process' in order to produce certain 'outputs'. Inputs include raw materials, power and energy and people's labour. Processes include manufacturing, processing, sorting, construction and refining. Different combinations of inputs and processes will produce different outputs. For example:

- A combination of knowledge, skill and labour could produce a haircut
- A combination of wood, graphite and machinery could produce a pencil
- A combination of metals, rubber, technology, machinery, energy and labour could produce a car

Products may be either goods or services. A good is something that can be touched and used. Sometimes goods are 'consumables'. This means that they are quickly used up and cannot be used again. Examples include items such as soap and shampoo and all food and drink. Other goods are more lasting and are called consumer 'durables'. These can be used many times over without really losing value. Examples of these include refrigerators, washing machines, dishwashers and freezers (so-called 'white' goods), cars, furniture, tools, household goods and machinery of all sorts. Services are provided to individuals and organisations and cannot be touched. Examples include transport, insurance and education, and personal services such as haircuts and manicures.

Have a go!

Group activity

Make a list of all the skills that you have in your group. Examples could include writing, speaking, drawing, spelling, sewing, painting, playing an instrument, cooking, remembering stuff, being a good footballer, swimming, etc., etc. If more than one person has the same skills, then rank them, or subdivide the skill so, while one swimmer might be faster, the other might have more stamina. When you have a list of skills, rank them in order of the ones you think are most useful to your survival.

Would your group survive as a society?

Do you think that you could exchange skills with another group to help survival?

Discussion

Are some skills more important than others? Discuss why this might be the case, or in what circumstances a skill might become useful. What are the skills that entertainers and sportspeople have that make them worth so much? Are these skills any use in helping with survival?

Web-based activity

Businessman Duncan Goose quit his city job to ride round the world on a motorbike. On his travels, he saw the real hardship caused to the people who do not have clean drinking water. One billion people do not have the basic 'need' of clean water. Two million die each year from dirty-water-related diseases. He set up bottled water company One, and ploughed all the profits into providing clean water in developing countries. The profits are used to build PlayPumps in remote areas. Basically, these are roundabouts that, when kids play on them, pump clean water up from below the surface. 'We can't change the world overnight, but we can improve the life of one person, one day at a time' is the motto of the company. Visit the websites below and then answer the questions.

www.execdigital.co.uk/Driven-to-Drink—Duncan-Goose-talks-about-One-Water,-PlayPumps-and-social-entrepreneurship-_5860.aspx

www.beaconfellowship.org.uk/biography2007_dgoose.asp

Many businesses are set up for profit. Explain Duncan Goose's reason for setting up One. Do you think that this is a better model than a profit-based business? Give reasons for your views.

The One Water Playpump

Quickfire questions

1 What is a need?
2 What is a want?
3 What is meant by specialisation?
4 What is barter?
5 What is the difference between a good and a service?
6 What is meant by consumer durable?
7 What is primary production?
8 What is secondary production?
9 What is tertiary production?
10 What is a social enterprise?

Hit the spot

> Give two reasons why someone might want to specialise.

>> Explain the input-process-output model, with at least one example.

>>> Give three reasons why someone might want to set up in business. Choose which you think is the best reason. Justify your choice.

Cracking the code

Business Providing products that people want, usually for profit. Learn this, it is a word that is commonly misspelt!

Primary 'First' – the first stage of production: extraction, quarrying, farming, mining, etc.

Secondary 'Second' – the second stage of production: manufacturing, refining, processing, etc.

Tertiary 'Third' – the third stage of production: i.e. the provision of services and support.

Chapter 2
The nature of markets

IN THE NEWS

Not long before you were born a loaf of bread (the government uses a standard 800 gram loaf for comparisons) cost just 50p. In February of 2007, according to *The Grocer* magazine, it topped £1 for the first time. By 2008 it had continued to rise and, even though cheaper and 'own brand' bread could be had, the cost for a 'normal' loaf was close to £1.20. Pasta, too, has been on the rise, with 500 g of pasta shapes costing up to £2, almost twice as much as ten years ago. Such price rises are important to us when they involve foods that are a staple part of our diet – things that we shop for on a regular basis. We are particularly affected when the price of a basic ingredient goes up. In this case, the price of bread and pasta is closely linked to the main ingredient in their manufacture – flour – and flour is made from wheat. Wheat is also a basic ingredient for some types of beer, for cereals and for pastry.

The price of wheat more than doubled in the year up to Spring 2008, when it hit $12.00 a bushel (the weight used to measure wholesale wheat – 60 lb. or approximately 27 kilos). As recently as October 2006 it had been less than $5.00 but, as demand has risen and supply been reduced, prices have continued to rise. The demand for wheat from growing nations like China and India has hit the market at the same time as bad weather has destroyed crops in Argentina and India. Even Canada, with its hundreds of miles of rolling wheat fields, has been hit by bad weather. In addition, there has been a new source of demand, as wheat (and products that can be grown instead of wheat) are harnessed for biofuels.

Higher prices may take a while to work their way through into every wheat-based product as big food businesses like Kellogg's and Kraft will have long-term supply contracts. But consumers are already not being offered bread with soup in restaurants, and prices of pizzas and pasta have risen. But what causes prices to rise (and sometimes fall), and how do these changes affect businesses?

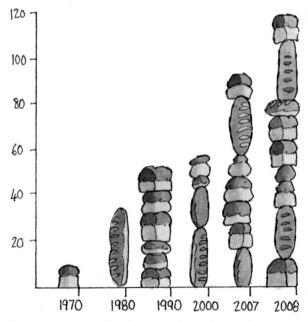

Changes in bread prices

@ Go to **statistics.gov.uk** for the latest information about prices – search for 'inflation' and 'retail price index'.
The Intellectual Property Office at **www.ipo.gov.uk/whatis.htm** tells you how a business can protect ideas, designs and trademarks.

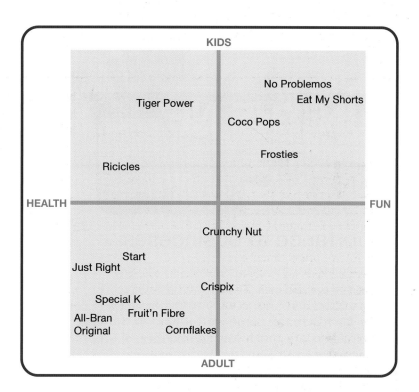

Market map for Kellogg's cereals

Markets and prices

All businesses operate in markets. A market is any way by which buyers and sellers are brought together. Sometimes this is physical – an actual place, like a farmers' market, Saturday market or craft fair. A supermarket is just a very large market, where any number of goods (and services) are offered for sale. Sometimes the market takes place 'virtually'. Buyers and sellers meet over a telephone connection, or via computer. In an auction market, people making telephone bids from abroad are still taking part in the market. Someone buying shares via a website and internet connection is still taking part in the stock market. New technology has opened up many more markets, and many more ways for people to operate businesses (and some more problems, as we shall see later). Prices in a market are determined by the number of people who want to buy and the number who want to sell. The amount people want to buy is called **demand**. The amount sellers want to sell is called **supply**.

Price changes

If too many sellers enter a market, then there will be too much supply. If every farmer saw that the price of wheat had gone up, and switched to wheat production, what do you think would happen to the price? If there are many buyers in a market, and it is not easy to increase supply, then the price will be pushed up. What do you think happens to the price of concert or Cup Final tickets if everyone wants one but there are only so many seats? The way that markets operate is to find the price where buyers and sellers agree on the amount to be exchanged.

Importance to businesses

This is vital to businesses because they all operate in markets. Some are highly competitive – in other words, there are a lot of other businesses trying to reach the same customers. In some cases markets are much less competitive. If you are the only person who supplies something, and it's something people want, you can probably ask a very high price.

Competition

In a competitive market, businesses can try to attract customers in a number of ways. The main two ways may be defined as

- **price competition** – where the business attracts customers by setting a particular price;

- **non-price competition** – where the business uses other means such as promotions and special offers or competes by providing extra or better services.

In some markets, there is very little competition. If someone has a good idea for a new product, they can actually protect it from competition by using things like patents, trademarks and copyright. In other markets, a few businesses may have grown large by taking over other businesses, and therefore getting rid of the

competition. Sometimes they even have enough power to prevent other businesses from setting up in competition with them. In the interests of fairness, governments sometimes intervene in markets to provide goods or services that people would be unwilling or unable to pay for, or to try to make markets more competitive.

Mass or niche

Some markets are huge and are called mass markets. For example, millions of cars are sold every day, all over the world. Some markets are tiny and are called niche markets. A limited edition, special model of a particular car will have a very small market (and be very expensive). Some businesses will try to attract as many customers as possible, some will be happy to attract just a few customers, but with a highly-priced item.

Gaps in the market

Businesses look for changes and gaps in the market. Businesses can try to create a gap in the market, or they can try to find a gap, and fill it with a product. Alternatively, they could expand into other markets. Kellogg's could, for example, look for products that are not wheat-based to

A product for a niche market

bolster its range. Or it could move into completely different markets, like chocolate, or car production. (This is not as far-fetched as it sounds – Mars, for example, make pet food, coffee and pasta sauce, as well as being a leading confectionery firm.)

Summary

- All businesses operate in markets
- Prices in a market are set by how many people want something, and how many people are willing to supply it
- Prices move up or down as supply and demand changes
- In some markets there is a lot of competition, in others, very little
- Businesses compete in markets by charging different prices, or through non-price competition
- Markets may be very large (mass) or very small (niche)
- Businesses try to change market conditions to their own advantage

Core knowledge

All businesses operate in markets. In a market, price is set by how many people want a good or service, and how many will supply it. Buyers will want something because they have a need for it – we have already come across this idea. But they can also be persuaded that they have a 'need'. Businesses will try to persuade customers through advertising, promoting and branding. One method is to find a gap in the market or, if there is no gap, to create one by creating desire and therefore demand for a product.

Kellogg's brand strength lies in its most popular cereal products. Kellogg's could try various ways to sell more of these. It could lower price, it could increase advertising or it could promote the products in other ways. Also, Kellogg's could bring out new products to cover those areas where it doesn't feel it is strong. To do this, it can draw up a '**market map**'. This divides the market into four, with each part showing one part of the market at which a product might be aimed. One of the skills of market mapping, for a business, is to be able to define the key parts of their market. These could, for example, be men, women, young or old people, luxury products or everyday necessities, low- or high-priced products, healthy or 'indulgent' products, and so on. You can see from Kellogg's market map that they market their range at both young and old, and have some products whose strength is their 'healthy' message, while others are strong because they are more 'fun'. 'Fun' products are, of course, one way to get young people to eat healthily. You can see that adult, healthy cereals are very strong, with Kellogg's cornflakes central to this. The two Bart Simpson brands (top right quarter) have been added in the last few years to strengthen this part of the market. There is still, however, quite a gap in the market for a 'fun' product for adults. Kellogg's could move Crunchy Nut more in that direction (by advertising), or come up with another product to fill this gap.

And more

Many markets now take place 'virtually', i.e. with the buyer and seller never meeting. This has opened up a lot of new opportunities for businesses. Businesses can use new technology to advertise products and to provide ways for people to buy. Most businesses now have a website operation, which will include ways to order products. Many small businesses are run using websites like eBay and using protected payment systems like PayPal.

Of course, the major problem with a technology-based market, is that you do not meet the person from whom you are buying/to whom you are selling, so the exchange and payment cannot take place at the same time. If you think about a normal, non-technology-based transaction, you often hand over your money at the same time as you receive the goods. Sometimes there is a delay, particularly in business-to-business (B2B) transactions, while orders are made (purchase orders), deliveries are made and paper requests for payment (invoices) follow, but even this process is nowadays often electronic and therefore much faster. There is also the growing problem of fraud and identity theft. There are ways to reduce these problems – for example by using a third party to hold funds until goods are delivered (this is how PayPal works), by using secure servers and by having good firewalls. Nevertheless, e-crime is a growth area.

Technology helps businesses in other ways. There is now little need for businesses to handle large amounts of cash (and many businesses now even refuse to take cheques) as transfers can be made safely and efficiently by **EFTPOS** and chip and pin cards. Businesses can also collect a lot of information on customers and their buying habits, through data gathered at electronic checkouts.

Have a go!

Group activity

Make a list of the top five advertising campaigns that are taking place at the moment. Compare your list with other members of your group and decide on an agreed top five. For each campaign, say what you think the business is trying to do. Is it trying to enter a new market or expand an existing one? Perhaps it is just trying to reposition a product in a different market segment. Rank the businesses according to which you think have the most effective advertising.

Discussion

Discuss the reasons why you think your chosen advertisers have decided to go in this direction. What do you think is happening to the market in each of the cases at which you have looked that would make the business try this particular tactic? Do you agree with them or could you recommend another course of action?

Web-based activity

Biofuels are an area where there is some argument. Some people say that they are putting up the price of wheat (and other foods) so that poor people cannot afford food. Other people say that there are benefits to the environment that outweigh any problems. Use a search engine to find out about biofuels and decide if you are for or against them. Put together a folder, poster or display that supports your argument.

Quickfire questions

1 What is a market?
2 What forces in a market determine price?
3 What is a 'virtual' market?
4 In which two ways do businesses compete?
5 How could a new business protect itself against competition?
6 What is a mass market?
7 What is a niche market?
8 What is a gap in a market?
9 What is a 'market map'?
10 What is meant by 'identity theft'?

Hit the spot

> Give an example of a competitive market. Describe the features that make it competitive.

>> Explain why non-price competition might be the main way to compete in a highly competitive market.

>>> Suggest three possible problems with markets and new technology. Evaluate ways to limit these problems.

Cracking the code

Demand The amount people want to buy.

EFTPOS (Electronic Funds Transfer at Point of Sale) Moving funds directly from one account to another (e.g. your bank to a shop's bank).

Market mapping A way of dividing the market into key areas.

Non-price competition Using ways other than price to compete.

Price competition Setting a different price to your competitors.

Supply The amount that producers/businesses want to sell.

Chapter 3
Taking risks – enterprise

IN THE NEWS

Superjam

Fraser Doherty decided, at the age of 14, that he would like to make some extra pocket money. Looking around, he saw that many boys and girls of the same age group as himself were working long hours at jobs that were anything but rewarding. In fact, the figures show that a third of under-16s hold down a part-time job, with the most popular being car washing and newspaper deliveries. Once over 16, they can earn more by waiting tables, babysitting or shop work. None of this attracted Fraser, however, so he decided to look around for other opportunities. With the help of his grandmother, he began to produce jam, finding a ready local market in friends and neighbours. Market research showed him that jam was a market in decline, but only because it was seen as such an unhealthy product. His grandmother's wartime jams had contained a minimum of sugar – due to shortages – so used other ingredients to produce sweetness. Fraser's jams are sweetened with grape juice, making them much healthier. In addition, everyone, he thought, does strawberry and blackberry, so I'm going to try something different. He experimented with different fruits and produced many more unusual jams, concentrating on the so-called 'superfruits' such as cranberries and blueberries and ingredients such as ginger. Friends and neighbours spread the word and sales rapidly increased. Fraser found himself selling at farmers' markets and to delicatessens as demand grew.

By the time he was 16, Fraser was producing 1000 jars a week, as demand rocketed after appearances on

SuperJam

the UK Food Channel, BBC TV's Working Lunch and C4's Tricky Business.

In early 2007 Fraser gained a huge order from national supermarket chain Waitrose. He had to say goodbye to the home kitchen and set up proper production facilities in order to supply most of Waitrose's 183 stores. In October, giant retailer Tesco took up further supply.

Current success, however, is built on immense hard work and long hours. A teenager's social life was sacrificed for 60-hour weeks making jam and weekends spent selling it at farmers' markets, often with little success when bad weather kept customers indoors. Early losses and setbacks, however, just made Fraser more determined to get the product and the market right.

The result? Fraser is well on his way to becoming Scotland's first jam millionaire!

www.realbusiness.co.uk
http://news.Scotsman.com
www.bbc.co.uk/dragonsden/

Enterprise

Fraser has shown the qualities of an **entrepreneur** and of **enterprise**. These are both words that you will come across often in your study of business because what they represent is so central to the success of a business. Enterprise means taking risks and developing new ideas. It means finding the money to try products and ideas out on the market. Without enterprise, and without entrepreneurs, there would be no new business ideas. Without entrepreneurs we would have no electricity, no motor cars, no air travel, no computers (or computer games), no mobile phones ... The invention of each of these is not enough to ensure its success. Each needed an entrepreneur – a person who was willing to take a risk and hope that people would buy the product. Take the motor car, for example. Without Henry Ford's idea of factory-led mass production, the car would probably still be a luxury item for the very few. He didn't invent the car, but he did make sure that ordinary people could afford to buy it.

Enterprise therefore involves:

- *New ideas*: Entrepreneurs think of new products, of new ways to use old products, or new markets to which they can sell products. The key ideas of the entrepreneur are to do with bringing products to market.

- *Money*: To do this, entrepreneurs need money – in business we call this finance – in order to develop products, test products, make changes to products and tell people about products (and all the good things about them). They may need to set up production, for instance in a factory. They may need to employ people (who will then want paying). They may need to buy **raw materials** before they can start making a product. Many entrepreneurs do not have enough of their own money, so have to convince other people of the value of their product. Sometimes they may borrow money. Sometimes they may persuade other people or organisations to risk money on their idea.

- *Risk*: Entrepreneurs risk their own money, other people's money, and their own reputations. Taking a risk is probably the hardest part of enterprise. The entrepreneur must be prepared to lose – and then to try again.

- *Reward:* Of course this is what drives all entrepreneurs. Seeing a product on sale and being used may be reward enough. But the reward that most entrepreneurs seek is profit. This means making more in **revenue** than it costs to produce the product.

Qualities of an entrepreneur

The typical qualities of an entrepreneur are a bit like those of an old-time explorer. They must really believe that they can succeed and, as well, must be:

- *Willing to take advice*: Entrepreneurs need to listen to people who can help them. This may be professional advice, such as from a bank or marketing company. It may be advice from

Entrepreneurs take risks …

friends and colleagues. It may be advice from customers about the product that the entrepreneur is selling.

● *Enthusiastic*: Entrepreneurs need energy and enthusiasm. This is linked to self-belief. They must really believe in the product that they are selling and be keen to persuade people to buy it.

● *Hard working*: Entrepreneurs cannot afford to be lazy. They are risking both their own money and, often, that of other people. Often success means putting in long hours. (Look at the 60-hour weeks Fraser had to put in on top of anything else he wanted to do, like socialise or study.)

● *Persistent*: (meaning 'keeps on trying'). This is really important. Entrepreneurs will not always have a smooth ride. They will encounter many obstacles and have to face setbacks as well as enjoy successes. To become a success, they must be prepared to keep trying.

Did you know…?

Many entrepreneurs started as really small businesses – Virgin's Richard Branson started with a student magazine; Body Shop founder Anita Roddick with a single shop; Tesco started in 1924 when founder Jack Cohen combined the first two letters of his surname with the initials of TE Stockwell, from whom he bought a delivery of tea.

Summary

● Business relies on people with new ideas
● These new ideas can be turned into new products, or new uses for existing products
● People willing to test these ideas in the market are called entrepreneurs
● The quality that these people show is enterprise
● Enterprise involves many other qualities, such as hard work and enthusiasm

Core knowledge

All businesses start with new ideas. In general these can be split into two. First, completely new products, second, existing products, but aimed at a different part or segment of a market. Let's first understand the terms.

A *product* is the result of business activity. It can be either a good or a service. A good is a physical product like a car, a mobile phone, a bicycle, a computer game or a loaf of bread. A service is something that is done for a person or organisation like a haircut, a car service, insurance or transport. A taxi driver owns a product (the cab) and provides a service (the cab ride).

A *market* is anywhere where a product may be bought or sold. A traditional market (like a farmers' market) has stalls and stallholders offering goods for sale, but a car showroom is as much a market as this, and businesses like eBay show that a market can exist anywhere – even in cyberspace. Markets are broken down by businesses into smaller parts or segments, so that each segment can be more accurately targeted.

Enterprise may therefore involve:

- A completely new good. One inventor developed a glue that didn't stick very well. The entrepreneur in him turned it into the highly successful Post-it notes business.
- A completely new service. When personal music players first came out, a number of businesses were established to turn people's record collections into digital media.
- An improved or better good. Cars are a good example, many now have as standard airbags, electric windows, abs braking, lower carbon emissions, etc.
- An improved or better service. Silverjet saw that there was a demand for business class flights so launched an airline where all seats were business class. Unfortunately, like many new businesses, it failed!

The Post-it note was a completely new idea

And more

Modern successful entrepreneurs recognise that there are other vital qualities that they will need. Being a successful entrepreneur isn't just about taking risks, it is about being able to manage those risks. Risk management is the skill of judging how important or dangerous a risk is, and then making sure that it is minimised wherever possible. For example, there is much less risk involved in bringing a product to a small part of a market in order to test it than there is in trying to hit the whole possible market first. Many entrepreneurs therefore introduce ideas in small ways or small markets, just to test them out.

Success also involves the ability to solve problems. Problem-solving skills mean that the entrepreneur can see a way through difficulties that other people cannot. It means identifying the problem, coming up with possible solutions, deciding on the best solution (linked to risk management) and then putting the solution into effect.

Entrepreneurs must also have team-working skills. They must be able to get the best out of those around them, making good use of people's different qualities. As well as being able to lead teams, they must have good listening skills, and be prepared to act on advice given by team members.

Some entrepreneurs, having been successful, try to help other entrepreneurs by investing in them. This is called providing risk capital. Such entrepreneurs are also called venture capitalists. Watch any episode of the BBC programme *Dragons' Den* and you will meet successful entrepreneurs (the panel) and up-and-coming ones (those with ideas and products).

Have a go!

Group activity

Working in a group, you are going to manage a risk. Think of an activity that you, or a group of friends, could undertake. This could be something simple like going to the cinema or travelling to the next town. It could be something more adventurous, like an outdoor pursuits weekend or even a trip abroad. Once you have decided, carry out a risk assessment on the activity. Break it down into small steps, decide what the risk is for each step and then say how this risk could be minimised. Finally, explain why such risk management is really important to businesses.

There is risk in the simplest action

Some activities are high risk

Discussion

What do you think is the single most important quality for an entrepreneur? Which entrepreneurs can you use as evidence to support your decision?

Web-based activity

Visit the BBC's website for *Dragons' Den* at **www.bbc.co.uk/dragonsden/**. Listen to the opening credits. These will tell you how the 'dragons' made their money. Then watch the first part of any of the 'pitches'. When the pitch is over, pause the broadcast and write down three of the sort of questions that you would ask. Decide what answers you would like to hear, then decide whether you would be 'in' or 'out' with this particular entrepreneur. Then play the rest of the broadcast to see what the dragons asked and decided.

Quickfire questions

1　What is the business quality shown by the entrepreneur?
2　What do entrepreneurs take? What do they develop?
3　What was Henry Ford's winning idea?
4　Entrepreneurs can bring new products to market. How else can they make products successful?
5　Define revenue.
6　Define profit.
7　Give three key qualities of an entrepreneur.
8　Suggest two sources of professional advice for entrepreneurs.
9　Describe what is meant by venture capital.
10　Name one successful entrepreneur and suggest one factor that made him/her a success.

Hit the spot

> Give two reasons why a successful entrepreneur might support other entrepreneurs.

>> Explain how important enterprise skills are to business.

>>> Which quality of an entrepreneur do you think is most important to success? Explain why you think this.

Cracking the code

Enterprise **Taking risks and developing new ideas for successful businesses.**

Entrepreneur **The person who shows enterprise qualities.**

Raw materials **Basic material and components used to make a product (like wood used to make tables).**

Revenue **Money received by a business from sales.**

Chapter 4
Reducing the risks of starting a business: Franchising

IN THE NEWS

What is the world's biggest fast-food franchise operation? McDonald's? Pizza Hut? Perhaps KFC? In fact, it is the hugely successful Subway chain, which makes its own bread daily and specialises in fresh ingredients and healthy alternatives. Subway – now not just the biggest fast-food franchise, but the biggest franchise operation of any sort in the world – started in 1965 when two friends decided to set up a sandwich-making enterprise. Once it was a success, they decided to expand. They could have done this by opening up new stores themselves but, instead, decided to franchise the idea.

In 2008 Subway opened its 28,000th store worldwide. By the middle of the year it had overtaken McDonald's in terms of the number of stores operating, opening them at a rate of almost one a day. The year before it had reached its thousandth store in Australia and its thousandth in Britain and Ireland when it opened three new franchises on the same day (in Manchester, Southend and Donegal, Ireland). It currently operates in 86 countries worldwide. Unlike many of its competitors, it is also experimenting with a different cultural 'mix' and offering sandwiches made according to religious and dietary rules such as halal and kosher. This will allow it access to even more markets in Asia and Africa.

Subway makes fresh sandwiches (in submarine-shaped rolls – hence the name) so has no need for fryers or grills, making it a more attractive proposition to many than its hot food competitors such as KFC, Burger King, Pizza Hut and McDonald's. Because it does not need cooking facilities, Subways have many more possible venues available to them than cooked food outlets and can be found in an enormous variety of venues, apart from the high street.

The world's biggest fast-food franchise

It has also been more easily able to adapt its menus to healthy eating, having no fried products and being able to substitute low fat and low calorie ingredients where possible. Its range of fresh sandwiches and salads now includes an 'under 6 g of fat' line that has become very popular. Part of the success is down to the levels of support available to franchisees. They receive advice from Subway consultants on all aspects of the operation, from choosing a site to training the staff and from buying in ingredients to marketing. The formula is so successful that many franchisees have opened multiple outlets.

@ www.subway.co.uk/about_latest_details.asp?press_news_id=32
www.thefranchisemagazine.net/
www.TheUKFranchiseDirectory.net
www.FranchiseDirect.co.uk

Franchises

Franchising is often classed as a type of business ownership. It is, however, a type of business organisation, rather than ownership. Franchises may be bought and sold by sole traders, partnerships, companies, cooperatives and charities. (One Subway branch, for example, is owned and operated by a church and sited in the church in Buffalo, New York, where it is part of a drive to help underprivileged kids by providing work opportunities.) A franchise is when a business sells the right to use its trade marks, brand, image, logo, etc. to another business. In effect, the buyer buys the right to trade using the successful ideas of another business.

How a franchise works

When a successful business decides that it would like to expand, it can do this in a number of different ways. It could, if it were a retail business, open more branches, or expand into internet sales. A manufacturing business could move into larger premises. Any business could expand by buying out its rivals. Alternatively, it can sell its successful business idea or format to others that want to profit from it.

The successful business that decides to expand in this way is called the **franchiser**. It sells the **franchise** to a **franchisee**. This will be for a certain sum of money called a **fee** (ranging from a few hundred to tens of thousands of pounds) plus, usually, a percentage share of the **turnover** or profits of the franchisee, called a **royalty**.

Franchisers may also gain by selling products to franchisees at higher prices than if they bought them elsewhere. There are advantages and disadvantages to both franchiser and franchisee.

Advantages of franchising

The franchiser

- is able to carefully select franchisees, and only sell to those who it thinks will add value to the brand;
- knows that franchisees, who have risked their own money, will be keen and enthusiastic to make the business a success;
- can expand more rapidly;
- receives money from the franchisee, so does not risk its own money on expansion;
- can gain from *economies of scale*, through being able to buy in bulk (one of the advantages of expansion).

The franchisee

- has had some of the financial hard work done in advance as the franchiser has a good idea of what setting up the business will cost, and reflects this in the franchise fee;
- receives support from the franchiser when setting up and ongoing support in terms of advice, marketing, advertising, etc. For Subway, this is reckoned to be one of its real strengths and includes financial, marketing and training advice.

Disadvantages of franchising

The franchisee

- may be restricted in terms of what they can do with the business. Some franchisers, for example, insist that they only sell their own brands, and that they only use certain suppliers. Subway is more flexible on this than many of its rivals;

- may feel that royalties are too high and they are not being rewarded for their effort;

- are unable to sell the franchise on without the agreement of the franchiser.

The franchiser

- is risking the business brand and reputation, and may end up with a franchisee that damages both.

A franchise, therefore, provides a safer route into business for many and a more certain route to expansion for many businesses.

The franchiser can offer advice and support

Did you know...

Some businesses take both routes to expansion – opening new branches themselves and franchising. McDonald's, for example, has both its own branch network and tens of thousands of franchised branches. Control over stock, cooking, training, service, etc. is such that you will never be able to tell which is franchised and which is not!

Summary

- A franchise is where a successful business expands by selling the right to use its business model
- The franchiser is the business selling the franchise
- The franchisee is the business buying the franchise
- Franchises are usually bought for a fee, plus a royalty
- Some advantages of franchising include, for the franchiser, easier expansion and more certain financial flows; for the franchisee, a successful model and lower risk
- Some disadvantages include, for the franchiser, the possibility of a franchisee damaging its reputation; for the franchisee, higher costs and restrictions on the business
- Statistically, franchises are more likely to succeed than other independent start-ups, so remain popular

The process of franchising

Firstly, a business has to be a success. Secondly, it has to have a business model or type that will lend itself to franchising. A car manufacturer or oil refining business is unlikely to be able to attract franchisees. Costs and risks will be far too high. In addition, the franchiser needs to know that the franchise will add to his own business, rather than compete with it. If a car manufacturer were to sell a franchise, the cars produced would compete in the market with its own vehicles. A franchiser must therefore have a business model that

- can easily be transferred;
- does not cost too much to set up;
- can be kept from competing with itself or other franchisees.

This is why many franchise operations are found in the fast-food market. Premises are reasonably small and therefore easier to find. With Subway, they are even more flexible as frying facilities are not needed. Costs to set up can be kept at a competitive level. As with many franchises, exclusive areas can be given so that one franchise is not in competition with another.

The franchiser will advertise the availability of a franchise through one of the franchise magazines (such as *The Franchise Magazine*) or through a website, such as **www.TheUKFranchiseDirectory.net** or **www.FranchiseDirect.co.uk**

Franchisees can then see what it will cost to buy the franchise, the likely rewards, and the restrictions that the franchiser puts on the business. The franchiser will also be careful to vet applicants and many, who it does not think would be good for the image of the business, or where it is not convinced there is sufficient business knowledge, will be rejected. With a popular franchise, like Subway, there are often waiting lists of those who wish to apply.

Comparing a franchise with an independent business

Although many people have the dream of starting their own business, few actually make it. Many people are put off by the risk of failure. Franchisees are buying a successful business idea, so there is less chance of failure. According to the Office for National Statistics (ONS) around 50 per cent of new businesses fail in the first two years of operation. For franchises, this figure plummets to less than 10 per cent. In addition, over 90 per cent of franchises are in profit – and stay that way. The British Household Panel Survey 2008, based on 6000 households, says that only one in seven of those who wish to start a business actually do and, although some will eventually make it, more than two-thirds never manage to realise their dream.

Standards

The franchisee must convince the franchiser that s/he has enthusiasm and business knowledge, and can run the business to the standards required. Once an application is accepted, the franchiser will then provide some or all of the stock, advertising (including national advertising for the brand, from which every outlet benefits), marketing and point of sale materials, financial advice, training, insurance, legal advice, design and shop fitting and even loans.

Both the commercial TV station and the product advertised are franchises

Other franchises

Not all franchise operations are in retail. Regional TV stations in the UK (commercial stations like TV South West and Yorkshire Television) buy a 'right to broadcast' in a particular area from the Independent Broadcasting Authority. Train companies like Virgin and National Express buy a franchise for the right to run trains on Network Rail's tracks.

Have a go!

Group activity

Visit your local High Street or shopping centre and map the shops that you find there. You should try to map between 20 and 30 shops. Now try to find out which are franchises. Divide the number of shops between the members of your group and, by using the internet, or by interviewing shop staff, find out which are franchises. Once you have put all the information together, produce a chart to show which are franchises.

Discussion

Discuss the reasons that you can give for these businesses being franchises. Which of them did you expect to be franchises (refer to the Core Knowledge on page 23)? Which of them were you surprised to find were franchises?

Web-based activity

Imagine that you had £10,000 to invest in a new business. Visit either **www.TheUKFranchise Directory.net** or **www.FranchiseDirect.co.uk** and decide which business you would like to buy. If you need more money, you could go into partnership with a classmate if you can persuade him or her that your idea is better than theirs!

Quickfire questions

1   Define 'franchise'.
2   Explain the difference between the franchiser and the franchisee.
3   What is a 'royalty'?
4   Name five fast food franchise operations.
5   Name five other franchise operations.
6   List five types of support that the franchiser might give to the franchisee.
7   Give three advantages of franchising to the franchiser.
8   Give three advantages of franchising to the franchisee.
9   Name at least three disadvantages, to either franchiser or franchisee.
10   Give three things a franchise needs for it to be a success.

Hit the spot

Outline what is meant by a franchise.

What is the difference between a royalty and a fee?

Explain whether you would rather have a royalty charged on turnover or profit, and why.

Give three benefits of a franchise to either the franchiser or the franchisee.

Give three drawbacks of a franchise to either the franchiser or the franchisee.

Explain why a franchise start-up might be a better bet than an independent business start-up.

Read the information on Subway. Which part of their business model is it that makes the franchise operation such a success? Give reasons for your answer.

Cracking the code

Fee The price of the franchise.

Franchise When a business sells the right to use its successful business model in order to expand.

Franchisee The person or business buying the franchise.

Franchiser The person or business selling the franchise.

Royalty In relation to franchises, a percentage of the turnover of the franchisee, paid to the franchiser.

Turnover The number of products sold times the price of each.

Chapter 5
Business aims and objectives

IN THE NEWS

Antonio Carluccio was surprised to receive an early seventieth birthday present when the Queen presented him with an honorary OBE. 'I didn't think an Italian citizen could get a British honour,' he said in a later interview. But Antonio shouldn't have been surprised at his award for 'services to hospitality' as he is one of the most successful chefs and restaurant owners of the past 20 years. At each stage of his business career, he has had clear aims and objectives – targets that he wanted to reach. Having reached these targets, Antonio then moved on to harder or higher objectives. As a successful chef in the 1990s, Antonio had found it frustrating that he could not obtain the fresh ingredients that he needed for the high quality food that he wanted to cook. He had been taught, in his childhood in Italy, to recognise the 'free' foods of the countryside such as berries, leaves and, especially, edible fungi such as mushrooms and truffles. He opened his first shop, with the aim of providing fresh ingredients, in 1991. The overall aim of the shop was 'to provide great quality, authentic Italian food at sensible prices. We also wanted to allow informal but excellent service to our customers.' Other aims have to be financial – obviously the shop had to survive and then, hopefully, make a profit. It did, and then growth became an aim as a wholesale business and other shops were opened. In November 1999 a new concept was launched when a combined food shop and 'caffè' was opened. These are restaurants with a food shop attached. Each restaurant is based on the idea that the

Chef and entrepreneur Antonio Carluccio

ingredients are as important as the finished meal, so each has a specialist food shop attached to it where customers can buy the ingredients for the Italian dishes served. There is also a wide range of coffees. Carluccio's can now be found all around the country, and the company is quoted on AIM (AIM is the Alternative Investment Market, the little brother of the Stock Exchange). A further aim is to expand internationally, and the first shop outside the UK was opened in Dublin in 2008.

All through the process, however, the original aim – the 'mission statement' – has remained the same: good quality produce, authentic Italian food, sensible prices, excellent service. By staying true to this target, Carluccio's has continued to grow and thrive from its beginnings as a single shop run by a chef and his wife.

@

- You can read the 'five minute interview' with Antonio Carluccio at **www.independent.co.uk/ news/people/the-5minute-interview-antonio-carluccio-chef-and- restaurateur-396967.html**

- The Federation of Small Businesses has surveyed UK business to see who follows a policy of corporate social responsibility (CSR). Read the report at **www.fsb.org.uk/data/ default.asp?ID=82&loc=policy**

- Go to the government's support site for businesses, called Business Link, and see what they have to say about acting responsibly being good for business. You will find the site at **www.businesslink.gov.uk**

Did you know...

Many small businesses are in business for reasons other than profit. A business may want to provide a service, or exist because the person running it prefers to work for himself or herself.

Aims and objectives

Both **aims** and **objectives** are types of target, so a business needs to distinguish between them. The aim of the business is usually defined as its long-term target. Sometimes these may be impossible to measure (Carluccio's 'excellent service', for example) or so far into the future that they may never be reached (Coca-Cola's aim is to be 'the beverage of choice' all around the world, replacing water, tea and coffee; Heinz's aim for its tomato ketchup is to be 'the world's favourite ketchup, on every table').

These aims may be stated as '**mission statements**' and, although they may not be attainable, give a good idea of what drives the business. The objectives of the business are the shorter-term targets that it hits on the way to its aim. They are like stepping stones on the way and can be further broken down into targets.

Did you know...

Businesses will try to quantify targets where possible. For instance, for customer service they will keep a record of the number of complaints and the speed with which they were resolved. They may also record if, and how often, a customer returns.

SMART targets

Targets are smaller steps, and need to be measurable so that progress can be seen. Businesses usually set themselves what are called SMART targets. These are:

- SPECIFIC – the target should be as definite as possible

- MEASURABLE – it should be quantifiable, so often involves figures or percentages

- ATTAINABLE – it should be a target that it is possible to reach

- RELEVANT – it should form a logical part of the overall strategy of the business

- TIME-RELATED – there should be a set time for the achievement of the target.

Types

Business objectives can, broadly speaking, be put into three categories:

- being satisfied

- wanting to reach a maximum

- wanting to reach a minimum.

For small businesses, in particular, the idea of 'being satisfied' as a target is a very common one. Many small-business owners are happy working for themselves, providing a certain level of service, or making a certain level of income. For them the idea of doing more, or of expanding, just means extra work. They are happy with what they have. Often one of the main objectives of a small business is to maintain its independence.

Maximising

The most commonly quoted 'maximum' that a business might want to reach is profit. This is the difference between costs and revenues. This is not, however, the only area that a business might wish to maximise. It could want to maximise:

- *Productivity* – to look for the maximum efficiency of its workers and machines and combinations of them;

- *Manpower* – to employ the best possible people, at the best rates;

- *Innovation* – to be the first to market, always at the cutting edge of technology;

- *Management expertise* – to make sure it has the most efficient and loyal managers with the highest levels of knowledge and training;

- *Marketing* – to have the biggest slice or most control over the market in which it operates;

- *Resources* – to use the most reliable sources and achieve the best value for money;

- ***Social responsibility*** – to have the best reputation of the business in the community.

Of course, any or all of these are likely to have the effect of making the business more efficient, or its products more desirable, and will therefore contribute to greater profitability.

Minimising

Minimising objectives are those where a business wants to make the least, rather than the most, of something. A firm might, for example, want to minimise **labour turnover** due to the expense of appointing and training new workers. They may want to have as small an impact on the environment as possible. Usually these can be turned into 'maximising' aims – such as labour efficiency or social responsibility.

Did you know...?

Social enterprises are likely to have targets that are not related to profit. They may, for example, want to bring the maximum benefit to a community, or to help as many people as possible. They are still, therefore, likely to have efficiency targets.

Summary

- Businesses set themselves targets
- Aims are long-term targets
- Objectives are shorter-term targets, steps to reaching aims
- Targets should be SMART
- Targets are often set to maximise something
- Sometimes a business aims to make the 'least' of a negative target

Core knowledge

Aims and objectives may both be thought of as types of targets. Businesses need to measure whether or not they are succeeding in what they are doing, so need to set targets. Objectives are not just 'set' however. They need to be carefully thought out as the effort to achieve objectives is a key part of running a business. Businesses must decide which objectives are more important in terms of which will contribute most to the future of the business. The success of a business may be judged by how clear and appropriate its objectives are, and how successful it is in reaching them.

Businesses therefore need ways by which they can measure progress. Sometimes this is easy, as figures are involved. Sometimes it is much harder. How do you know, for example, that customer satisfaction has improved? One way is to turn these into SMART targets. Most small businesses will start with the main aim of surviving, only then can they look to the future. The business would want to break even (meaning that they earn in revenue at least as much as they have spent) or make a small profit. Many small enterprises do not want to expand once they have reached this point. Owners and other stakeholders (who are discussed in the following chapter) need to know what they are aiming for, and whether they are reaching it. The most common targets are

- *Profit* – usually measured as a percentage of turnover;
- *Growth* – for those businesses that want to expand either in their current market or into new markets;
- *Market share* – the bigger the share of the market owned by a business, the more power they have in that market;
- *Customer satisfaction* – do customers come back a second time, are complaints kept to a minimum, is feedback from customers good?

And more

One area in which there has been growth in the past few years is that of corporate social responsibility. This (often shortened to CSR) has become a central part of the aims of many businesses. Businesses work in communities, they need supplies of labour or raw materials, they need to transport finished goods. CSR is all about carrying out these activities with as little negative impact as possible. Media interest in businesses making a profit on the back of child labour, or poorly paid and overworked third-world workers, led to a response by consumers. Businesses that damaged the communities in which they worked – environmentally or socially – or who underpaid suppliers, lost customers. In some cases, they also lost the support of their own investors. Many businesses have decided that it is better to act **ethically** than to maximise profit on the back of anti-social practice. They have therefore written into their corporate aims the idea of at least giving back to communities as much as they take out, treating workers fairly and being careful of their use of resources. There are a number of key areas that these policies cover:

- *Fairtrade* – making sure that suppliers receive a fair price for their crops;
- *Sustainability* – making sure that the environment is not harmed – recycling, reusing and replacing, and using alternative energy sources where possible;
- *Food miles* – making the distance between food producer and shop as small as possible;
- *Carbon footprint* – this is the measure of the impact of an activity on the environment; businesses can offset this through 'green' policies;
- *Ethical investment* – investors may only want to invest in those businesses where they are assured that the business has a high standard of ethics.

Energy use leaves a carbon footprint

Have a go

Group activity

Look at the possible 'maximising' targets for businesses. Name a business that you think is aiming for each target. What can you say about the different kinds of business?

Discussion

Visit the websites of some top businesses and make a list of their mission statements. What similarities are there between them? Can you spot any current trends from this? Discuss what you think they have in common and what you think makes them different.

Web-based activity

Visit:
www.guardian.co.uk/environment/2007/may/17/rupertmurdoch.broadcasting
and read what Rupert Murdoch intends to do with the Sky media and publishing empire. Explain why you think he has set this target.

Quickfire questions

1 What is a business 'aim'?
2 What is a business 'objective'?
3 What is a 'mission statement'?
4 What does SMART stand for?
5 Outline why a business should always have SMART targets.
6 Name the three broad types of business objective.
7 List three things that a business might aim to maximise.
8 List three things that a business might aim to minimise.
9 List one objective of a small business that may not be appropriate for a larger business.
10 What is meant by 'social responsibility'?

Hit the spot

> Choose three businesses. Find out as much as you can about each business. Which do you think is the most successful? By what measure?

>> Measure your own carbon footprint at **www.carbonfootprint.com** and then set your own aims and objectives so that you have your own environmental responsibility programme.

>>> Explain why businesses feel that it is necessary to set themselves targets. Which target do you think is the most important for a small business? Give reasons for your answer.

Cracking the code

Aim **Long-term target.**

Ethical **Doing what is morally the right thing to do.**

Labour turnover **The number of people leaving and being replaced in a time period.**

Mission statement **A 'what we do and how we do it' long-term aim of a business.**

Objective **Shorter-term target, on the way to reaching an aim.**

Social responsibility **(often called corporate social responsibility or CSR) Environmental or social aims usually written into a CSR policy.**

STARTING A BUSINESS

Chapter 6
Stakeholders

Coffee Nation

The founders of Coffee Nation were dissatisfied by the inconsistent quality of coffee found in the UK. They recognised that the high street coffee shops cropping up in towns around the country had created a taste for premium quality coffee amongst the consumer.

In 1999, Coffee Nation's founders set to work developing a self-service coffee machine concept that combined barista coffee, using fresh, quality ingredients, with the consistency, availability and ease of vending. This would eliminate the possibility for human error and allow retail, travel and leisure outlets to offer their customers great-tasting coffee.

Coffee Nation now has 60 employees. There are currently 650 sites where Coffee Nation drinks are sold. Each machine is connected to the internet and monitored by a dedicated helpline, so when machine faults are recorded, service engineers are on site within a matter of hours, whatever the time of day, to fix the problem.

Coffee Nation has a **policy** of fair trade and sources selected beans for its blend from Rainforest Alliance certified farms. This means the business will always pay a fair price for coffee beans and not use its buying strength to force down the price it has to pay, as well as supporting coffee farmers to preserve their natural eco-systems in their local area.

Persuading people to pay more to receive gourmet coffee has been cracked by Starbucks. Once people get used to drinking quality coffee, they are willing to return time and time again. Coffee Nation believes enough people will do this, even if this means paying a higher price for a much better quality product.

Coffee Nation's main challenge was to convince customers that good coffee can be obtained from a machine. Although some consumers are still resistant, Coffee Nation is successfully re-inventing its brand identity to engage consumers with the message that its coffee is made using fresh milk and real beans.

High-quality coffee 24 hours a day

@ Visit the Coffee Nation website at:
www.coffeenation.com

Stakeholder

A **stakeholder** is an individual or group of people that have an interest in a business. Stakeholders want the business to do well, because if it does, they benefit. Similarly, if the business fails, then stakeholders suffer in some way.

The main stakeholders are usually thought to be:

Employees

These are the people who work for a business in return for a wage or a salary. Quite often employees work for more than just money. A job might bring status and a sense of purpose to someone. If a business were to close, its employees would lose their incomes and have to look elsewhere for their livelihood. On the other hand, a successful business can afford to pay higher wages to its employees. A successful business could also afford to train employees to a higher standard. So, workers have an interest, or stake, in their employer doing well. This is particularly true when there is **unemployment** in the country. Someone who loses his or her job might find it very difficult to get another one.

Shareholders

A shareholder is someone who has bought a small part of a business. The shareholder will receive a share certificate for the money paid. In return, the shareholder will get a share of the profits that the business makes. This payment is usually called a **dividend**. A business that is doing well will be able to afford to pay a high dividend to its shareholders. If the business is making a loss, there will be no shareholders' dividend.

Customers

A successful business might be able to reduce the prices it charges customers. It will also be able to afford to buy better standard materials, or pay for better training for its employees. These would help to improve the quality of the products that customers buy. A failing business might try to cut corners with its product, reducing its quality.

An employee is a stakeholder

Once a business has closed down, of course, there will be less choice for customers.

Suppliers

When a business buys materials from a supplier it will usually receive credit. This means the business does not have to pay its bill straightaway. This allows the business time to make the money to pay the supplier. If the business is not successful, it might not be able to pay the supplier. Therefore, suppliers want the business to do well so they will get their bills paid! Coffee Nation takes its responsibility further than this. The business believes that it has a responsibility to pay a fair price for the coffee it uses. The business could buy coffee cheaper from other suppliers, but will only deal with responsible suppliers who ensure the growers receive a good income.

Creditors

Suppliers are a type of **creditor**, as the business owes them money. There are other types however. If a business has borrowed money from a bank, and most businesses do, the bank is a creditor.

The local community

This is a very general term that tends to cover the people within the area the business operates. Businesses have to pay taxes that are called rates to local councils. This money is used to provide services, such as street lighting and road maintenance in the area. If a business fails, the local council will no longer receive the rates from this business. There will be less money available for the council to spend on improving the **local community**.

Many businesses employ people who live in the area they operate. Wages paid to these employees will often be spent in local shops. This creates even more money for the local community.

Internal and external stakeholders

The different types of stakeholders can be seen as being internal or external Internal stakeholders are those directly connected with the business. These include employees and shareholders.

External stakeholders have an interest in the business, but are not actually part of the organisation. These would include suppliers, customers and the local community.

Everyone in the local area is a stakeholder

Did you know...

Many businesses now like to state publicly who their stakeholders are. Business web pages will often have details of stakeholders. It's almost compulsory, it seems!

Summary

- Stakeholders are people who are affected by a business's success
- Stakeholders who are part of the business are said to be internal stakeholders
- Businesses have different views about which stakeholders are more important
- In the past, many businesses were only really been concerned about their owners, the shareholders

Core knowledge

When a business takes off, the person who starts it is probably going to be the person who also runs, or manages, it. The entrepreneur has put his or her money and time into the venture and obviously wants the business to do well. In most cases, 'doing well' means making a healthy profit.

Being successful, however, will not just depend on the owner and manager. There are other people that the business should not forget. Customers are important. Without customers, the business will not be able to sell its product or service and will soon be forced to close. A business that treats its customers badly will find it hard to keep them. Selling poor quality or even dangerous products will put customers off. They will probably go elsewhere next time. A plumber who regularly turned up late, for example, would get a poor reputation and find it harder to get business in the future.

Employees are another group the business should consider. In many businesses the employees are the people the customer deals with. If employees are not seen as being very important they will be unhappy working for the business. They will come across as not bothered, which will reflect badly on the business. Respecting employees is not just about paying them good wages. As with all humans, employees want to feel they belong and are doing a worthwhile job.

And more

Increasingly these days, businesses are taking a wider view of their stakeholders.

People are becoming more concerned about global warming and other environmental issues. Businesses need to be seen to be caring about these issues too, otherwise they could lose valuable customers. Many businesses have written statements or policies on what they will do to reduce their impact on the environment. So, the environment can also be seen as a stakeholder.

At one time, businesses didn't really think they had a commitment to the local community in which they operated. They provided jobs to local people and paid local taxes, and many thought that was all they needed to do.

Some people would argue that businesses are not genuinely concerned about issues such as the local community and environmental harm. Being environmentally friendly and caring for the local community costs money. If a business is not to lose out, then the extra money it receives from attracting additional customers with its caring image should be greater than the money it spends getting the caring image.

Business has an impact on the environment

Have a go!

Group activity

Working in a group, consider a business that believes that its most important stakeholders are:

● its employees, and

● the local community.

Describe what the business might do to look after these stakeholders. Are your suggestions free, or will they cost the business money? What will be the benefits to the business, if any?

Now, consider how the actions that you have described in your previous answer could affect these stakeholders:

● the owners of the business, and

● customers.

Discussion

These days, many businesses like to be seen to be supporting local charities. This was unusual 20 years ago. Does this mean that businesses are becoming more generous?

Web-based activity

Go to the Coffee Nation web pages at **www.coffeenation.com**. Say which of the business's stakeholders are mentioned on the pages. Write a report stating what Coffee Nation is doing to help its stakeholders.

Quickfire questions

1 What is a stakeholder?
2 How are Coffee Nation's vending machines different from other vending machines?
3 List three of Coffee Nation's stakeholders.
4 How does Coffee Nation look after its customers?
5 What is a creditor?
6 Is an employee an internal or external stakeholder?
7 What is meant by fairtrade?
8 How might buying fairtrade coffee actually help Coffee Nation?
9 List three ways consumers would be affected if Coffee Nation were to go out of business.
10 Give three ways the local community might be affected when a business closes.

Hit the spot

> Give two reasons why a business might give money to a local school.

>> Explain how the quality of a product or service can depend on how much interest the business takes in its employees

>>> Discuss whether shareholders are the more important than other stakeholders.

Cracking the code

Creditor A person or organisation that is owed money by a business. A bank that lends money becomes a creditor of the business.

Dividend The share of the profit a shareholder receives.

Local community The people and institutions that are associated with an area. There is often a sense of belonging.

Policy Rules or a set of guidelines used by a business.

Stakeholder Someone who has an interest in the success of a business.

Unemployment Those people who are seeking work, but unable to find suitable jobs are classed as unemployed. The government counts how many people are claiming job seekers' allowances to calculate the level of unemployment.

Chapter 7
Planning an enterprise

IN THE NEWS

Bigger Feet

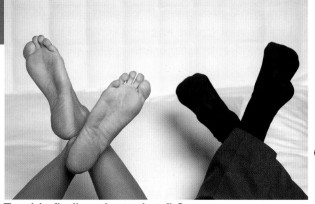

Trouble finding shoes that fit?

While many of his friends were concerned about music and the latest fashions, Oliver Bridge found himself in front of BBC and CNN cameras. Oliver had just started a new business and the media were interested. What attracted them was that Oliver was a 15-year-old successful businessman. Oliver's success was no accident. The planning of his enterprise had been thought through carefully. He had taken advice and produced a detailed **business plan**.

Oliver understood that the media would be interested in his story and gaining **publicity** was an important part of his plan. After appearing on television, sales greatly improved.

Oliver's business, Bigger Feet, is an online shoe retailer for people who need much larger than average shoes. The business came about from Oliver's own frustration in trying to buy big enough shoes for his large feet. His complaints led to his mother suggesting that he started up his own business. The idea grew on him and he put together a plan.

After realising that several people at school also required large shoes, Bridge undertook some **market research**. He found that about a million people in the UK have large feet. Bigger Feet produce men's shoes from size 12 and ladies' shoes from size 9.

One problem Oliver did have was getting banks to lend him money. People under 18 cannot be sued for not repaying a loan. So banks require someone older to agree to pay if the young person defaults. Such a person is called a **guarantor**.

Oliver planned to do all the work, or to use willing family members to help. This way there was no need to employ staff, with the problems that can come with them. Oliver reasoned that if the business did take off, then he could hire any staff that he needed. Oliver's plan was to keep costs down as much as possible. His family house was used to provide a small office and storage space for the shoes. There was no need for expensive shops and staff.

Oliver said, 'A website allows you to put something across very professionally at a very low cost. Our website probably rivals a medium-sized business, when in fact we're working from a tiny office.' Oliver also found that when he goes on holiday, the internet gives him the flexibility to continue his business without interruption.

Oliver's research took him to trade shows in Europe to find out more about the market. He also managed to negotiate a deal with Leicestershire wholesaler, UK Distributors, to buy just the shoes he needed. This way he rarely has more than 30 to 40 pairs of shoes in his possession. Not buying in bulk meant that Bigger Shoes was not a credit risk to the wholesaler.

The business plan

Having a good business idea is not enough to make an entrepreneur successful. What needs to be done is to put the idea into practice. Before this can happen, the entrepreneur needs to check that the business will work. What equipment will be needed? What about employees? What is the market like? Where can materials be bought? All this needs careful planning.

One important resource is money. Unless the entrepreneur is fortunate enough to fund the project out of his or her own pocket, the money will have to be borrowed. Before banks give a loan, they will want to know that there is a good chance of the business being successful. Banks want to be reasonably confident that they will get their money back. The usual way to persuade banks to lend money is for the entrepreneur to produce a business plan.

Oliver's success in getting Bigger Feet started lay with his willingness to plan the business. A business plan is a document that outlines how the business will run during the first year or two. It should have enough detail, so any problems can be identified before it is too late. Some of the details are bound to be guesswork. It is impossible to say for sure, for example, whether people will like the product or service. It may be the best thing since sliced bread, or it could fall flat. The entrepreneur can only make a reasonable estimate of sales.

So, what is in a business plan? Business plans can be written in different ways, but most will contain this information each in its own section.

The business idea

What exactly is the product or service? How will it be different from what is already out there?

Management

Banks will want to be confident that the business will be well managed. If they have doubts about the managers they will be unwilling to put money into the venture. Details of the managers would include their business experience. Do the managers have a track record in the key areas of

business, such as finance, marketing and managing employees?

The market

This section will probably include some information about who is likely to buy the product or service. Details on the competition and what makes this product different – its unique selling point.

Selling the product

How will the product be sold? Will it be sold through a retail outlet, like a shop or market stall, or through the internet?

Finances

This is the section that finds out if the idea is likely to be profitable and, if so, how long it will be before a profit is made. A key part of this section will be a forecast cash flow statement. This is a list of the money coming into and out of the business each month over the next year or so. All money needs to be there, including how much the owners of the business will be taking out for their own living expenses.

Summary

● A business plan is a document that tries to find out if an entrepreneur's idea is likely to be successful

● A business plan will usually include information about the product and its market, management, competition and cash flow

● Most investors will want evidence that a business has a good chance of success. They will usually ask to see the business plan.

Core knowledge

A successful entrepreneur is not just someone who can come up with a great business idea. It is also a person who has the self-discipline to work out and check the details of the project before getting started, putting them down on paper. Only by doing this will the entrepreneur know that he or she has a business that can survive. The temptation might be to start up the idea before other entrepreneurs beat you to it and capture the market. Careful planning is important if you want to avoid losing a lot of money.

Very few businesses can be started for next to nothing. Start up costs have to be paid: advertisements even in local papers are expensive, the entrepreneur might need to buy a van, or other vehicle. Even a painter and decorator will spend hundreds, if not thousands, of pounds on ladders, a roof rack to carry the ladders, brushes, a storage place, and so on. Some of this money can be recovered if the business does not work out, but other costs will be lost.

There is also the entrepreneur's time to consider. Entrepreneurs are known for being hard working and prepared to put long hours into their business to help them become successful. If the business fails, then this time has been wasted and probably unrewarded.

Some entrepreneurs might write a business plan as a way of attracting investors or getting a loan from the bank. They may be tempted to exaggerate the details of the plan to make the project look better than it is. A careful investor will study the plan in detail and be worried about any aspect that looks unreasonable.

And more

A business plan is never an exact document. Much of it can best be described as educated guesswork. There will be things the entrepreneur will have a good idea about. The costs of materials can be negotiated from suppliers before the business starts. The entrepreneur will know the costs of advertising and how much an employee will cost. Some figures will be less reliable. An entrepreneur will have to 'speculate' how well the product will sell. Market research will provide some guidance on how well the product will be received by the market. But tastes change and there is no way of determining whether someone else has the same idea as you and is about to start a similar business.

All an entrepreneur can do in his or her business plan is to be honest, realistic and base as much on fact as possible.

Have a go!

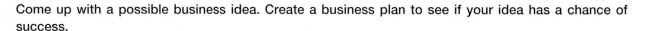

Activity

Come up with a possible business idea. Create a business plan to see if your idea has a chance of success.

Your teacher may even be able to invite a manager from a local bank to come into your school and give you feedback on your plan.

Quickfire questions

1   What is a business plan?
2   Who is likely to be interested in reading a business plan?
3   What are the main sections of a business plan?
4   Why do banks need guarantors?
5   What was different about Oliver Bridge's business?
6   What risks did Oliver take when starting his business?
7   Give two ways Oliver Bridge reduces the risks of failure.
8   Why would it be difficult for a new business to produce a cash flow forecast for the next three years?
9   Why do banks want to know about the previous management experience of an entrepreneur before giving him or her a loan?
10   What is meant by a credit risk?

Hit the spot

> Give three sections that a business plan is likely to have.

>> Explain two things that a bank would look for within a business plan.

>>> Discuss whether a well-written business plan is more important that a good business idea.

Cracking the code

Business plan A detailed document that looks at the workings of a new business. It can be used to find out if the business has a chance of becoming successful.

Guarantor Someone who agrees to pay another person's debt.

Market research Finding out about competition and people's attitude towards a new product or service.

Publicity Using the media to raise people's interest in a product as a form of free advertising. Newspapers writing about a new film, and chat show hosts interviewing the film's stars, are examples of publicity.

IN THE NEWS

Paula Vika Hair Designs

Paula Vika came to the UK from Angola in September 1999 with her six-year-old daughter. She was forced to leave the African state because of the civil war that was raging there. When she arrived in Britain she had nothing to her name. She recognised that if she was going to get on in her new country, she needed to learn how to speak English. So one of the first things she did was to enrol at a local college on an English-speaking course.

Paula was determined that she did not want to receive handouts, so set about finding a job for herself. At this point in her life, her only concern was to survive. She didn't expect to be running her own business within a short time. The **Job Centre** tried to place her in lots of different office jobs, but she couldn't get on because of her poor English. The Job Centre suggested that she should think about starting her own business. She looked into this but found it hard to get a loan from banks. She had no references and she was thought to be too great a risk to them.

She managed to find funding eventually from **The Prince's Trust**. Someone from the Trust interviewed her and offered her help writing a business plan. Paula had always styled friends' hair in Angola. Hairdressing seemed to be the obvious business route for her to take. Paula undertook some market research to see if the business had a chance of surviving. The Prince's Trust gave her a loan and her advisor suggested that she rent a chair at a local salon in Great Yarmouth. The Trust also pointed her in the direction of the **New Entrepreneur Scholarship**, where she could learn basic business skills.

Paula operated her own chair at somebody else's salon for 12 months. Her customers kept coming back asking for Paula to style their hair. She was always busy and she felt that it was now time to expand. Paula found a vacant salon in Norwich. She now employs two staff. One person works four days a week; the other works two. She also trains a young girl who comes in on Saturdays and school holidays.

Paula draws on her Angolan hairdressing experience in her salon. She offers a range of Afro-Portuguese contemporary and traditional styles. She is able to explain the services available to non-English speakers in five languages.

Visit Paula's website at:
www.paulavika.co.uk

What does unlimited liability mean for the entrepreneur?

Running your own business is not without risk. Getting a business off the ground requires money to buy equipment, materials and to pay wages. It can often be some time before the business is bringing in more money than it is costing the entrepreneur. The business will still have to pay its regular bills for items like rent, phones and electricity, even if it has not got many customers. An entrepreneur will often be allowed **credit** by suppliers. This means that when the business owner buys materials, the bill will not have to be paid for a month or two. So, it is quite possible for the business to build up large debts.

If the business idea was not as good as the entrepreneur first thought, the money coming in – the **revenue** – might dry up. Entrepreneurs in this position might find it increasingly difficult to pay their bills. The point may be reached when it is clear the business is never going to recover in the foreseeable future. The entrepreneur might decide at this point that it is no longer worth carrying on.

When this happens there is still the problem of unpaid bills. The debts owed to the business's **creditors** still have to be paid. The owner of the business is liable for the debts that he or she has built up. The owner is said to have unlimited liability. This means that even if the business fails, the owner has to settle the bills. The laws on unlimited liability are very old. They lay down rules on what personal possessions the owner must sell to get the money needed to pay off creditors.

Bankruptcy

If an entrepreneur is not paying his or her bills, creditors might even decide to go to court to have the entrepreneur declared **bankrupt**. This only happens when they feel there is no chance that the business will recover. Creditors are unlikely to get all of their money back if this happens. They know, however, that it will stop things getting worse. Once an entrepreneur is declared bankrupt by court, the business will probably stop trading and any possessions – or **assets** – will be sold.

In some cases, an unsuccessful entrepreneur can even make himself/herself bankrupt. This is known as voluntary bankruptcy.

Someone who has been declared bankrupt will be freed from most of his or her debts. The bankrupt person will be banned from running another business for a number of years, but will then have the opportunity to have a fresh start.

Sole traders and partnerships

One entrepreneur who owns a business is a **sole trader**. When two or more people set up and run a business together it is a **partnership** and they are called business partners. Partnerships have several benefits:

- The partners may have *more funds* to put into the business than a single entrepreneur.
- Partners can give each other *moral support* and discuss ideas and solutions to problems.
- The partners will have a *greater range of skills*.
- The *flexibility* to cover if one partner is on holiday or ill.

Each partner is legally responsible for the debts of the business. Partnerships usually have unlimited liability, so one partner could lose his or her personal property if the other is irresponsible in business.

Summary

- Having a good business idea is no guarantee that the business will be successful
- Most small businesses have unlimited liability, which means the owners are responsible for all the debts they build up
- Unlimited liability means the owner of the business still needs to pay outstanding bills, even if the business closes down
- If a person is declared bankrupt, he or she is no longer responsible for debts

Core knowledge

Some people believe that anyone who runs a business must be rich. This is far from the truth. Everyone who starts a business runs a risk. If the business fails the owner still has to pay off the debts that have built up. If things go wrong, a business idea could be very costly. This is what puts many people off starting their own business.

There are ways an entrepreneur can avoid losing a great deal of money. In fact, a good entrepreneur will not rush into business without trying to reduce the chances of failure and bankruptcy.

Finding out if customers will actually buy the entrepreneur's product rather than that of a competitor is important. This process is known as market research and will be studied in a later chapter.

There are other things can be done to minimise risk. Starting small and expanding when the idea has proved it can work makes sense. This is advice that Paula Vika followed. Rather than opening up her own salon straightaway, Paula rented a chair in another salon. Only when she was sure she had a good chance of success did she look for her own salon.

And more

Having unlimited liability can put people off starting a business. Many will consider the benefits of becoming a limited company very attractive and complete the necessary paperwork to achieve this. The process is discussed in the next chapter.

Another way for an entrepreneur to minimise risk is to lease equipment. Leasing simply means renting, rather than buying outright. The entrepreneur doesn't actually own this equipment but if things do not work out, it can be sent back to the leaser. There won't be any loan repayment to worry about if the business fails. There are other advantages of leasing. The equipment can be exchanged when more up-to-date equipment becomes available. Often this newer equipment will be no more expensive to lease. In addition, the lease contract will probably include

Essential equipment for business may be bought or leased

maintenance and repairing faults. This means the entrepreneur can plan a budget without having to worry about repair or replacement bills.

Keeping the number of employees to a minimum is another strategy. Employees have to be paid even if there is very little business coming in. There are also laws giving redundancy payments to unneeded employees when they have to leave. This will probably mean the owner having to work long hours, but the risks are reduced.

Have a go!

Activity: Bankruptcy

Find out what the laws on bankruptcy are. Produce an information leaflet or poster containing this information. Imagine someone thinking of starting a new business will read the poster/leaflet. Try not to put the person off starting up, but make sure it contains a clear outline of the law.

You will find the information on the internet. **www.insolvency.gov.uk** and **www.insolvencyhelpline.co.uk/bankruptcy** are just two sites.

Quickfire questions

1 What is meant by unlimited liability?
2 Give two ways an entrepreneur might lose money when a business fails.
3 How did Paula Vika create a unique selling point for her business?
4 Why are banks often reluctant to lend money to new businesses?
5 What is voluntary bankruptcy?
6 What is leasing?
7 Outline how leasing works.
8 Explain why creditors may not want to declare a poor payer bankrupt.
9 Why might an entrepreneur still find it difficult to pay bills even if the business is selling many goods?
10 Does bankruptcy mean an entrepreneur has failed?

Hit the spot

> Describe two reasons why a new business might not make as much revenue as the entrepreneur expected it to make.

>> Explain two ways Paula Vika helped reduce the chances of failing in business.

>>> Discuss whether the risks of starting a business are greater than the possible rewards.

Cracking the code

Assets Property or possessions owned by an entrepreneur or a business.

Bankrupt An entrepreneur who is unable to pay his/her bills. Receivers will take control of the business and sell off its assets. Creditors may then receive some of the money the business owes them.

Credit Buying goods or services and paying after they have been received.

Creditor Someone to whom a business owes money.

Job Centre A government-funded organisation that tries to find suitable work for job seekers.

New Entrepreneur Scholarship An organisation that helps people from disadvantaged backgrounds and areas to get started in business.

The Prince's Trust A charity started by the Prince of Wales that provides funding and support to unemployed young people who want to start their own businesses.

Revenue The money coming in from the sale of goods. This is sometimes called turnover.

Sole trader A business organisation owned and managed by a single person.

Partnership A business owned and run by two or more people.

IN THE NEWS

Innocent Smoothies

A spectacular success

Three young university friends started Innocent in 1999. None of them had any experience in drink manufacturing, nor did they have any financial backing. Despite these things Innocent's success has been spectacular.

Innocent's three founders, Richard Reed, Adam Balon and Jon Wright, had wanted to run a business together since their days at university. When they graduated they went their separate ways into jobs in business. But they still held on to their dream and it was always the main topic of conversation whenever they met.

The idea for Innocent Drinks came from looking at their own hectic urban lifestyles. As busy professionals they were working long hours, not finding the time to visit the gym and relying on fast food. After considering many possible products, the entrepreneurs came up with the idea of selling fruit smoothies.

They knew that people were becoming more health conscious, but they were not sure that people would be prepared to pay £2 for a 250ml drink. To find out if the idea would work, in 1999 they took their drinks to a jazz festival. By their stall they had a sign that asked the question: Do you think we should give up our jobs to make smoothies? Customers were asked to place their empty cups in one of two bins: Yes or No. There were far more cups in the Yes bin, so they took the plunge and resigned from their jobs.

As they had absolutely no experience in fruit or the drinks market, going from idea to reality obviously involved doing some research. 'We went away and just kept buying fruit and making up recipes that we thought tasted good,' recalls Reed. 'Then, once we had these drinks that we liked and our friends liked, we just needed to know if other people would go for it.'

However, the move to self-employment wasn't, well, a smooth one. One of the key obstacles was securing finance. Not only did they have a relatively expensive product with a short shelf life and no experience in the sector, it seemed they were in the wrong place at the wrong time. The three entrepreneurs were unable to pay themselves salaries at first. Times were very tight: their overdraft was getting bigger and bigger and they ended up having to pay their bills using their credit cards.

In the end, Innocent secured the funding it needed from a **business angel** but there were still obstacles to overcome. As a limited company, the investor knew that at worst, he would only lose as much

The moment of choice

money as he had invested into Innocent. He would not have to sell his personal possessions to pay any outstanding debts if Innocent failed.

Five years on and 10 million sales later, Innocent drinks are in shops across the country and word is spreading. But despite the overwhelming growth, until last summer Innocent hadn't spent a penny on advertising.

Innocent also gives away drinks to the homeless, plants trees, encourages recycling and donates to the third world, while its entire staff are treated to a snow boarding trip every year, awarded £2000 for the birth of each child and invited to apply for a £1000 scholarship to achieve something they've always wanted to do. 'Like recording a single or going surfing,' explains Reid.

The three founders gave up their jobs in 1999 and Innocent became a limited company in June 2000.

 Check out Innocent's website at:
www.innocentdrinks.co.uk

Did you know...

The multinational Virgin Group is a private limited company. Its main owner, Richard Branson, turned the business into a public limited company is 1984. However, Branson was so dissatisfied with public investors that he brought Virgin back to a private limited company two years later.

Limiting liability

A small business will always remain small unless the owner can raise capital to expand. A retailer, for example, might expand by buying or renting new shops. Alternatively, the retailer could buy out another business and increase in size this way. However it is done, it will need money. Probably this will be more money than the original business is able to provide from its trading.

Entrepreneurs will try to persuade others to put in **capital**, in return for a share of any future profits the business might make. These **shareholders** will often have very little to do with the running of the business. They have to trust that the managers are controlling things in a way that keeps their investment safe and gives them a decent dividend. Shareholders do not want to find that the company is losing money or, worse still, they are liable for debts of the company. After all, it is not because of them that the business is going under.

Clearly, shareholders would be reluctant to lend money if the risks are too high. They would not want to lose their house and car because managers were not running the business properly. For this reason, a law was passed many years ago that restricted just how much a shareholder could lose. If a business is found to be operating in a sound way, the shareholders could be granted limited liability status. This means that the most the owners of the business, the shareholders, could lose is the money they used to buy their shares. They will not be called upon to sell their personal possessions to pay the business's debts.

Creating a private limited company

A business goes through a process called **incorporation** in order to gain limited liability status. This involves giving information to the authorities, proving the business is operating properly and is secure. A business can be identified as a limited company by the abbreviation Ltd after its name. Another type of limited company is a public limited company, plc, which will be looked at in another book.

A private limited company must show that it has limited liability. This is usually done by putting Ltd after its name, which is an abbreviation for limited. This warns suppliers that they might not receive all of their money if the business fails. There are restrictions on who can buy shares in the company. The shares cannot be sold to the general public. It is often just immediate family who have shares, or people who work in the business.

A sign of limited liability

Summary

- The owners of a business with unlimited liability are responsible for all of its debts. The owners may be required to sell their own personal possessions to pay off **creditors**.
- If the business goes through the process of incorporation it can be granted limited liability status. This means the owners, the shareholders, can only lose the money they put into the business. They are not required to sell their personal possessions to pay the company's debts if the business fails.
- Private limited companies cannot sell shares to the general public

Core knowledge

If somebody asked you to put money into his or her business, you would expect to have a say in how the business was being run – it is your money you are investing, after all! You may, however, have neither the time nor the expertise to monitor the business closely. You have to trust the entrepreneur is running the business properly, so your money is safe.

So what happens if the business does not do well? You took a risk when you lent the money, so you should be prepared to accept you might lose some, or all of it. What you wouldn't want is to find that not only have you lost all the money you put into the business, but you are also expected to sell off your house to pay the business's debts. This is what could happen with a business with unlimited liability. The owners, which include you, would have to sell their personal possessions to pay the creditors.

If you put money into a limited business, however, you would only lose up to the value of your investment. There would be no need to sell your own personal assets to settle the debts of the business. Limited liability was introduced to protect investors from losing their own property, even though they were not responsible for the failure of the business.

Limited companies will have one or more directors who look after the shareholders' interests.

And more

It is for this reason that many businesses choose to become 'incorporated', particularly if they are expanding. It is not a particularly difficult or an expensive process, but it does make it easier for a business to attract investors. People will be more inclined to put money into a business if they know the size of the risk, or their liability, that they are taking.

Incorporation means that a business is given a separate legal status from its owners. A limited business can be sued in its own right, rather than the owner taken to court, if something goes wrong. The business can also sue others, such as someone who owes it money, but is reluctant to pay. Property can also be held in the business's name.

To become a limited business, two documents have to be written. These are the Memorandum of Association and the Articles of Association. The first document, the Memorandum, just describes the business, giving basic details: its address, names of shareholders, and so on. The Articles document contains more information. It includes how decisions will be made in the business: details about the regular meeting with shareholders – the AGM – and how profits will be shared.

Unlike an unlimited business that can keep its financial affairs to itself, a limited company must send its accounts to Companies House. These can then be seen by anyone who is interested, including competitors. It is for this reason that some unlimited businesses prefer to remain unlimited.

Have a go!

Web-based activities   @

Go on the internet and find local businesses that have limited liability. Mark on a map of the area in which you live where these businesses are located.

Use the internet to research more about Innocent Smoothies. Produce an information sheet about the company's involvement in good causes. The sheet should be written for young readers and contain suitable illustrations.

Quickfire questions

1   What is a creditor?
2   What does the abbreviation Ltd stand for?
3   What is a shareholder?
4   Why would investors be more willing to put money into a limited company?
5   What do we mean by a business angel?
6   How did the three men who started Innocent find out whether the idea of selling smoothies was likely to succeed?
7   What is the role of a director?
8   Why might a business find it difficult to expand without limited liability status?
9   Why might a business not want its financial accounts to be available to the general public?
10 Why might a member of the public be reluctant to buy shares in a private limited company?

Hit the spot

> Describe two benefits the owners of Innocent Ltd had when they gained limited liability status.

>> Explain why a supplier would want to know if a business that had placed an order was a limited company.

>> Discuss: If limited liability is such a good thing, why do not all businesses become limited companies?

Cracking the code

Business angel A private investor who is willing to put money into a new business, where a bank would probably not take the risk.

Capital The value of the funds put into a business. Capital is what is used to buy the equipment the business needs to operate.

Creditor Someone to whom a business owes money. This could be a supplier or even an employee who is paid a week or month in arrears.

Shareholder A person who owns a share of a business.

Chapter 10
Business location decisions

Welsh entrepreneurs, brothers Graham and Ian Pugh and Carl Hitchings, planned to open a garden centre and were looking for a suitable location. Pugh was already an established name in the garden centre business. The brothers' grandfather opened a small nursery in Rhiwbina, Cardiff in the 1930s. Their father Colin established a garden centre at Cardiff in 1968 followed by a nursery and growing centre at Caerphilly. So the entrepreneurs knew the importance of location when it came to deciding where to site their enterprise.

The site of old, but rundown, nurseries at Wenvoe on the main gateway to the Vale of Glamorgan road was eventually chosen. There was enough space for future expansion on the 7-acre site. The A4050 road which bordered the site is one of the busiest roads in Wales. The Wenvoe location was attractive, being on the main route to and from Barry, the Vale and Cardiff Airport. It was conveniently placed for attracting **passing trade**, and just a few minutes' drive from Cardiff.

Despite the site having housed a nursery before, much had to be done to update it to attract customers.

Their new company, Style Gardens, started a £1 million transformation of the site. This involved clearing the land, erecting new buildings and extensive landscaping works, including a new frontage on to the Port Road. It was no good having a good location if the garden centre did not look attractive and inviting to customers.

The company now employs 25 full- and part-time staff – most of whom were taken on in the past two years to keep pace with expansion. It plans to double its workforce and the whole site's current £3.5 million turnover within five years.

 Take a look at the Style Gardens website at:
www.stylegardens.co.uk

Locating a business

One of the most important decisions that an entrepreneur has to make is where his or her business is to be based. Many entrepreneurs will choose to run their businesses from their own homes, in order to keep costs down. Others might recognise that to get the best chances of success, it may be necessary to move somewhere else. This might even mean moving to a different part of the country, or abroad.

The growth of internet shopping has reduced the importance of location for many businesses. The internet has allowed even the smallest business to access a global market. Items can be bought by customers using the internet and then delivered to them using a courier or the postal service. Of course, the internet would not be suitable if a personal service, such as hairdressing or plumbing, was being offered. It would also be difficult if the products being sold were very fragile or perishable.

Running a business at home

There are several factors that a new business might need to take into account when the owner decides where to locate his or her business.

The owners of Style Gardens Limited took care to ensure that they chose the right location for their new business venture. South Wales was somewhere they were familiar with and family members had been successful in setting up similar businesses in the area. The Wenvoe site was big enough to allow for future expansion without moving to larger **premises**. Wenvoe was also close to the large population of Cardiff.

The market

Some businesses have to be located close to their markets. This could be because the product they sell costs a lot to transport. Having a nearby market is important to service providers, such as shops. Customers would not travel vast distances just to go to one particular supermarket, if there were others much closer. Also, a plumber who lived 30 miles from his main market would spend a long time each day travelling.

Road system

A good road system, or infrastructure, allows a business to be located further afield. Time can be saved if a business is located close to a major road or a motorway. Goods can be transported more quickly and customers can reach the business without a difficult journey. It is for this reason that many industrial estates and shopping malls are located near to good road systems.

Available employees

Businesses need employees, so there needs to be suitable people living locally. If the business needs employees with particular skills, local people should have these skills, or they will need to be trained. If low-skilled workers are needed, a suitable number should live within easy reach of the business. Low-skilled workers are less likely to own a car, so they will need a place of work on a bus route, or within walking distance.

Competition

Having a lot of similar businesses in an area often seems a bad thing for a business. Competition tends to bring prices down as one business tries to attract customers from another. Even so, an entrepreneur might still want to move into a location where there are several other similar businesses. The product or service being offered must be popular to attract several businesses. It is possible that one more business could survive in the market.

Many businesses rely on a good road system

Summary

- The location of a business is important and can make the difference between success and failure
- There are many things that businesses need to take into account to work out which is the best location. These include: how close customers live, how easy it is to get goods in and out, the level of competition in the area and whether suitable employees can be obtained.
- The internet has transformed where businesses are located. Any business can produce a web page that can be used to attract customers and gain orders. Buying goods through the internet is becoming increasingly popular.
- For some entrepreneurs it is more important to operate close to where they live than move to where the business might be more profitable

Core knowledge

Many new businesses will operate close to where the entrepreneur lives. The business may actually be based in the owner's house. A builder may, for example, use a room in his or her own house as an office, and possibly own a yard where the building materials are stored. Work may be undertaken within, let's say, a 20-mile radius of one of these places. Any more and too much time could be spent travelling to the site each day. The range in which our builder can operate will depend on how good the roads are in the area. A motorway system might make it realistic to travel much further to a job.

If there were a lot of competition for builders in a particular area, a new builder might find it more profitable to move to a new town where there is less competition. Too many competitors means the business will have to look harder for work and accept a lower price for the job. Having a **USP** (a unique selling point) might help to attract customers.

If the product is expensive to buy with a target market of wealthy consumers, such as the expensive coffee vending machines produced by Coffee Nation (in Chapter 6), it will need to be placed in a suitable location. It would be no good having an expensive coffee vending machine at a day centre for the unemployed.

And more

Some businesses are more mobile than others. By that we mean they find it easier to move to and operate in other locations. If a business is selling a product that can be delivered by post or courier, then the actual location of the factory or storage facility is not that important. Orders can be parcelled and sent off from a nearby post office each day, or collected by a courier service. Such a business will probably choose to be located where the costs are cheapest.

Service providers, on the other hand, need to be close to the market. It would be difficult to operate a hairdressing salon, for example, in an industrial estate on the edge of a town. It will need to be in the high street where it would be seen by potential customers. Few people would like to travel a long way to have their hair cut.

There is a theory that businesses will tend to be located where they can make the most profit. Not everyone believes that is true though. Many entrepreneurs would not be prepared, for instance, to move to the other side of the country. They might prefer to remain close to where they were brought up, even if this means that their costs are higher and there is more competition. Also, established businesses cannot easily uproot and go somewhere else that would be more profitable. This is sometimes called **industrial inertia**.

Have a go!

Group activity

If possible visit an industrial estate. If a visit is difficult then a virtual visit can take place by going to a website, such as **www.manor-industrial-estate.co.uk** or **www.youngsindustrialestate.co.uk**

Study the industrial estate and produce a report identifying:

- The type of businesses located there;
- Where the likely markets for the products are;
- What the communication systems are like – such as roads, motorways, railway stations and airports.

Find a map on the internet of the area in which Style Gardens is located. The postcode is CF5 6AD. On this map clearly mark the reasons that makes the location suitable for a garden centre.

Quickfire questions

1 What is a garden centre?
2 What is an industrial estate?
3 What is meant by a market?
4 What is a courier?
5 Why do many entrepreneurs prefer to run their businesses from their own homes?
6 Explain why prices tend to be cheaper when there are several businesses in an area selling the same good or service.
7 How does the closeness of Cardiff help Style Gardens?
8 Why are some people still reluctant to buy goods on the internet?
9 Describe how businesses might benefit from being close to an airport.
10 Explain why many industrial estates are found on the outskirts of towns, rather than the centre of them.

Hit the spot

⟩ Give two reasons why a business might want to set up in an area with many competitors.

⟩⟩ Explain how a good motorway system can make it cheaper for a business to operate.

⟩⟩⟩ Discuss whether it is a good idea to locate a business in an area where there is high unemployment.

Cracking the code

Industrial inertia A term used when a business remains in a location when the reasons why it started there no longer exist.

Passing trade Custom that comes from people who happen to notice the business when they are in the area.

Premises The buildings and land belonging to a business.

USP Unique Selling Point, the things that make one business stand out from its competitors.

MARKETING

IN THE NEWS

V2Go

Entrepreneurs Stephen Marsden and James Whittaker spotted a gap in the market when they tried to find a vegetarian or vegan fast-food outlet in their local town centre. Surrounded by burger bars, meat pizzas and fried chicken outlets, they decided that there was a place for a vegetarian-based outlet. They tried looking for similar outlets, but their research revealed that the competition was not particularly strong and, in some cases, there was no competition at all. For instance, in the Trafford Centre in Manchester, there were no vegetarian options. This, then, was a good place to put the first of what they hoped would be many branches. They contacted the Vegetarian Society, which was happy to back the project.

V2Go was established as the first real vegetarian fast-food operation to open in a shopping centre in the UK. Whittaker is quoted as saying: 'We were acutely aware of the lack of choice available to veggie consumers and for those seeking a healthier meal option. Although most fast-food outlets have a vegetarian option the choice is somewhat limited. We want to provide delicious and wholesome meals and snacks which as well as being vegetarian are healthy. We believe we've now got a product range which will appeal to most tastes. We will also be introducing low fat symbols for the calorie aware consumer.' After securing the success of the first branch, they looked at expanding. 'Our ultimate aim,' he said, 'is to have a V2Go in every city of the UK.' Market research has also shown that the business has to cater for a range of tastes. Research has shown that V2Go has broad appeal with non-vegetarians as well as veggie customers. In an interview in the *Manchester Evening News*, James said: 'Many of our customers are vegetarian though we know from research up to 40 per cent are what we call "fair weather veggies" who succumb to the odd bacon sandwich now and then but, for whatever reason, are fussy about eating meat and enjoy soya or Quorn-based foods. Up to 80 per cent of our customers are women who are both calorie and health conscious and love the fact they can enjoy fast food without high fat content.' V2Go has now expanded, become a private limited company, and gone international with an outlet in Belfast.

Source: Trafford Centre Publicity Material;
Manchester Evening News

V2Go set up its first branch at Manchester's Trafford Centre

@ The Vegetarian Society can be found at **www.vegsoc.org**. What help do you think organisations such as this can give to particular businesses?
Read the article, published in *The Independent* newspaper, at **www.independent.co.uk/ life-style/food-and-drink/ features/fast-food-neednt-be-junk-food-523835.html**. If you were setting up a food business, what information from this would be useful to you?

Market research

Purpose

The purpose of market research is to find out if a product, or idea, is viable in a market. It is important that the business does not confuse promotion with research. Research requires feedback – in other words, there must be a response in terms of data collected. Handing out flyers or putting up posters is promotion, not market research. Both sides of a market need researching.

- *Looking at demand*: if there is high demand for a good or service, it is likely that there are already many competitors. If research shows good levels of demand, and few competitors, then there is a gap in the market.

- *Looking at supply*: if there are few or no competitors in a market, this could mean that there is a **gap in the market**. Equally, it could mean that there is little demand. It could also mean that the existing businesses are able to stop others from entering the market. Maybe they have all the supply tied up? Or are able to keep customers loyal?

Methods

A small business is limited in the market research it can carry out. It would be pointless (and expensive) for example, to conduct a survey in several cities. To find out about the supply side, the business could use local telephone and business directories to see if competition existed. It could also obtain information from its suppliers (a supplier survey), to find out who else they supplied, and whether any of these were local and likely to be competitors. It could also use internet search engines. If competitors are found, this does not mean that there is no room for the business and a visit to a competitor (as a customer) could give good information about the best way to compete.

To find out if there is any demand is harder. This is because, to be accurate, the research needs to target the right customers. One method could be to telephone a selection of customers (a telephone survey), but there would need to be help in identifying who to telephone. V2Go, for instance, could have contacted members of the Vegetarian Society in Manchester. Other methods could include door-to-door surveys and approaching people on the street or in the shopping centre where they intended to put the business.

New technology

Small businesses have the problem of a limited budget for research, and a difficulty in targeting it effectively. New technology can be a great help in collecting information and keeping down costs. Professional market research information is available on the internet, but is costly to collect and present, so tends to be expensive. The small business can, however, carry out competitor surveys using internet search engines. It can also, for free, visit the websites of competitors to

Primary research: a door-to-door survey

to give feedback – these are extensively used in hotels and other service industries. V2Go could ask, for instance, what else customers would like to see on the menu. By collecting customers' email addresses, the business can carry out email surveys at a fraction of the cost of a postal survey.

Primary research: asking for customer feedback

compare prices, product ranges, special offers, etc. Research will be much more accurate if competitor websites are actually visited. The business can then see exactly what is offered, how it is priced, and judge levels of customer service.

Continuing research

Market research does not stop once the business is established. It helps the business to decide not only what to sell, but also what direction its products should take. What changes or developments would attract customers and/or help the business to compete more effectively? Comment sheets could be issued for customers

Did you know...

There is a difference between data and information. Data is raw facts, figures, statistics, etc. Information is when this data has been turned into a form that can be easily understood.

Summary

- Market research is used to find out if a product will sell
- Market research needs to look at possible demand and at competition
- Research may be either primary (first-hand) or secondary (already published)
- Small businesses can carry out only limited market research
- Some research information, such as directories, is freely available
- New technology can help small businesses to find out about competition
- Research needs to be ongoing, to check if customer demand or competition is changing

Core knowledge

Primary research (also called 'field' research) is data that has not been collected before. It is 'first-hand' information. Primary research may be expensive, but it can be targeted to collect exactly the information needed. Methods include:

- Questionnaires and surveys carried out among customers (or potential customers) and suppliers – there is a whole science to asking both the right question and the right type of question so that responses can be sufficiently easy to analyse, or sufficiently detailed to provide the information being sought.
- Observation – traffic counts, footfall counts, watching customer behaviour.
- Interviews – either face to face or via telephone (face to face is more effective but more expensive).
- Focus groups – small groups of people who are asked in-depth questions to measure their reactions to products; a new advertisement may, for example, be shown first to a focus group so that they can react and comment on it; a new product may be 'tasted and tested' by such a group.
- Electronic information – usually only available to large businesses, such as till roll and loyalty card information (e.g. who bought what, when; who came back; how often?).

Secondary research is research that has been previously published. There are very good sources of secondary data such as government figures and statistics and numerous less reliable sources. The problem with secondary research is that, while some of it may be cheap (it may even be free – government collected statistics are available at **www.statistics.gov.uk**) much of it may not be exactly what the business wants. Often secondary research may only provide background information. For example, secondary data may provide evidence of a demand trend in the direction of healthy living. It would need the focused primary research of a business to be able to see if it could take advantage of such a trend.

Primary research: a survey of passers-by

And more

Research can also look at what potential customers may or may not be prepared to pay for. A **customer analysis** is useful in this respect. A business needs to have a good idea of its 'ideal customer' and may be able to draw up a picture of 'the person' that they want to attract. To whom is the product or service going to appeal? This is called 'customer profiling' and is used to help target customers. Example questions that could help to build a customer profile are:

- what age should the customer be?
- what income group?
- what interests and hobbies should they have?
- what level of education will they have reached?
- where do we expect them to live?
- do they have access to the internet?
- what sort of added value will they respond to?

Often such research is disguised as something else – many competition entries ask for basic information about the entrant while warranties and guarantees will often only be validated by the purchaser filling in details on a guarantee card.

The data collected may be, as with all research, either quantitative or qualitative. Quantitative data consist of figures, graphs, tables and statistics. Usually, the bigger the sample, the more accurate the data, but this tends to make collecting such data expensive. National data is collected by the Office of National Statistics and published on the web. Qualitative data consists of opinions and views. It is unlikely to be statistically accurate but will help to give a complete picture. In some cases, qualitative data (the opinions of local residents, for example) may be more powerful than quantitative.

Have a go

Group activity

Decide on a new product or idea for which you think there will be a demand. Draw up a mini-questionnaire for use in your group. Ask just ten questions. Try out the questionnaire on your group and draw up the answers. You should then, between you, decide two things:

1 Were the questions correctly phrased and did they give useful information?
2 Is there demand for the product that you have suggested?

Discussion

Draw up a map of your local village centre or shopping centre. Shade in the different types of business, e.g. hairdressers, newsagents, estate agents, different types of retail outlet. Decide what you think is missing from the area and would therefore be a good business to set up. Try to convince the other members of your class or group that this is a good business idea for the area by collecting appropriate evidence.

Web-based activity

Reviews of V2Go in Manchester (and other restaurants) can be read at **www.veggieheaven.com/ uk/england/manchester/29/V2GO/**. How helpful do you think such review sites are to the business, to other customers, to competitors? Would such reviews form part of market research?

Quickfire questions

1   What is the purpose of market research?
2   What are the two general areas that should be researched?
3   Suggest three ways for a small business to carry out research.
4   What could a business research using the internet?
5   Name one problem that small businesses have with market research.
6   Give two circumstances where a business should carry out market research.
7   What is meant by 'primary' research?
8   Give three examples of primary research methods.
9   What is meant by 'secondary' research?
10 Give one example of secondary market research information that is free.

Hit the spot

> Describe the two main areas where market research should be carried out.

>> Explain the difference between data and information.

>>> Which do you think is more effective, primary or secondary research? Explain the reasons that you think so.

Cracking the code

Customer analysis Building a picture of the 'ideal' customer from customer behaviour.

Gap in the market Where demand exists in a market but there is no product to fulfil it.

Primary research Field research; research that has not been carried out before.

Questionnaires A list of questions used for primary information.

Secondary research Desk research; research that has been previously carried out or published for another body or purpose.

Chapter 12
Marketing mix elements and price

IN THE NEWS

Despite recent problems in the air industry as a whole, easyJet and Ryanair continue to make a profit on the back of their low price model of air transport. easyJet has been in operation since 1995 and in 2007 made over £200 million profit carrying over 37 million passengers. As consumer demand for low cost travel has increased, both airlines have expanded. Ryanair, which started in 1997, is Europe's biggest low price carrier and the third largest airline in Europe measured by passenger numbers. Measured in terms of international passenger numbers, it is the largest airline in the world.

Costs – and prices – are kept low through quick turn round times for planes and by cutting out 'frills' and 'extras' such as complimentary food and drink. Charges are also made for many of the services that air travellers might take for granted, such as baggage carrying and check-in. The marketing mix for these carriers also includes a different product, in that they fly direct from city to city (or to outlying airports of cities) rather than using a 'hub and spoke' system. Many airlines carry passengers on what may be loss-making short services to their 'hub' airport, from which they then fly to long haul international destinations. For instance, Heathrow is British Airways' major hub, Amsterdam Schiphol is KLM's and Chicago that of United Airlines.

Both carriers have also been quick to see the cost-saving benefits of new technology, such as internet booking, with easyJet being the first to introduce web booking (in 1998) and then to abandon any other form of booking. Ryanair's website was introduced in 2000. By 2001 it was taking 75 per cent of all bookings and, like easyJet's, now takes all bookings. Ryanair has also been at the forefront of promotion offering, in 2007, 1 million seats at 1 penny each.

Other changes have squeezed airlines in general. While the low cost, low price model is still succeeding, but at a much slower pace, other models have gone out of business. Silverjet decided on a very different marketing mix – a luxury product and high price, promoted to business travellers. It established as a business-class only airline in 2004, flying to Dubai and New York, but went out of business in 2008, hit by the fall in demand for air transport that was causing all the airlines to look again at their business model and current marketing mix.

'No frills' air travel has been very successful

@ Airlines don't have to be huge but can be quite small businesses. Do a search to see what you can find out about Danny Reilly, who set up an airline – Nexus – when he was just 18.
easyJet and Ryanair each have their own websites where you can find information about the businesses.

Marketing mix

The **marketing mix** is the term given to the way that an entrepreneur sells a product. It is the mixture, or balance, of the various elements that go into making a sale. A successful business depends on its product being offered to customers at the right price, in the right place and with appropriate and effective promotion methods. This is often called 'the Four Ps' – product, price, promotion and place. Different businesses will adopt different mixes – some leading on product, some (like the low-price airlines above) leading on price. Some will rely heavily on advertising, while some will rely on reputation and 'word-of-mouth'. For others, it is the convenience of distribution that is the most important factor (such as banking services made available 24/7 over the internet). Most small businesses will have a limited budget for their marketing mix, so will have to share it out with care.

Dividing the budget

The marketing budget needs to be divided between the four areas of product, price, promotion and place. The product refers to the goods or services that are produced by the business. If the product is not good enough, no amount of promotion or pricing tactics will lead to its being successful so it is central to the mix. Price has to be set somewhere near the customer's perceived value for the product. A customer will have an idea of what a particular product should cost. While an airline ticket to New York could be acceptably priced at £300 it would be unlikely to get many takers at £3000. There will be a range of prices that the average consumer considers to be fair and reasonable for a product. The customer might be willing, in certain circumstances, to pay £600 or £700 for a seat on the plane, but is likely to be unwilling to pay more. Customers have an idea of **'value for money'** for a good or service. Promotion covers the various ways in which a business brings its product to the notice of the potential customer and tries to persuade them to buy it. This includes advertising, special offers, publicity stunts and other tactics. Place refers to where the product is sold, and how it gets there, so includes distribution.

Price

A key part of the mix is price. It is important to understand the basic relationship between price and demand. In general, the higher the price, the less a product will be demanded. Fewer people can afford it, and for many, it may fall outside their acceptable 'price range' or their idea of value for money. They may also switch to cheaper **substitutes**, if these are available. Lower prices, in general, encourage an increase in demand. Again, however, if a price drops too low, the customer might be suspicious of value. If a jeweller lowered the price of gold rings so that they were really cheap, customers would just assume that they were not gold!

Cost plus pricing

The most common form of pricing is probably cost plus pricing. This is where the business adds up the various costs of producing the good or service – raw materials components, power, labour, etc. and then adds on a percentage for profit (called a mark-up). Businesses will link mark-up to the price that they feel a consumer will be willing to pay for the product. If consumers see a product as having a high value (designer clothes, for example) then a big mark-up can be added to the actual costs of production. Most methods of pricing can be called competitive, as they involve pricing in such a way that a product sells at a similar price to those with which it is in competition.

Some customers will pay a high price for designer clothes

A price can be too low

Did you know...

Some pricing strategies are more promotional. A loss leader, for example, is where a product is priced so low that it does not even cover its costs. It is often a staple product (such as bread or milk) priced to attract customers into the shop so that they spend money on other products.

Summary

- The marketing mix is the mixture of factors needed in order to sell a product
- It has four parts: product, price, promotion and place
- The four parts are often referred to as 'the four Ps'
- Getting the right balance is more important than any one part
- The marketing mix will need to change over time, and as other factors change
- Price is a key part of the mix
- Price should be set to cover costs
- Customers have an idea of 'value for money; price must be set in this range

Core knowledge

The business needs to keep an eye on all parts of the marketing mix, as the relative importance of the parts will change over time, particularly over the lifetime of a product. When a product is first launched, for example, it may be important to have a lot of promotion, to let customers know of its existence and where to buy it. Whatever is happening, some businesses will find it offers opportunities – even a hurricane makes work for roofers! As an example, let's look at three current trends that have been around for long enough to be regarded as established, and their possible effect on three businesses. Current trends include:

● a fall in the number of houses being built due to changes in the economy;
● trends towards more healthy eating and drinking habits;
● increased internet usage (and increased speeds through broadband).

Our three example businesses are a small building firm, a luxury restaurant and a local newspaper.

● The building firm needs to find new ways of finding work. Its excellent internet access, and the fact that planning applications are now published on the web, allows the owner to see when planning applications are approved. He can then promote his services to people who need them directly, using leaflets or even visiting.

● The restaurant could alter its product, by changing menus to healthier alternatives, organic produce and seasonal foods. It may also have to lower prices in order to attract different people.

● The local newspaper could change its product by carrying more advertising. It could also lower prices to advertisers. Increased advertising revenue could allow it to lower its cover price. Some newspapers are free, paid for by advertising.

And more

More important than allocating funds or efforts to each individual part of the mix is getting the balance right. The key to a successful business is not just a well-balanced marketing mix but one that is appropriate for the business and that responds appropriately to change. A small business could respond to a change in demand in a number of ways, depending on the change and on the type of business. If demand falls, a business may seek to revive sales by lowering price – knowing that lower prices should lead to an increase in demand. But there could be a catch. Some products are sold in very competitive markets, where it is easy for customers to switch from one seller to another. In these markets, the business is probably already charging the lowest price it can in order to compete. Lowering price could lead to lower profits, or even losses. It may therefore be better for the business to try to alter another part of the marketing mix. Perhaps new distribution channels could be opened, or changes made to the product. In other markets, the business may have a product that is so special and unique there is little competition, and there are no substitutes available. In this case, the business might be able to raise price and still not lose custom.

Have a go

Group activity

Changes in a market bring some benefits and some drawbacks. Each person in your group should list three businesses which have gained from cheap air travel, and three that have lost. Decide which you think has lost the most. Decide on a pricing strategy to help them recover.

Discussion

The low cost, low price model used by Ryanair and easyJet has led to a lot more air travel taking place. Discuss whether or not increased air travel is a good thing or not, and why.

Web-based activity

List five current products that might go on your wish list for a birthday. Search the web to see how cheaply you could buy them. List the top and bottom prices for each product and note the difference. How much could you save by 'shopping around'? Explain why you think there is this difference in price.

Quickfire questions

1   What is meant by the 'Four Ps'?
2   What is the most important element of the marketing mix?
3   Why do small businesses have to be careful about marketing?
4   Why do different businesses have different marketing mixes?
5   What is meant by 'value for money'?
6   What is meant by a customer's 'price range'?
7   What happens to the marketing mix over time?
8   What usually happens to demand if price goes up?
9   What is cost plus pricing?
10 What is competitive pricing?

Hit the spot

> Define the marketing mix.
>> Explain the link between 'price' and 'value for money'.
>>> Explain the relationship between price and demand. Under what circumstances might that relationship break down? Explain why you think so.

Cracking the code

Substitutes Products that can be bought instead of something, e.g. tinned fruit instead of fresh fruit.

Marketing mix The mixture or balance of the four key elements of marketing.

Value for money Nothing to do with the 'value' of the product, but linked to what the customer thinks it is worth; this may be different for different customers.

Chapter 13
Marketing mix elements and product

The BBC iPlayer is a development of technology that the BBC was already running to allow people to listen to the radio over the internet. This takes up little bandwidth, and also allows users to listen to programmes that have already been broadcast, as well as listening to 'live' broadcasts. The iPlayer allows users with certain operating systems to download programmes, and watch them for up to 30 days. Other system users can watch TV programmes for up to seven days after broadcast, but not download them. Digital Rights Management (DRM) software is used to protect copyright and the commercial value of programmes so that they 'expire' after a set period of time and can no longer be played. Only users with a UK-based IP address can access the service, restricting it to Britain.

This version of the iPlayer was, when launched, only available to Windows XP users, leading to complaints that this was unfair to other users. A petition, sent to 10 Downing Street, demanded that the service be made available to people who did not use Windows. The petition reached over 16,000 signatures and brought a response from the BBC Trust (the governing body of the BBC) that: 'it noted the strong public demand for the service to be available on a variety of operating systems. The BBC Trust made it a condition of approval for the BBC's on-demand services that the iPlayer is available to

BBC iPlayer

The BBC iPlayer

users of a range of operating systems, and has given a commitment that it will ensure that the BBC meets this demand as soon as possible.' By the Spring of 2008, the service was also available to Mac and Linux users and people using other browsers, such as Firefox and Safari.

The product has been a phenomenal success, and by 2008 was accounting for over 5 per cent of all internet traffic, and rising.

The BBC iPlayer can be found at **www.bbc.co.uk/iplayer**. Follow this link **www.independent.co.uk/news/business/news/internet-groups-warn-bbc-over-iplayer-plans-461167.html** and read the article published in *The Independent* newspaper. What changes do you think broadband providers are going to have to make to their product?

Watch this 1958 Persil advertisement on YouTube at **www.youtube.com/watch?v=L6880aSkS08**. Has Persil made real or superficial changes?

Did you know...

Video streaming and internet rental has not succeeded in killing off the cinema. This is because the product they provide is different. Widescreen, surround sound and the 'experience' of cinema are not easily created in a home setting.

Responding to change

Businesses may fail or get into difficulty because they are unable to change their business model as circumstances change. It is important for businesses to be able to respond to change. They may be able to respond by changing any element of the marketing mix. Often it is most effective (and necessary) to change product. The BBC (and other broadcasters) had noted a significant change in demand so developed a new product in order to take advantage of this change.

Trends and markets

What they had seen happening in the market was a change in viewing habits, brought about by various advances in technology. The first change was the introduction of video recorders that could be programmed. These were used most often to 'time shift' programmes, so that people could watch them at times that were convenient to them. DVD recorders and 'Plus 1' channels, along with multiple repeats, also helped to drive this

trend. At the same time, better and faster computer technology was allowing viewers to download films and video from the web. In 2006, Google launched a video service for people to buy video on demand, but it lasted less than a year, as the technology was not sufficiently developed. The BBC was the first to successfully develop a product that recognised viewers' changing habits and wants, and came out at the right time to make use of new technology.

Small businesses

Small businesses can learn many lessons from the BBC's success. They spent a long time getting the **product** right, and testing it in smaller markets, before going ahead with the national launch. The product itself has also had a knock-on effect on some small businesses, making the demand for video and DVD rentals fall.

Competition

Businesses need to be able to change in response to competition. If a competitor introduces a new

---

Did you know...

Businesses can make even better use of new technology through, for example, integrating different technologies. For example, you can programme your Sky+ box with a mobile phone if you've forgotten to do it at home.

New technology can change the market

product, or changes their product, then to stay successful the business will need to match this. Trends in markets will also mean that changes are necessary. Businesses can pick up current trends from press and media reports and, in their own industry, through specialist magazines (like *The Grocer*, *Farmers Weekly* and *Heating, Ventilating and Plumbing* magazine). Competing businesses that spot a trend or change first, and are flexible enough to be able to take advantage of it, tend to succeed. Businesses can change the product itself, the product range, or the product mix.

Changing the product is generally done by adding value – such as additional features or benefits. Sometimes these are real changes, sometimes only **cosmetic** (see 'And more' box).

- The **product range** refers to the different product lines which a business sells. For example, the range in a bakers is likely to include bread, rolls, cakes, pastries and pies.

- The **product mix** refers to the variety of product types. A narrow mix means that the business is dependent on a particular market segment and so may be heavily affected by changes in that market. A baker who sells only bread products is not in as strong a position as one who also sells sandwiches, crisps and pies.

Technology

Businesses may also have to change a product due to changes in technology. When videotapes first became available, many specialist shops opened in order to provide rental services, which, as technology moved on, became DVD rental services. Now, some successful rental businesses have moved from physical premises to providing a postal service. The next stage is likely to be an internet only service, where films are streamed or downloaded. This will rely on appropriate technology being in place for consumers to download and pay for films and for producers to protect them from pirate copying.

Did you know...

Products are usually bought for a combination of core reasons and secondary reasons. The core reason for buying an item of clothing may be to stay warm. Colour and style give secondary benefits. A third layer of benefits comes from the promise of quality provided by the brand. This is known as the augmented product.

Summary

- Product is just one part of the marketing mix
- Businesses may respond to change by changing the product
- Some changes are caused by changes in technology
- Some changes are caused by competitors
- Businesses need to respond to changes by competitors
- Products can be changed by adding value
- Some changes are 'real' others may be cosmetic

Core knowledge

A product can be either a good or service. Goods are either for consumption or production. **Consumer goods** are either durable (lasting, like a car or freezer) or non-durable (quickly used up, like food, or toothpaste). Industrial or **producer goods** are those that are going to be used as part of the production process. These include tools, parts, factories and equipment. Services include services to individuals like haircutting, entertainment or car valeting and services that support business, like insurance, transport and banking.

Products go through a '**product life cycle**'. This describes the stages through which a product passes in a market. In the first stage, the product is researched and developed, before it is even brought to market. Many products do not survive this stage. Once the product is launched, it may need supporting with heavy promotion. If it is a good product, competitors will begin to bring out their own versions and the market can become crowded. At this point, changes can be made to the product to try to attract new markets, or to make it different to the competition. As long as further changes to the product can keep people buying it, this is worth doing, but with most products there comes a point when it is no longer worth the support, and it can then be allowed to die. In terms of time, product life cycles can be extremely short-lived – a matter of weeks – or carry on over a number of years.

And more

Customers buy products because of the benefits that they will get from them. These benefits are either real (or tangible) benefits or extra (or intangible) benefits. For example, buying (and wearing) an Adidas hat gives the real benefit of keeping your head warm. It also gives the extra benefit of you looking fashionable. Sometimes, the extra benefits are of more importance to a consumer than real benefits. A fashionable pair of shoes may not be as comfortable or as waterproof as unfashionable ones, but we may still prefer to wear them. The use of branding is a key way in which businesses try to make 'extra' benefits important. Where a business tries to make its product different to those of its competitors, this is called product differentiation. Big businesses can achieve this through the use of a brand.

Choosing style over comfort

Changes to a product will also be of two types. There may be real changes, so that the product actually does perform better, or provide greater 'real' benefits. Increasing the power of a washing powder to clean or whiten would fall into this category. Other changes may be 'cosmetic'. Sometimes a product is repackaged or rebranded and not really changed at all. Calling something 'new' or 'improved' or saying it works 'better' is meaningless unless it is possible to compare performance. Putting it in a bag instead of a box, or a packet instead of a tin does not change the 'real' product and sometimes is an excuse to decrease value. A 'new, convenient size', for example, may disguise an increase in price.

Have a go

Group activity

Each person in your group should list three products that have been changed in order to increase demand. Look at all the products that you have listed between you and decide which change has been the most successful. Decide why you think this is the case.

Discussion

Look at the changes that have been made to Ariel over the years (see diagram). Which of these do you think are real changes and which cosmetic? Why do you think that soap powders, in particular, are always changing?

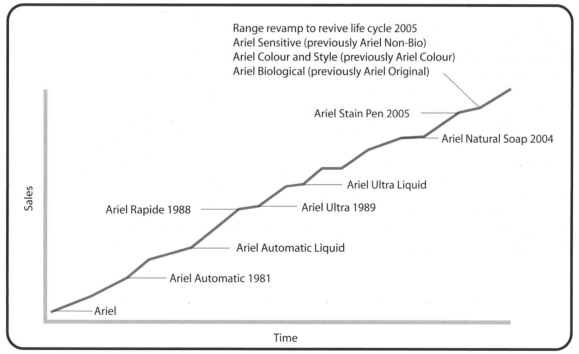

Range revamp to revive life cycle 2005
Ariel Sensitive (previously Ariel Non-Bio)
Ariel Colour and Style (previously Ariel Colour)
Ariel Biological (previously Ariel Original)

Ariel Stain Pen 2005

Ariel Natural Soap 2004

Ariel Ultra Liquid

Ariel Rapide 1988

Ariel Ultra 1989

Ariel Automatic Liquid

Ariel Automatic 1981

Ariel

Sales

Time

Revamping Ariel

Web-based activity

List five current market changes that are affecting demand. Collect media cuttings or clips to illustrate your choice. Suggest which of these factors is having the biggest effect on demand, and for what. Suggest how this market could change its product (or another part of its marketing mix) to take advantage of the change.

Quickfire questions

1   Why is it important that a business can respond to change?
2   What is meant by a 'trend' in a market?
3   Name three current trends that could be important to a business.
4   What is the difference between a real change to a product and a cosmetic change?
5   What is meant by 'product range'?
6   What is meant by 'product mix'?
7   What is meant by 'adding value' to a product?
8   What is the difference between a good and a service?
9   What is meant by a 'consumer durable'?
10 What is a 'product life cycle'?

Hit the spot

> Define 'product' as part of the marketing mix.

> Explain why a wide product mix might be better than a narrow one.

> Which single part of new technology do you think has had the greatest effect on demand? Explain the reasons why you think this is the case.

Cracking the code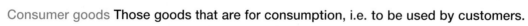

Consumer goods Those goods that are for consumption, i.e. to be used by customers.

Cosmetic Cosmetic changes are changes to the look or feel of a product that are basically surface changes, rather than a real change in the product.

Producer goods Those goods that will be used in production, like tools, machines, components.

Product The output of a business; what is produced for sale: this could be either a good or a service.

Product life cycle The stages a product passes through from research and launch to eventual withdrawal.

Product mix The variety of product lines offered by the business, therefore targeting several markets.

Product range The different product lines within a targeted market.

Chapter 14
Marketing mix elements and promotion

IN THE NEWS

Levi Roots ran a small business, on a limited budget, based on his grandmother's recipe and with production in his own kitchen. He operated as a sole trader, with limited capital, and limited opportunities for expansion. His opportunities to promote the product were – as with most small businesses – also fairly limited. His biggest sales were seasonal, made at the Notting Hill Carnival, which he had supplied with both music and Caribbean sauce for over 20 years. In fact, Levi's first career was as a musician, having played with some of the greats like Bob Marley, and being recognised at the MOBO awards. With the help of his seven children, Levi produced 65 bottles of the sauce a day in his kitchen. He packaged it himself and sold it at Brixton market, carrying it in a bag on his back. Demand from the Caribbean community became strong enough for Levi to set up a website to promote the sauce and take orders.

In 2006, Levi was spotted by a BBC researcher and invited to appear on *Dragons' Den*, the BBC programme where rich investors decide whether or not to support new ideas. Levi Roots sang his message to the entrepreneurs – the possible investors – and three pulled out straight away. Two – Peter Jones and Richard Fairleigh – could see the potential of the product and offered £25,000 each for a 20 per cent stake in the business.

Levi Roots and his Reggae Reggae Sauce

Within a few weeks of appearing on the programme, production had increased to 150,000 bottles a day and had to be moved to a factory. Peter Jones helped to secure a major order from supermarket Sainsbury's, and the sauce became its fastest selling brand, selling 40,000 to 50,000 bottles a week in over 600 stores.

What Levi Roots really needed was a promotional boost, to let the wider world know about his sauce. This came from the programme (which is watched by over 3 million people), so provided peak time advertising for a fraction of what it would cost on a commercial channel. His 'dragon' partners were also able to promote the sauce directly to big business, leading to its phenomenal success in a short space of time. Levi has also been able to use the success of the sauce, and his own talents for promotion, to promote his music career.

You can find Levi Roots' website at **www.reggae-reggae.co.uk/**. Look at this site and list the ways in which it covers all of the elements of the marketing mix.

http://video.google.com/videoplay?docid=-5382825371553385541&q. This link takes you to a film of Levi talking and singing at an Enterprise event. What are the main points of his message to students?

You will find seven promotion methods on this site:
www.canadaone.com/ezine/may99/promote.html. Put them in order of which you think is most/least effective, and why.

Did you know...

The BBC does not carry any paid-for advertising. The BBC will often run promotional trailers for its own programmes, but will not accept advertising from commercial organisations. Instead the BBC is funded by government and the television licence fee.

Promoting a product

The product – Reggae Reggae Sauce – already existed, and was a good product. Levi Roots had already started to promote it, via his website. He also used the traditional promotional routes of the small business, such as recommendation and 'word-of-mouth' from satisfied customers. **Promotion** is just one part of the marketing mix, and it should be balanced against the other parts. It is no use having a huge budget for promotion and nothing left over for product development or distribution. The promotional methods chosen must be suitable for the business and the product that it is selling. Promotion is important but is also one area where the balance is sometimes wrong. A business can find that it has spent all of its money on promotion, but that there is no real effect on sales. Promotion can be expensive but, if it is not the right sort of promotion, can be ineffective. On the other hand, it is sometimes true that promotion that is free, or very cheap, can be just as effective as an expensive promotional campaign.

Above and below

Promotion consists of both 'above-the-line' and 'below-the-line' expenditure. **Advertising** is paid-for publicity for a product called 'above-the-line' expenditure. Other methods of promotion are called 'below-the-line' expenditure and include **public relations** and sponsorship. A suitable promotion method for a business will depend on the size of the business, the type and range of products that it is selling and on its market. A suitable budget for promotion should also be set, linked to:

- *Size*: A smaller business will obviously have less of a promotional budget than a larger one. This will limit it to certain media.

- *Products*: Some services can only be delivered personally. For example, you cannot sell a haircut to anyone other than the person in the chair! Industrial goods will be promoted through trained salespeople who can describe and demonstrate benefits at trade fairs and exhibitions or directly to the customer.

Did you know...

Some short-term prices are called 'promotional' prices, as they have been lowered temporarily. We recognise these through flashes saying 'sale' or 'reduced'.

Advertising

Small businesses

For a small business, the most suitable forms of promotion are likely to be:

- *Local newspapers*: these cover a precise geographical area so the business knows exactly who it is targeting. Using the government statistics site at **www.statistics.gov.uk** the business can carry out a postcode search and find out about the sort of customers that live in the area. Profiles will reveal house prices, average income, household size, patterns of expenditure and other information of use to a business. Just as important, perhaps, is the fact that such information is free.

- *Personal recommendation*: it is said that people tell ten others of every bad service experience they have, and just two of the good experiences. 'Word-of-mouth' is therefore very powerful and 'good reviews' are important.

- *Stationery and business cards*: these can carry product descriptions or be designed in such a way as to give a certain image to a business. Cards can also be placed in shop and newsagent windows and on notice boards.

- *Flyers, posters and leaflets*: online printing businesses have made these cheap to produce, but they still have to be designed and

- *Market*: Media are priced according to their 'reach', i.e. the number of potential customers reached. Many small businesses serve only a local market, so the use of TV, radio and national press advertising is not appropriate. The make up of the target market is also important. For example, if your product is aimed at teenagers, then promoting it to any other group is pointless.

Local sponsorship

distributed. Distribution can be targeted using postcodes.

- *Sponsorship*: this is available, but on a smaller scale. A business might, for example, sponsor the kit of a local or school football team, who then carry publicity on their kit.

- *Popular promotional techniques*: such as BOGOF (Buy One Get One Free) and other special offers can also be used by small businesses. They do, however, have to keep a very close eye on what these are costing them.

Is the promotion effective?

A business has to take all the costs and benefits of advertising into account when trying to see if a promotion has been effective. This is usually done by comparing the costs of the promotion with any increase in sales. It is not worth advertising if the benefits do not outweigh the costs. For example, if £1000 spent on promotion only resulted in £500 worth of increased sales revenue, then the promotion would be judged to be ineffective.

Did you know...

The main case in favour of advertising is that it informs – without it customers would not know what was on offer and would therefore not be able to make a choice. The case against advertising is that it is an unnecessary cost that is passed on to the consumer.

Summary

- Promotion is just one part of the marketing mix
- It consists of advertising and public relations
- AIDA (see Core) is the acronym used to remember what advertising should do
- Promotion is only effective if it is appropriate
- It needs to be appropriate to the size of the business, the type of product and the target market
- Small businesses can have effective advertising if they use the right media and hit the right target market

Core knowledge

Promotion covers all those methods that a business uses to communicate to consumers:

- that its product/s exist/s;
- that the product has features and benefits for the customer;
- that the customer should buy it.

The first aim is to make customers aware of a product. The second aim is to persuade consumers to buy it. The main ways in which businesses carry out these aims is through advertising and public relations.

Advertising is used to promote products through broadcast and print media of various types. **AIDA** is used as a way to remember the qualities that advertising should possess. It should attract

Sponsorship in action

Attention; create Interest; develop Desire and lead to Action. Once advertising is successful in attracting attention, it can then create interest by telling customers about the benefits and features of a product. Businesses will try to convince the consumer that the product is something that they need, or will derive pleasure or use from. Once 'desire' has been created, the action of buying the product should follow.

Public relations is any way of generating publicity for a business. Methods include events, press conferences, sponsorship, endorsement and product placement. Sponsorship is used to link a product with a certain event, person or sport. A strawberry grower might wish to be associated with Wimbledon tennis for example. Endorsement is when someone well-known is persuaded to say or show that they think a particular product is worth having. Product placement involves giving products away to celebrities, or for use on films or television, in the hope that the product will be used on screen.

And more

Some new forms of advertising have emerged as new media has become more widely available. For example, a business may send advertisements directly to your mobile phone. A number of new ways of advertising also involve the internet. Internet sites carry banners for other sites that link to them directly by 'clicking through' and are rewarded every time a user is directed to the site. They may also carry other advertisements that load automatically before a page loads. These advertisements may be effective because they are bold and animated but may be ineffective if they cause irritation to the user.

Viral advertising relies on people to 'spread the word' to other people via the internet. This has now become a part of mainstream advertising campaigns. Businesses will set up fake websites or blogs that 'reveal' new products. The 'secret' word then spreads across the internet as people pass on the message. By the time the actual promotion is launched, there is already a huge level of interest. Viral advertising will reach yet another part of the market. For a small business, advertising on the internet is reasonably inexpensive. However, it may lead to problems of distribution. The internet is an international medium, so it should be made clear on the website of the business whether the business is willing to distribute its product outside the UK.

Have a go

Group activity

Each person in your group should list three advertisements that they have found persuasive, or amusing. For each one say what it was that was particularly good. Rank the advertisements in order and agree on which is the best, and why.

Discussion

Choose three recent advertisements that you think have been effective and, for each, say how well you think it fulfils 'AIDA'. Suggest ways in which each promotion could be improved.

Web-based activity

Find five major events or sports that are sponsored by businesses. Sporting examples could include cricket and football leagues, motor racing and golf. Events could include concerts and festivals. You could even find TV programmes and series that are sponsored. For each say why you think the sponsor backs the event and what benefits they will gain from it. Which do you think is the most effective, and why?

Quickfire questions

1   Describe 'above the line' promotion.
2   Describe 'below the line' promotion.
3   Name the two parts to promotion.
4   Name three sponsored events.
5   Name the three main factors that make for a suitable promotion.
6   What is meant by 'reach'?
7   Give one benefit of advertising in a local newspaper.
8   Why are postcodes important to small businesses?
9   How would a business judge if a promotion had been effective?
10   What does AIDA stand for?

Hit the spot

> Describe three suitable promotion methods for a small business.

>> Explain the factors that are important in making a promotion suitable for a business.

>>> Using examples, explain why a particular business is sponsoring a particular event or sport. Judge whether or not the sponsorship is effective and say why you think so.

Cracking the code

Promotion That part of the marketing mix used to inform and persuade customers about products.

Advertising 'Above-the-line' promotion that is directly paid for.

Public relations (PR) 'Below-the-line' promotion – ways to attract attention and interest in a product that are not direct advertising.

AIDA The way to remember the qualities of effective promotion: it should attract Attention; create Interest; develop Desire and lead to Action.

Chapter 15
Marketing mix elements and place

IN THE NEWS

In April 2006 a music track by Gnarls Barkley made musical history by being the first to reach the Number One spot without selling any physical copies of the track. The track, called 'Crazy', was not released on tape or CD, single or album, but only as digital music, available via hugely successful music sites such as Apple's iTunes. It sold over 30,000 copies in a matter of hours, having already been made popular on Radio 1 as a jingle. It was bound to happen sooner or later as chart compilers and publishers decided that downloads had become so popular that they had to include them in the charts. They changed the rules so that this distribution channel was recognised as being as important as physical channels. After all, people were still buying the track, even if only digitally. Under the rule changes, as long as physical copies were going to go on sale up to a week later, downloads could count.

One month later Planet Funk used another 'new' distribution channel, made available by the growth of new technology, and released a track purely via mobile phone downloads. At the time, such downloads accounted for one in every 20 sales of tracks in the UK singles charts. '3', a mobile phone network, sold downloads at just 99p a track to both mobile phone and computer. 'I predict a riot' from the Kaiser Chiefs and 'Dare' from Gorillaz, each sold over 5000 copies once released via the mobile network.

Since then, many tracks have succeeded via downloads and it has become established as a new method of distribution. In other words, it is a new way to get the product to the consumer. The next step is to make even more use of the channel. Since downloads were made widely available, a number of illegal file-sharing or 'peer-to-peer' sites have appeared, where downloads of music are shared and therefore free. Producers do not want to lose the distribution channel, however, so are busy thinking up ways to make the product free, but also make money. In 2008, Universal, the world's largest recording company (home to the likes of Mariah Carey and U2) signed a deal to make millions of tracks available for free, on a site funded by advertising. The site (Qtrax) has also signed up the Beggars Group, the largest independent record producer in the UK (White Stripes, Radiohead, The Charlatans, Jarvis Cocker, Basement Jaxx) and industry giants Sony and EMI.

@

British group Coldplay hit the top of both the US and UK charts with a download-only single. Read about their success at:
www.mtv.co.uk/channel/ mtvuk/news/23062008/ 426592/coldplay_top_both_ charts
Look at three websites, chosen at random. How do they fulfil the idea of 'place'? How will they distribute products to you?

Finding the right place

The correct '**place**' (or mixture of places) and the ways to get a product to that place, will be linked to various factors. The most important of these are the product itself, the market at which it is targeted and the costs of **distribution**. In the case of a music track the product is easily transported but needs to be delivered quickly (and accurately), its target market is large, but easily accessed via technology, costs of distribution can be kept to a minimum. All businesses face the same decisions with their products.

Product

Products have different properties, all of which affect where they can be sold and how they are delivered. Look at the difference, for example, between coal and diamonds. Coal is heavy, bulky and dirty. Diamonds are small, valuable and clean. Neither has to be delivered with particular speed, but there are obviously security issues which make the transport of diamonds more expensive than coal. They will also be sold in very different places. Retail outlets range from the small, corner store or convenience outlet, up to huge hypermarkets and high street chains and department stores. Many still specialise in a particular product or line while others offer a more general range. Outlets need to consider which products will sell best, which offer the best profit margins and which products they actually have room to stock. Sales may need to be made in specialist surroundings, or with expert help, assistance or advice.

For neither of these products, however, is there a particular rush to reach a market. For something that is perishable, or new, this might be the prime concern. The first Beaujolais Nouveau of the season (a French red wine) is flown into the UK and sold at a high price; the first game birds shot at the start of the grouse season are delivered by helicopter to top London restaurants. Other foods may need to be processed or frozen. Transport may be arranged in such a way that the product arrives in a different condition, ready for sale. Bananas, for example, are packed into ships when still green, and ripen on the journey (they are too heavy and bulky to be flown).

Not the way to transport diamonds!

Bananas start their journey unripe

Market

The **target market** for the product may range from the very large – a mass market – to the very small – a niche market. Whatever the size of the market, the business has to consider how to reach it. It has to think about how the target market would access the product. For example, if the target market was older people, then making the product available via the internet would not be a good idea, as many older people do not use new technology. They may also mistrust payment systems. On the other hand, making a product like a music track available via mobile phone and internet hits exactly the market at which it is aimed.

Costs

Distribution costs will depend on the size of the market and on factors linked to the product such as whether it needs to be delivered quickly, or securely, individually or in bulk amounts. Remember that 'place' is just one part of the marketing mix. If the distribution costs mean that price has to be increased, this may be enough to stop the product being viable.

E-commerce

Although businesses can create a website for what is essentially a very small outlay, they need to make sure that the site is properly built and maintained. There are costs involved in designing the site, hosting it, and maintaining it. The website may be the most 'public' part of the business, so it needs to be accurate and kept up-to-date. Internet sales are a growing market with many large grocery stores now offering an online service of ordering backed up by home delivery.

Home delivery: orders are placed online

Did you know...

Place is both distribution and the places where products are sold. It therefore includes outlets such as shops. There are also non-shop outlets such as direct sales, postal and internet sales and vending machines. Most industrial products, for instance, are sold by an agent, via direct sales. Other well-known products such as Tupperware are sold directly through party sales and Avon through door-to-door sales. Postal sales may be responses to mailshots or direct advertising or could be through mail order or catalogue sales.

Summary

- Place is just one part of the marketing mix
- The term 'place' refers to the place where a product is sold
- 'Place' also means the way that the product gets to that place: this is called distribution
- Distribution traditionally went through several phases – the long chain (see Core knowledge)
- Much shorter routes are now more popular
- The main factors that determine the right place and distribution are the product, its market and the costs of distribution
- E-commerce is a growing and important part of 'place'

Core knowledge

'Place' is one part of the marketing mix. It refers both to the premises or other outlets where a product may be sold and to distribution channels. These channels are the way that a product is delivered either to such outlets or directly to the final consumer. The traditional distribution strategy was via what was called 'long channel' distribution. This meant that the product followed a **chain of distribution** as follows:

producer → manufacturer → wholesaler → retailer → consumer

Each person in the chain tended to deal only with the person before or after them. Each also carried out a particular job. The wholesaler, for instance, bought large amounts, provided storage facilities and sold smaller amounts on to the retailer. The problem with such a long chain is that it is both costly and slow. Each person in the chain provides a service, and adds to the cost of the product as they take their fee. It can also take a product a long time to pass through all the stages. Shorter channels can be achieved by cutting out parts of this chain and the shortest channel is direct from producer to consumer. If this can also be achieved at little or no cost – as with digital downloads – this can make the product much cheaper than if it had to be transported to a shop from where the customer then bought it.

And more

E-commerce refers to transactions that take place over the internet. To take place it needs a website – a place on the web where a potential customer can browse products and then buy remotely for delivery. It is a rapidly growing marketplace and as such yet another 'place' where products may be sold. There are two distinct and different routes into business on the internet. The first strategy is to set up as a pure 'dot com' business. This means that you only take orders via the web, and only distribute that way. One of the first companies to do this was Dell computers. This strategy gives access to a large market but removes the costs of shops, displays, sales staff and so on. The second strategy is to build on an existing successful business by adding an internet dimension. This is often referred to as 'bricks and clicks'. This is very much an area of growth and the majority of businesses now have a web presence. While the web may provide an inexpensive additional distribution channel, it should not be forgotten that most products still have to be delivered. The most successful web businesses are those that can sell the same product over and over again – commercial photo agencies, for example, or that provide a service that can be delivered via the web. These include advertising services, other services that can be carried out at a distance, such as share buying or tracing family histories and businesses that act as 'go-betweens', e.g. dating agencies, estate agencies and sites like Friends Reunited.

Have a go

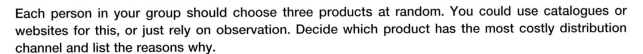

Group activity

Each person in your group should choose three products at random. You could use catalogues or websites for this, or just rely on observation. Decide which product has the most costly distribution channel and list the reasons why.

Discussion

There is a huge market in illegal downloads – basically, people sharing music between each other, without paying for it. This is one of the reasons that downloads are now tending to be 'free'. Do you agree that this is the direction that music distribution should go in? Give reasons why you think so (or not).

Web-based activity

Find out all you can about Qtrax, such as who they have signed up and what tracks will be available. Explain how you think that their model of distribution will work.

Quickfire questions

1 Describe the steps in traditional 'long chain' distribution.
2 Give an example of one retail outlet that is not a shop.
3 Name three properties that a product might have that would affect how it is transported.
4 Name three different types of retail outlet.
5 Name the three main factors that go to make up the correct 'place'.
6 What are the biggest and smallest markets called?
7 Give one advantage of using a website to sell products.
8 Give one disadvantage of using a website to sell products.
9 What does a wholesaler do?
10 What is meant by 'bricks and clicks'?

Hit the spot

> Describe how 'place' is an important part of the marketing mix.

>> Explain how and why distribution for a mass market will need to differ from that for a niche market.

>>> Choose three products. For each product suggest one appropriate and one inappropriate 'place' to sell it. Justify your suggestions by referring to the product, its market and the costs of distribution.

Cracking the code

Chain of distribution The stages that a product passes through from producer to consumer.

Distribution The part of place that deals with making the product available to the consumer.

Place The part of the marketing mix that refers to where a product is sold and how it gets to that place.

Target market That part of a market at which the product is aimed.

FINANCE

Chapter 16
Sources of finance

IN THE NEWS

The National House Building Council reported in Spring 2008 that housing starts were well down on the previous year. Over 20,000 houses were started in May 2007, with around three-quarters of these in the private sector. By May 2008 this had fallen to 9600, a fall of around 60 per cent. The fall has affected big and small businesses alike.

Taylor Wimpey is one of Britain's biggest building firms. It was formed in 2007 through the merger of Taylor Woodrow and Wimpey. Despite its size, it has still been hard hit by the 'double whammy' of increased credit costs and a declining housing market. It is in an industry where borrowing and debt is important. Houses and flats have to be built before they can be sold, so payments for land, labour, materials and services have to be made before any revenue can be collected from house sales. On small building sites, where only a few houses are being built, costs are often not recouped until the last house is sold. On bigger sites, there may be a 'rolling programme' of sales, with 'Phase 1' sales being used to finance 'Phase 2', and so on. Those building commercial properties like offices and shops are no better off – they still have to find businesses to rent the space. Taylor Wimpey has had to take action to bring its costs down and has cut 600 jobs while closing 13 of its regional offices. It has also stopped expanding, put some developments on 'hold' and put off starting new ones. The company has almost £2 billion of debt, held against its assets (what it owns). The trick is to keep lenders confident so that the debt can be managed.

Craig and Sean Deering both followed their father into the building trade. They are builders on a much

For sale
Plot 18
George Wimpey

smaller scale than Taylor Wimpey but face the same sort of problems. Deering Brothers Builders has debt held on credit cards and through trade accounts with their local building supply agency. They also have a business bank loan with monthly repayments that have to be met. To stay in work, as the housing market contracted, they have used some of their own savings to continue projects. They have also been forced to dramatically reduce the price of the houses they are building. As Sean says, 'We have a lot of debt, but hope that we can keep on top of it until the market picks up.'

@ Visit the Bank of England's site at **www.bankofengland.co.uk** to find out the latest figures for interest rates and for inflation. Work out what effect these will have on the housing market. Why is this important?

Visit estate agents' websites in your area. What can you tell about the housing market from these sites?

Look at **www.angelsden.com**. Would this be a suitable place for a business to look for finance? Can you say why you think so?

How much? Where from?

Probably the most frequently asked question for the small business start-up is 'Where do I get the money from?' The answer to the question generally comes in two halves. Firstly, before deciding on possible sources for the finance, how much do I need? Only then can the entrepreneur begin to look for suitable sources. The 'how much?' needs to cover fixed costs, variable costs and any possible **contingencies** (things that might happen in the future). Details of these are covered in Chapter 19. Small businesses will not have shareholders and, while they may have the option to become a private limited company, raising money via a stock exchange issue is not a route that is open to them.

Small businesses

For many small businesses the major form of finance will be the **owner's own funds**. These will come from personal savings and income. The owner may also raise money from friends and family, without the need for any formal agreement or payment of interest. It is up to them if they want to risk their money! These funds may also include the profits of the business. Profits that are kept for this purpose are called '**retained profits**'.

In addition, businesses will have to borrow money. This may be short term, to cover immediate payments, medium term, or long term to cover expensive items that are going to take a long time to pay for.

Short-term loans

Short-term loans are usually measured in terms of weeks or months, or even just days. While these are obviously short term, anything up to a maximum of three years is also considered to be short term. Sources for such loans are banks, or through various forms of credit. The main short-term borrowing from banks is through overdrafts or loans.

- An **overdraft** is when the bank allows a business to take more out of a current account than it has in it. It is a flexible way to borrow as the business can borrow as much or as little as it needs up to the overdraft limit. The business only pays interest on the amount of money actually borrowed at any time.

- A loan is a fixed amount borrowed over a set period. The business would borrow the whole amount it needed, and then pay this, and the interest, in set instalments. It is not as flexible as an overdraft but can be better for a business wanting to keep control of its budget as the business knows exactly how much it needs to pay and when.

Medium-term loans

Medium-term finance is defined as loans taken out over a period of between three and ten years. Medium-term loans are likely to be used to buy fixed assets such as machines and vehicles. The bank will often have a call on the particular asset as security for the loan. This means that if the business fails, or cannot pay for the loan, the bank can take the asset and sell it.

A delivery vehicle is an asset

Long-term loans

Long-term finance is reckoned to be loans from ten years upwards. These are usually taken out from banks that specialise in commercial loans. The alternative is to go to a bank or building society and take out a mortgage on factories, land or property. A **mortgage** is a long-term loan with property or land as **security**.

Venture capital

Businesses may also be able to take out loans from private investors. Successful entrepreneurs may wish to back a particular business venture if they think that it will be a success. They may also want to take part in running the business. This source is known as 'venture capital' and the individuals who provide it are often known as business 'angels'.

Finance may also be raised through government grants or related schemes. These are covered in the next chapter.

Did you know...

Debt is not a problem for most businesses as long as it can be managed. Actually borrowing money, or using credit, is a necessary step for the majority of businesses. Problems only arise if payments are not made, or the business cannot afford the interest. It is vital for a business to manage its debt properly.

Summary

- The main source of finance for a small business is the owner's own funds
- Issuing shares is not an option for the small business
- Most businesses need to borrow funds, or use credit
- Borrowing will be for the short, medium or long term
- Overdrafts provide flexible short-term borrowing
- Medium-term borrowing is usually secured against an asset
- Long-term borrowing is often in the form of a mortgage
- Trade credit is a common way for businesses to borrow
- All borrowing comes with a cost attached
- Borrowing is necessary for most businesses, what is important is that the debt is properly managed

Core knowledge

Small businesses have to use whatever sources they can for finance. While these businesses can apply for overdrafts or loans, small businesses and new businesses often have great difficulty in raising the money that they need. This is because the future for many businesses is uncertain. They can have a good idea, or what they think is a good product, and still not be a success. Banks and building societies know the failure rate of small businesses and may therefore be very careful about the loans that they make to them – or put strong conditions on them. Sometimes the conditions – such as high interest rates, or wanting security on the assets of a business – are enough to put the business off. Many entrepreneurs setting up a new business find that the most reliable source of finance is their own savings. They may also borrow from friends and family who are willing to take the risk. Banks and other lending institutions will want much more solid guarantees

Re-mortgaging the house can fund a business start-up

as they have the interests of their own depositors and shareholders to take into account. Entrepreneurs may also raise money on those assets that they already own. A householder can remortgage a house, for instance, in pursuit of a business dream.

Businesses can find it easier to raise money if they have a clear business plan, good market research and a really good idea of the amount of risk involved. Of course, if they are successful, there will be high levels of reward – but what happens if the business is not a success?

And more

One way for a business to raise finance is through various forms of credit. Credit is, essentially, borrowing something and paying for it later. It is a form of loan, but one that will have different conditions and costs to a bank loan. Credit may come through the trade, through using credit cards or through buying machinery, vehicles, tools or other capital equipment on **hire purchase**.

Trade credit is common in a number of industries. Small building firms, like the Deerings, will have agreements with building trade suppliers so that they can collect material, timber, sand, cement and so on as and when they need it, settling up at the end of the month or another pre-agreed period, Such credit is often free – it helps the suppliers to keep sales up and helps the buyers to budget. In other businesses, for example retail, stock may be bought on credit. This is because the trader hopes to have sold the stock before it must be paid for. In some cases stock is bought on a 'sale-or-return' basis. If the business can't sell it, it is sent back and does not have to be paid for. Small or new businesses may also use credit cards to finance their purchase of stock. If very carefully managed, this can provide an interest free way of borrowing money. To be interest free, the business would have to pay off all of what is owed by the monthly due date. While this can provide up to 56 days of free credit, the penalties for failing to pay it off are extremely high, with interest rates way above those of a bank loan.

Have a go

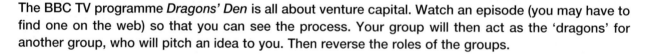

Group activity

The BBC TV programme *Dragons' Den* is all about venture capital. Watch an episode (you may have to find one on the web) so that you can see the process. Your group will then act as the 'dragons' for another group, who will pitch an idea to you. Then reverse the roles of the groups.

Discussion

Why do small businesses often have trouble raising the finance they need? Decide on a number of key steps that a business should take in order to make the raising of finance an easier process.

Web-based activity

Find out all you can about business angels and venture capital. (You could start at www.angelsden.com). If you were a small business, how would you go about raising venture capital?

Quickfire questions

1 Define 'owner's funds'.
2 What is meant by 'retained profit'?
3 Give three personal sources of finance for a small business entrepreneur.
4 Give one example of short-term borrowing.
5 Give one example of medium-term borrowing.
6 Give one example of long-term borrowing.
7 Define what is meant by 'security' in financial terms and give an example.
8 What is a mortgage?
9 Why do people make venture capital available?
10 What is meant by trade credit?

Hit the spot

> Outline the costs that a business will have to take into account before looking for funds.

>> Explain the difference between an overdraft and a loan. Give examples of when each would be appropriate.

>>> What could be the role of venture capital in small business finance? Would it be a good idea for a small business to seek venture capital? Give reasons for your answer.

Cracking the code

Contingencies Events that might cause costs in the future. A single one is a contingency.
Owner's own funds The owner's personal money.
Retained profits Profit kept from previous trading by a business.
Overdraft Permission to take more from a current account than is deposited.
Mortgage A long-term loan with property or land as security.
Security An asset that can be sold to repay a loan.
Hire purchase Buying something on instalments over a period of time.

Chapter 17
Business support

The Prince's Trust is one of a number of bodies that helps young people, including helping them into business. It concentrates on those who have had a rough deal – perhaps with disabilities, or failing at school, or from difficult family backgrounds. Much of its success is due to the support that it receives from the business communities where it operates. The Trust provides grants, advice and support to 18 to 30 year olds who need it. Its annual Celebrate Success Awards showcase success around the country.

- In Yorkshire, Oliver Griffiths, 24, unemployed, housebound and in a wheelchair, approached The Prince's Trust to set up a business helping young people into sport. A grant enabled him to attend coaching courses and then run courses for both able bodied and disabled youngsters. He also provides sports coaching for young people, both with and without disabilities.

- In London, Cat Byshiem, 29, was helped to set up Catherine Byshiem Jewellery Design. Originally from Norway, she designs jewellery based on Norwegian culture, patterns and stories. Her work has become well known enough for her to form part of a jewellery trade visit to New York. She received not just money from the Trust, however, but perhaps more importantly, support from two business mentors – successful business people who volunteer their services to help and advise young entrepreneurs.

- In the Midlands, Nyree Clark studied animal care at college but could not see how to turn this into a business until advised by the Trust. Again, it was not just money that was offered by the Trust, but sound business advice that led to her setting up Clark's Pet Couriers, offering a range of pet-related services. She now works with a number of local vets and has a small fleet of specialist vehicles for transporting pets.

- In the West Country, Claire Foster, 27, from Taunton, looked for a way of finding success on the back of the increase in demand for healthy food and drink. She saw that the market for smoothies was expanding, so set up a mobile juice bar called Superjuice. Set up with a grant from the Prince's Trust in 2005, it has expanded to include a hot range of healthy soups, porridge and even hot juices.

- In Norwich, Chinelo Brown was helped to set up a hair and beauty salon specialising in Afro-Caribbean styles. Starting with Chinelo's Hair Salon in 2006, it has already expanded into a high street beauty salon offering a range of services to men and women.

@ www.businesslink.gov.uk links to all parts of the UK governments business support network.
Follow the link to 'events' and see if you can find an event in your area that you could visit.
Listen to Claire Foster, owner of Superjuice, talking to *Dragons' Den* star Deborah Meaden on this link:
video.google.com/videoplay?docid=-8187285306371784895&hl=en. What do
you think of Deborah's ideas? What would you suggest yourself?
Visit **startups.co.uk** and click through 'entrepreneurs' to 'young entrepreneurs'. Choose which of
the examples you think is the most enterprising, and say why.

Did you know...

Informal support – that of friends and family, and of people you know with experience in business
– can be just as useful as the formal support offered by organisations. For example, local
knowledge of marketing opportunities may come from a friend or relative, rather than any official
resource.

Organised support

Support organisations, like the Prince's Trust, can help businesses in all stages of their development. The Prince's Trust (Prince's Youth Business Trust (PYBT), to give it its full name) provides grants and other assistance to young people under the age of 30 wanting to set up in business. It can help in market research, to find markets, and to develop products and services. Some bodies offer financial support. Others, just as importantly, offer advice and experience. Each successful business listed above was helped by an experienced business **mentor**. These are people with business knowledge who volunteer their time in order to support young people setting up new businesses. Many commercial organisations offer free advice and support as it is in their interest to have businesses run efficiently. High street banks, for example, will advise businesses on handling finance, and Citizens Advice Bureaux advise about business and employment regulations. The two main areas of business support are in finance and advice.

Advice and assistance

The government has a number of schemes in place which are designed to help small businesses. The Business Start Up Scheme, for example, is partnered with the Prince's Trust and is focused on deprived areas. It is aimed at helping the long-term unemployed find work through starting their own business. A visit to the business link site (**www.businesslink.gov.uk**) will show you that there are nearly two and a half thousand grants and support schemes available, as well as a wide range of training courses for both businesses and their staff. These include local, regional and national schemes as well as grants and support from outside bodies such as the European Union. Other bodies may encourage businesses of a particular type or group – such as The Arts Council for arts based businesses. Certain parts of government will also help with specific problems. HM Revenue and Customs will advise on taxation and customs rules, UK Trade and Investment will advise on overseas markets, the UK Intellectual Property Office (UKIPO) will advise on designs, trademarks, **patents** and **copyright**.

Did you know...

The government provides a series of guides to funding, finance and support. These can be
accessed through the **businesslink.gov.uk portal**. They are free to download.

An experienced business person can be a helpful mentor

Funding

The government helps by encouraging banks and other financial institutions to lend money to businesses. The Small Firms Loan Guarantee

Anyone who has an idea for a new or improved product, process or market can become an entrepreneur

scheme helps those businesses that have a good business idea, but do not have the assets to offer a bank as security. In this case, the government will guarantee up to 75 per cent of the loan, should the business fail.

In March 2008, as part of the Budget Report, a new Enterprise Strategy was launched. It is designed to help both new and existing businesses get the funding they need. It also helps businesses to understand and cope with business rules and regulation. The Strategy's central vision is to make the UK the most enterprising economy in the world and the best place to start and grow a business. It has five key aims:

● To create a culture of enterprise – where everyone who can be an entrepreneur is inspired to take up the challenge. There should be no barriers of age, gender, race or social background.

● To promote enterprise as a life-long journey, from primary school, through secondary school and into higher education.

● To provide access to funds so that entrepreneurs and small business owners can access the finance they need.

● To reduce and simplify the laws that govern businesses, to make this area easier to cope with.

● To help people to innovate, i.e. to develop new ideas and products.

Did you know...

If you are researching and developing a new product, your business may be allowed to set off some of the costs against tax. The government wants to encourage innovation, so provides **tax relief** in this area.

Summary

- There are many ways in which small and new businesses can gain support
- The majority of support is free
- Support may come in the form of advice or finance
- Advice is available formally and informally, locally, regionally and nationally
- The government has set up a network of websites and publications to provide advice
- Support may be available to help a business find finance through loans
- Financial support may also be available through grants
- Government is 100 per cent committed to enterprise, and therefore to supporting business

Core knowledge

Often the first place for a new business to visit will be the Local Authority where it is based. This will have a business support unit that can help it directly, or can put the business in touch with local Chambers of Commerce, Business Link or the Learning and Skills Council (LSC).

Chambers of Commerce are local organisations, made up of local businesses of all sizes and types. They link together to make a national network that will help and support business. British Chambers of Commerce (BCC), the national group, represents businesses that employ over 5 million people. Support is provided either from the national body, or at a local level. For example, to help new businesses BCC has developed a business start-up pack (**www.thebusiness-startup.co.uk**). Your local Chamber of Commerce can be found and accessed through **www.britishchambers.org.uk**. Chambers of Trade are similar locally based organisations.

Business Link is the government website that has been set up to help new business. Its sections include advice on starting up, finance and grants, employment, health and safety and taxation as well as advice on marketing, using e-commerce tools and expanding the business once it is established.

The LSC (Learning and Skills Council) can help the entrepreneur by providing the appropriate training – either to the owner or to employees. This includes access to an Adult Learning Grant. This is especially important for people who want to learn about new technology and how it can help their business to succeed.

And more

While businesses may have to borrow money or use their own funds, finance may also be raised through government grant or related schemes. The Grants and Support Directory (on **www.businesslink.gov.uk**) can be searched for grants specific to your area (such as rural businesses, or women into business) and to particular problems or issues – such as marketing, product development or expansion.

A grant is, in effect, a gift of money to a business. there is no interest, and the money does not have to be repaid. There are, however, fairly strict rules governing whether a grant may be available or not, and the application process may be complicated. It is also likely that certain conditions will have to be met (a minimum number of employees, for instance, or the grant may only be available to certain types of business). There is also likely to be competition for the grants available. Many grants involve '**matched funding**' where the grant is made only up to the amount of funding that the business is able to raise and risk itself. Grants may be made by national or local government and in such cases are often linked to particular areas where the government feels that help is needed. This may include areas of high unemployment (perhaps because a major local employer has failed) or government designated Enterprise Areas. There are 2000 Enterprise Areas in the UK situated in the most deprived areas of the country.

Have a go

Group activity

Go to the government's business link site (**www.businesslink.gov.uk**) and choose one of the support schemes available. Write a paragraph to explain the scheme. Make a leaflet to tell a local business about the various schemes by putting your paragraphs together. You should make it as attractive as possible, but also make sure that the advice is clear and accurate.

Discussion

Why do you think that the government is promoting a 'culture of enterprise'? What benefits will it bring to the economy? Are there any drawbacks?

Web-based activity

Visit the website of the UK Intellectual Property Office (UKIPO) at **www.ipaware.net/members/UKIPO.htm** and describe the process you would have to go through to register a new design or idea. How do you think that this helps new businesses?

Quickfire questions

1 What is meant by a grant?
2 What is the PYBT?
3 Give three sources of free advice for a business.
4 What is meant by 'tax relief'?
5 Describe the Business Start Up Scheme.
6 What is UKIPO and what does it do?
7 What is a Chamber of Commerce?
8 What is the LSC? What does it do?
9 What is a patent? How does it help a business?
10 What is meant by 'matched funding'?

Hit the spot

> Describe the work of the Prince's Trust.

> Explain how the Small Firms Loan Guarantee scheme works.

> Support for new businesses can come in the form of funds – money – or advice from experienced business people. Which of these do you think is most important? Give reasons for your answer.

Cracking the code

Copyright **Protection of the written word from being copied.**

Matched funding **When the business is expected to put in the same amount as a grant – so that for every £1 of grant, the business matches this funding. In this way, the business is half funded by grant and half by the business.**

Mentor **Person with business knowledge who helps to guide businesses.**

Patent **Protection from copying for an original design.**

Tax relief **When the government decides not to take tax on certain earnings.**

Chapter 18
Keeping accounts

IN THE NEWS

Business Active is a colour print magazine aimed at students, like you, studying business, finance or economics. For the magazine to be in profit means that it would have to take enough in revenue to cover all of its costs. This sounds easy, but, for Business Active, there were many costs to take into account and only limited sources of revenue. For a publication, there are generally two possible revenue streams. These are the cover price of the magazine or newspaper, and advertising revenue. For many publications the most important of these is advertising revenue, and a large proportion of a publication will be taken up by advertisers. With some publications, there is so much advertising that the publication can be free and is given away. Many local newspapers follow this model. With Business Active being aimed at an educational market of 14–16 year olds, however, its owners did not feel that advertising was appropriate. This left them with just the one revenue stream and the problem of finding the right price to attract buyers.

Costs, however, were another matter. Some costs are linked to the production of the magazine, others to promoting it or distributing it. The magazine has to be written, designed and typeset, and photographs taken and inserted. This means payments to writers, designers, photographers and administrative staff. It has to be printed, meaning payments to printers, and it has to be distributed, meaning payments to a firm of packagers and finishers, and postal charges. But even before all of this, there are other costs, some of which may never be recovered. These include initial advertising, a mailshot (written, designed, printed and posted) to all 5600 secondary schools in the country. This is expensive, but no sales have yet been made,

Volume 3 Number 3 Summer 2008

Business active

Derrek Lee hits a home run on Wrigley Field

Can Mars hit Cadbury's out of the park with it's purchase of Wrigley's?

so this involved borrowing the money and therefore incurring another cost – interest.

Whether or not the magazine reaches its sales target makes little difference to those from whom office space is rented, or who provide telephone or other communications services. They will have to be paid however many copies are sold.

Without proper accounts it is impossible to see whether the magazine is in profit or not or where improvements can be made to try to make it more successful, or more profitable. Clear and accurate accounts are an essential part of running even the smallest business.

@

Visit your local estate agent's website and see how much it would cost to rent or buy a small office. What other costs do you think a business would face once they had chosen a property?

Choose a small business type that you might like to open. (Perhaps a hairdressers, or nail bar, perhaps a small builder or retail business, perhaps a computer-based business.) List everything that you will have to buy to set up. Search the web for suppliers and see what the total costs of your set-up will be. Look at **www.hsbc.co.uk/1/2/business/finance-borrowing/business-loan** or a similar site and work out how much your loan will cost you. Remember, interest payments are a cost!

Did you know...

It is almost possible, with new technology, to be completely mobile. You could operate an internet service from a laptop. In this case your 'land' is anywhere that you set the laptop down to use it. Of course, this may make the 'land' element free or very low cost.

Business accounts

Many businesses struggle to survive because they do not keep a proper account of how much is being spent and how much received. This sounds like such a simple thing that it is difficult to see how a business could overlook it. However, particularly with a small or new business, there may be many, many other jobs which are, or seem to be at the time, more important than recording income and expenditure. It is vital, however, that a business keeps track of what is going out, as well as what is coming in!

Revenue

A business would not be in business unless it was taking money. The cash that it takes is called sales **revenue**. It is measured as the price of a product multiplied by the number of sales. A common mistake is to confuse revenue with **profit**. Revenue just measures the money coming in from sales, and takes no account of cost. Imagine buying a magazine for £2.50 and

then selling it to a friend for £2. You have a revenue of £2, but have actually lost 50p on the deal. Revenue is the income a business receives for the sale of its goods or services. There could,

A small business owner must keep track of income and expenditure

Did you know...

One of the areas that makes keeping accounts difficult is that values do not stay constant. A machine or vehicle is worth more when it is first bought than six months or a year later. This fall in value is known as 'depreciation'. Eventually, what was once a brand new shiny asset will be worth nothing!

The assets of a business will include vehicles, stock, buildings, machinery, etc.

therefore, be several streams of revenue for a business from the different products and services that it offers. A magazine, for example, will have revenue from its sales of copies and its sales of advertising space.

Resources

Whatever the type of business, it will require certain resources in order to operate. These are referred to as 'factors of production'. Every business needs

- *Land* – meaning somewhere from where to operate the business; this may be a space to put a factory, store goods or park vehicles. Equally, for a small business, it could refer to the back bedroom being used as office space. You may think that somewhere like a mobile hairdressers doesn't need land, but you would be wrong. Whatever the business, it needs a 'home base', and even a mobile business has to have a fixed point to which mail is sent.

- *Labour* – someone to actually do the work. In the smallest businesses the labour is provided by the owner himself or herself. Whatever this person does, is counted as labour. So this includes planning and thinking along with anything physical. Obviously, in larger businesses, there will also be people employed. Also included in 'labour' can be the original ideas, innovation and hard work that goes into 'enterprise'.

- *Capital* – this is not money (although often wrongly referred to as money) but the **assets** of the business – machinery, vehicles, buildings, raw materials, tools. Even brands and things like reputation can have a figure put on them.

Wages, power and telecoms bills are running costs

Costs

All of these inputs cost money and so have to be accounted for. A typical business has rent or mortgage payments on premises, business rates and **costs** for power and communications. It has wages to pay (even in one-person businesses, where the owner needs to include his or her own 'wage' in the accounts). It has to pay for materials and other costs of producing its product. Some of these costs only need to be paid once, others keep having to be paid.

- **Start-up costs** are also called sunk costs. These are costs that have to be met before the business can start to produce its good or service. They include buying machinery, furniture, vehicles and office and other equipment. They might also include market research costs and initial marketing.

- **Running costs** are those costs that have to be paid to keep the business operational. Examples include raw materials, wages, power and telecoms bills. Some start-up costs become running costs, e.g. if the business buys a machine on credit, the initial deposit is a start-up cost, the continuing payments are running costs. Running costs have to be paid, or the business cannot function. Once the business is covering its running costs, any additional revenue can go towards offsetting the start-up costs.

Did you know...

Another way to divide costs is into 'fixed' and 'variable' costs. Fixed costs have to be paid whether or not the business is producing anything. Examples include rent and the fixed part of power bills. Variable costs are directly linked to production, such as the amount of paper or ink used to produce a magazine.

Summary

- Keeping accurate accounts is vital to the efficient running of a business
- All businesses receive revenue from sales
- Revenue is not profit
- All businesses have certain costs
- Businesses have to pay for their inputs: these are land, labour and capital
- Some costs are paid at start-up, before the business can operate
- Some costs are ongoing, and are called running costs

Core knowledge

You can practise the skills of accounting by drawing up a simple budget for yourself. This is a good way to plan spending and make sure that you can afford what you want. Like a business, you will have certain sources of income. You are probably not selling a good or service, so this is income, rather than sales revenue. (The minute you do sell something for money, it becomes sales revenue, and you are operating a business, even if it is only making cakes and selling them at the school fair.) Like a business, you could have different sources of income – perhaps some of it is earned: pocket money for doing jobs around the house, a paper round, a part-time job. Some of it will be gifts rather than earned (and may be irregular) such as birthday money or money for passing examinations. You will also have expenditure, again in various different ways. Some of your spending may be regular (like the rent or fixed power charges that a business has to pay). Some may be extraordinary 'one off' spending – buying an expensive present for a special birthday or occasion, for instance. Other spending may be regular – payments into a savings account, magazine or club subscriptions, bus or train fares or other travel costs. Some may go up or down unexpectedly. For instance, a problem or crisis (or even a new relationship) may cause you to use your mobile phone much more than usual. You can see from this that your own income and expenditure is complex, so it is no wonder that a business may find it even more so.

And more

In business, there are two different kinds of account, and therefore two different kinds of accountant. The difference is between those accountants who work with the figures produced now and in the past, and those who have the job of predicting and forecasting what might happen in the future. The first group are called financial accountants. These are in charge of accurately recording the costs and revenues of a business. They prepare the figures, balances and accounts to help the business to operate efficiently. In a small business set-up, such as a sole trader or partnership, these accounts could be quite simple. They are important for two sets of people – the tax authorities and the owners themselves. The tax authorities need to know how much income is earned so that they can charge income tax on individuals and corporation tax on profits. The owner needs to know so that they have a clear picture of what is happening in the business, and know if they need to cut costs or boost revenue.

Once a business becomes a limited company, there is a legal requirement to publish certain figures. These include balance sheets, showing a snapshot of what a business owns and owes at any one time, a profit and loss account, and, in public limited companies, a statement to show the flows of cash in and out of the company. These are all figures that relate to the past performance of the business.

The second group are called management accountants. These use internal business figures for forward planning. (See page 120.)

Have a go!

Group activity

Each of you should draw up a set of three 'rules' for a small business in terms of how and when to keep accounts. Put all the rules together and agree on the most important 'top five'. You could then draw up a leaflet or poster to illustrate these.

Discussion

Why do you think so many businesses – particularly small businesses - find it hard to keep accurate and up-to-date accounts? List the reasons and possible solutions. Suggest good practice that would help a business person.

Web-based activity

Use a spreadsheet to draw up a simple budget for yourself for the next six months. Use a search engine to find an online guide to your programme and make it interactive, so that you can change income and expenditure and see what happens.

Quickfire questions

1 Describe what is meant by 'revenue'.
2 Describe what is meant by 'profit'.
3 Name a business. Give three possible costs for this business.
4 Give one possible source of revenue for this business.
5 Define what is meant by 'land' as a factor of production.
6 Define what is meant by 'labour' as a factor of production.
7 Define what is meant by 'capital' as a factor of production.
8 What is an asset?
9 What is the difference between start-up and running costs?
10 Name the two different kinds of accountant.

Hit the spot

> Explain the difference between revenue and profit.

>> Which is the most important factor out of land, labour, capital and enterprise? Give reasons for your choice.

>>> Explain the difference between start-up costs and running costs. Which is most important to a business? Give reasons for your choice.

Cracking the code

Asset What the business owns, such as stock or equipment or vehicles.

Costs A precise business term, referring to the amount that has to be paid for a good or service that a business needs. Costs are then further subdivided.

Profit The difference between cost and revenue, when revenue is greater than cost.

Revenue Money received by a business as a result of sales.

Running costs (or operational costs) Those costs that arise out of the operation of the business.

Start-up costs Those costs paid once, when a business is first set up.

Chapter 19
Making a profit

IN THE NEWS

Joel Harrison is a sixth-form student at a large college in the North of England. As the son of a sheep farming family Joel had always thought of grass as being something of an asset. He knew that farmers actually had to pay for grazing if they could not rear sheep on their own land. This was an additional cost to many sheep farmers, including his father's farm. Joel knew that his father even had to rent fields from neighbouring landowners in order to be able to feed all of his flock. Working in the library at the college, Joel was disturbed one afternoon by the sound of heavy mowing equipment. He looked out of the library window to see two huge industrial mowing machines cutting the vast lawns of the college. He was immediately hit by a bright idea and contacted the college authorities.

Now Joel's father rents some of his sheep to the college. Sheep are good for lawns and they keep the lawns in good trim. On top of this, there is the added benefit of them providing a calming rural backdrop to the students' studies. Mr Harrison receives some rent from the college and, of course, gets to feed his sheep for free. The college saves money because it no longer has to hire noisy and expensive contractors. Students and staff can also see that it is getting closer to its environmental targets. Joel has made money out of the deal by acting as the 'middle man' between his father and the college. As a business, he is automatically a sole trader, as he has not chosen any other form of business (see Chapter 8). This means that not only does he get to keep any rewards, but he also carries all the risk and responsibility. He has looked at the possibility of providing the service to other organisations but needs first to know if he is making a profit.

His revenue comes from the college, which has paid him for setting up the service. However, he does not yet know if he is making a profit, as there are other costs involved. He has had to provide fencing, and has taken out insurance against any damage or nuisance that the sheep may cause. His father delivered the first flock, but he will be responsible for transport if he sells the service to other organisations. He also needs to include the costs of his own time taken to set up and manage the project.

Joel's unique business

@

The government's site for start-ups at **www.startups.co.uk/66788429117 18766542/making-a-profit.html** has a calculator for a business to see if it will make a profit. Input some costs for Joel (or a business of your choice) and see what sort of issues there might be.
On **www.mybusiness.co.uk/ YVM1eXBotKRAKg.html** you will find a long list of possible costs a business should include. See if you can think of any others.

Accounting and predictions

As with many small businesses, it is important that Joel looks to the future. It may be that he will make a loss in the first couple of years but is prepared to ride this out in order to make a profit once the business has built up. Businesses do not always make a profit in their first few months, or even years, of operation. Joel may have to borrow in order to cover his start-up costs and hope that future expansion will enable him to go into profit. He can only take this risk by 'looking into the future'. He has to use the figures and accounts that he has drawn up for the business and project what might happen in the future. Asking 'what if such-and-such happens' or 'what if such-and-such a cost rises' is called making 'what-if' predictions. Such predictions can only be made on the back of accurate accounts.

Target

Joel's first target is likely to be to break even. In other words, he needs to make enough revenue from selling his service to cover the costs of providing the service. If he was dealing with just one stream of revenue, and one set of costs, this would be easy. But, as with all businesses, there are various different costs to be taken into account.

Break even

Break even is the financial position where the total revenue of a business (the total amount of money coming into the business from sales and other activities) is equal to the total cost. At this point the business is making neither a profit nor

a loss. It can be shown on a break even chart which shows costs against revenues and includes fixed costs, variable costs, total costs and sales revenue. (See table.)

Number sold	Sales revenue	Fixed cost	Variable cost	Total cost
0	0	15	0	15
1	10	15	5	20
2	20	15	10	25
3	**30**	**15**	**15**	**30**
4	40	15	20	35
5	50	15	25	40

Profit and loss account

The profit and loss account shows what profit has been made, and where it has gone to. This is drawn up to show what has happened in the past (usually) six or twelve months of operation. It shows the past performance of the business. Here is a typical account for a small business, in this example a retailer called Rodney selling chocolate bars.

The first part of the account is called the 'trading' account. In this Rodney includes:

- Sales revenue to show the number of sales x price for the products sold in the period that the account covers. Rodney has sold 500 £1 bars.

- For any product that the business has sold, there will be an associated cost. For example, the raw materials or components used to make the product. For our retailer this is the price that he has paid for the chocolate bars. Rodney paid 50p each for the bars.

Trading Account

Sales revenue	500 × £1	500
Minus Cost of sales	opening stock 100	
	plus purchases 600	
	less closing stock	
	200 = 500 × 50p =	250
Gross profit		**250**

Profit and Loss Account

Gross profit	250
Minus Expenses	50
Net profit	**200**

- To know the cost of sales accurately, Rodney has to work out how much stock he actually bought in the period. Rodney has some stock at the start of the period (opening stock), bought more stock when he needed it (purchases) and has some stock left over (closing stock). The difference is the cost of the stock bought.

Gross profit shows the profit Rodney made on sales and is the first figure on the next part of the account, called the 'profit and loss' account.

Some of Rodney's stock

From this trading profit, Rodney takes the various other **expenses** that he has had to pay: rent for the shop, wages, electricity, petrol for his van, interest on loans, business rates, cleaning costs, telephone bills – in fact, all of the running costs (also called operating costs or **overheads**) of the business. In here, Rodney would also add in any other income of the business such as rent, interest on bank deposits or investment income. This gives him **net profit** for the period.

The third part of the account (called the 'appropriation' account, and not shown in our example) shows what happens to this profit. Some may go in taxation, some may be kept to reinvest, some may go to the owners.

Did you know...

Profit maximisation (the making of as much profit as possible) is often given as the central aim of businesses. Other aims, such as independence, or providing a service, may be more important and there are also not-for-profit business organisations such as charities (see Chapter 5).

Summary

- Profit is the reward for enterprise
- Profit is made when revenues are greater than costs
- When costs are greater than revenues the business is making a loss
- It is important to count in all costs
- Break even is when costs and revenues are equal
- A profit and loss account shows where money has come from, and where it has gone to

Core knowledge

What is profit? Profit is the reward for enterprise, or risk taking, and may be considered to be the main reason why many businesses are in business. Profit is defined as what is left once costs have been taken from revenue, as long as this is a positive figure. If costs are greater than revenue then this is a loss.

The important thing about calculating profit is to make sure that all costs have been taken into account. If this does not happen, then a false picture of profitability will emerge. Often, particularly in small or start-up businesses, the owner's own time is not costed in. In such cases it is easy to overestimate the amount of profit that has been made. Many small business owners and entrepreneurs are dedicated to their business, and put in long hours and a lot of hard work. This should be properly costed before deciding whether the business is worth operating. Against this, of course, go the benefits of working for yourself, setting your own hours and goals and reaping the rewards if the business is a success.

Profit is also a signal to other businesses that this is an area where they might be able to compete. If a business is making a profit in a market, then there is room for competition. If losses are being made, then this acts as a signal that one or more businesses should leave the market.

And more

The table earlier in this chapter shows the various elements in calculating break even. Building a break even graph from a chart is fairly straightforward. There are just four lines to consider. Fixed costs are those which do not alter as output alters, this is therefore shown on the graph as a horizontal line (FC). Variable costs are those that change as output changes and are therefore shown as rising as output rises (VC). Adding fixed costs to variable costs gives total costs (TC). Total revenue (TR) shows price x sales. The point where total cost is equal to total revenue is the break even point. To the left of this point, total costs are higher than total revenue, so the business is making a loss, to the right of this point, total costs are lower than total revenue, so the business is making a profit. The further away sales are from the break even point, the greater the profit or loss. Because there are so many different costs in most businesses, and of different types, it is not always easy to say which should be included and where, so it is often hard to be accurate about break even. This makes it a tool of limited use. It does, however, give clues as to the sort of methods that a business could use to reach or increase profit. Increasing price might increase revenue, lowering costs would enable break even to be reached earlier. Break even tables also show that fixed costs become less of an issue when spread over higher levels of output.

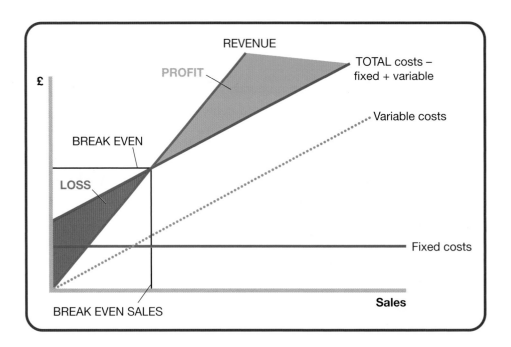

Have a go

Group activity

Draw up a profit and loss account from the following figures for a small business selling widgets. Wendy's Widgets has bought and sold 400 boxes of small, 250 boxes of medium and 22 boxes of large widgets in the past six months. She buys widgets at £8 for a box of small, £9 for a box of medium and £12 for a box of large. Wendy sells widgets at £10 for a box of small or medium and £13 for a box of large. Her expenses in the period include rent £200, labour £400, transport £350, power £50, and insurance £25. Has Wendy made a profit?

Profit and Loss Account	TOTAL
Sales revenue	
Cost of sales	
Gross profit	
Expenses	
Transport	
Labour	
Rent	
Power	
Insurance	
Net profit (before tax)	

Discussion

Looking at the figures for Wendy's Widgets, do you think it is worth Wendy staying in business? What advice would you give her regarding her business?

Web-based activity

Explain why 'what-ifs' are important to a business. Show how you could make use of a spreadsheet to work out 'what ifs'.

Quickfire questions

1 Describe what is meant by a 'what if' in business.
2 Give an example of a typical 'what if'.
3 Define break even.
4 What is 'gross profit'?
5 What is 'net profit'?
6 Explain what is meant by 'cost of sales'.
7 What is the 'trading account'?
8 List the typical expenses of a small business.
9 What are 'overheads'?
10 Explain how profit acts as a signal to other businesses.

Hit the spot

> Describe how a break even point can be calculated.

>> Explain how some businesses mistakenly calculate break even on output rather than sales. What problems is this likely to cause?

>>> Explain why profit is called the 'reward to enterprise'. What other rewards might be as important to the entrepreneur? Give reasons for your answer.

Cracking the code

Break even The point when costs equal revenues.

Expenses The costs to a business of all the services and other inputs used to run the business.

Gross profit Profit before expenses have been taken off.

Net profit Profit after expenses have been taken off.

Overheads Also called running costs: the day-to-day costs of operating the business.

Profit maximisation Making as much profit as possible.

Chapter 20
Managing cash flow

IN THE NEWS

Cash flow problems are likely with any small business, but especially with any business where cash comes in on an irregular basis. The Little Theatre, in Dale, is typical of many small community theatres which struggle to keep money coming through the doors all year round. Theatres find themselves in the position – as do all businesses – of having to pay fixed costs even when there is no performance. The Little Theatre has to pay its council tax and business rates, and standing charges to gas and electricity companies, whether or not it has a performance on. There are also some of its staff who are full time, as it is not possible (or desirable) to take on temporary staff for certain jobs. The caretaker, for example, needs to open the building in the morning, clean it and ensure that it is made secure and locked up at night. Even worse, its costs rise during a rehearsal period – staff and rooms are required and lighting and heating costs go up. Actors need to be paid once they are cast in a part and in rehearsal, props and costumes need to be bought or made and permissions to perform bought from the copyright holders of the play. All of this has to be paid before a single ticket is sold or even printed. (Ticket printing and publicity are even more costs that have to be paid before the doors open to the public.)

The Little Theatre's biggest money spinner is the annual Christmas pantomime. This starts its run in November and continues far into the New Year. In fact, it runs for as long as there is an audience coming to see it, and the theatre managers hope that, in most years, this will take them to the start of March. The pantomime does not always play to a full

Panto season

house, and eventually has to close as audiences dwindle. However, during its busiest four weeks, either side of Christmas Day, it is a sell-out, with both afternoon matinee and evening performances. Management has to try, each year, to take enough money in this period to support the theatre for the rest of the year. It also has to think of other ways to generate cash when the theatre is not staging a performance and to try to come up with ways of spreading or delaying payments to suppliers.

@ Go to **www.thisistheatre.com/ panto.html**. What performances are on in your area? List the ways in which each theatre is trying to spread cash flow.

Visit **www.fireworks.co.uk**. How many ways of increasing firework sales can you find? Can you think of any other ways?

Cash flow statement						
£	Month 1	Month 2	Month 3	Month 4	Month 5	Month 6
Balance brought forward	1000	−1000	−1000	−2000	2000	5000
Sales revenue	2000	2000	2000	4500	3500	4000
Cash in hand	3000	1000	1000	2500	5500	9000
Cash out	4000	2000	3000	500	500	1000
Balance carried forward	−1000	−1000	−2000	2000	5000	8000

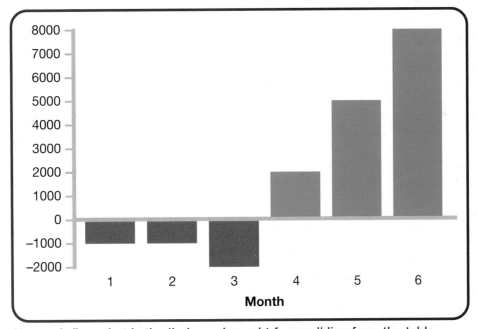

Net cash flow, that is the 'balance brought forward' line from the table

Cash flow

The Little Theatre can use the financial accounts that it has drawn up to see whether or not it is making a profit. This, however, shows it the position at the end of a period of time, rather than during it. It may be that, by the end of the year, the theatre is making a profit, but this does not show the full picture, or possible problems during the year. This is the case for many businesses that face uneven flows of cash into and out of their business. In the most extreme cases, for instance seasonal products, a business will have to make all its sales in a very short period and use this money to support itself for the rest of the time. Typical seasonal products include Christmas decorations, ice cream, fireworks, holidays and many different kinds of fruit and vegetable.

Seasonal sales of these products peak in December

Cash shortages

The Little Theatre needs to know when cash is going to come in and, just as importantly, when it needs to go out in terms of payments to suppliers and for services like **utilities**, marketing and communications. It is often a shortage of cash rather than a lack of orders that is the reason for the failure of a business. If a bill becomes due for payment, and the business does not have the cash to meet it, this can spell disaster. Imagine a delivery service that could not afford its fuel bill, or a retailer that does not have the money to pay the rent on the shop, or a farmer that doesn't have the money to pay for seed. In each case, even though the business may be a viable one – even a successful one – a lack of cash could see **creditors** forcing the business to close, so that they can be paid from the sale of its **assets**.

Cash flow table

A cash flow table shows the flows of money into and out of a business. Cash flow is often pictured as a bathtub, with cash flowing into it from the taps, and out again through the plughole. There are problems for the business if the tub overflows or runs dry! If it overflows, this means that the business has too much cash, which could be invested to make money. If it runs dry, then the business may not be able to pay its bills.

Cash flow forecast

A cash flow forecast shows predicted flows of cash into and out of a business. A detailed cash flow can show trends in costs and prices and be a useful management tool. It lets the business know when it will need to borrow money, how much it will need to borrow and for how long. This can help it not only to have financing in place, but to choose the most appropriate type of finance.

Managing cash flow

There are two ways for a business to manage cash flow. One is to increase revenue or, if this is not possible, to spread revenue, so that it comes in more evenly. The other is to reduce or spread costs. Many businesses that sell seasonal products will try to spread sales throughout the year, by making products popular at other times.

Solutions to cash flow problems

To spread revenue, the Little Theatre could sell advance tickets or season tickets to shows. This brings some revenue in ahead of actual ticket sales. It could also try to create new revenue streams. For example, the foyer space could be used for art exhibitions, or rented to another business as a coffee bar or café. It could try to bring its costs down or, if this is not possible, spread or reschedule payments. For example, it could pay utility bills monthly rather than in a lump sum.

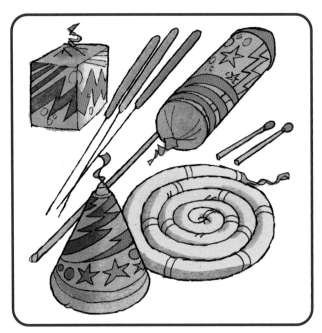

In the UK, seasonal sales of these products peak in November

Did you know...

Firework manufacturers have successfully moved some firework sales in the UK away from the run-up to 5 November by promoting them for weddings and other events and celebrations.

Summary

- A business needs to control flows of cash
- Cash flows into and out of a business exist both when it starts up and when it is operating
- Cash flow problems are one of the main causes of business failure
- Businesses can help cash flow by increasing or spreading revenue
- Businesses can help cash flow by decreasing or spreading costs
- Cash flow forecasts are a powerful management tool

Core knowledge

The main cash inflows happen firstly when the business is set up, and then when it starts operating. The first inflows are the cash used to start the business, for example owners' funds, loans and grants (see Chapter 16). Once the business is operating, there are then inflows of sales revenue. The main outflows are also in two parts. When setting up, the business will need to buy stock, premises, machinery, tools, etc. and to pay for marketing and promotion. Once operating, the outflows continue – buying stock, paying interest on loans, taxation, expenses such as rent, rates, wages, power and communication charges. If there is more flowing into a business than leaving it the business has a cash **surplus**. If there is more flowing out than in, there is a cash **deficit**. A cash flow statement shows flows in and out of the business in the past. A forecast estimates what those flows will be in the future. It is a month by month prediction of how much cash will be needed, so that the business can plan ahead and make sure that:

● it has enough cash to cover payments when they become due;

● it does not carry too much cash.

Carrying too much cash is as much of a problem as not having enough. Money that is in tills, or current accounts, could be earning interest for the business if it was invested.

And more

There are two different types of accountant. Financial accountants look after and record the costs and revenues of a business: its income and expenditure. They also make sure that its accounts are accurate for the people who need them, such as the tax authorities and the owners.

Management accountants use the internal financial information of the business. These figures are only available to the managers and owners of the business. (Many of the figures used by financial accountants are, especially in limited companies, available to the public.) They are figures and accounts that are used to work out how well the business is doing and how to move it forward. They involve managers in making forecasts and in planning for the future. These accounts are vital in planning the future direction of the business and are the major tools in strategic planning. The major tools used are budgets (working out future spending and income) and ratios, which measure one factor in terms of another (for instance how productive a machine is in terms of its cost) to show efficiency or effectiveness and forecasts. A management accountant would not be interested in a cash flow statement, for example, but would want to know about the forecast future cash flows of the business so that this could be managed. Management accountants are often found in positions of power and responsibility in a business, and rise to top management positions.

Have a go

Group activity

Each person in your group should set up a spreadsheet to calculate cash flow for an imaginary business. Look at how other people have used formulae and decide on the most efficient way to set up the spreadsheet.

Discussion

If a sole trader cannot pay a bill, creditors can take him or her to court. If the court decides to make the person bankrupt, it can force the sale of his or her possessions in order to pay the bill.
Do you think that creditors – which are often big companies like electricity suppliers - should be allowed to do this?

Web-based activity

Find out all you can about company 'receivers'. What is their role? What link do you think they have with cash flow problems?

Quickfire questions

1 Describe one possible cash inflow when a business is at start-up stage.
2 Describe one possible cash outflow when a business is at start-up stage.
3 Describe one possible cash inflow when a business is at operational stage.
4 Describe one possible cash outflow when a business is at operational stage.
5 Give three examples of products that have seasonal sales.
6 What is a creditor?
7 What is an asset?
8 Describe how a cash shortage could be a problem for a business.
9 Describe how a cash surplus could be a problem for a business.
10 Give two possible ways to solve a cash flow problem.

Hit the spot

➤ Before doing this exercise, you should decide what business Kingston and Webb are in. You can then repeat the exercise using different types of business.

➤➤ Look at the six month cash flow forecast for Kingston and Webb (page 117). Suggest ways to improve the forecast.

➤➤➤ Identify the months when Kingston and Webb may have problems of cash shortages and suggest what they should do to solve the problems.

➤➤➤ What is the problem from months 4 to 6? Explain why this is a problem, and suggest possible solutions.

Cracking the code

Assets What the business owns, such as stock or equipment or vehicles.

Creditor Someone, or a business, that is owed money.

Deficit When cash outflows are greater than inflows.

Surplus When cash inflows are greater than outflows.

Utilities Services such as water, gas and electricity.

PEOPLE IN BUSINESSES

Chapter 21
Recruiting staff

Education Sense

Probably all school students know what a supply teacher is. It's the person who replaces the full-time teacher when he or she is off ill or on a training course. Sometimes these teachers are called cover or relief teachers. Schools will often hire a supply teacher by phoning up an agency. Karl Gannon runs one of these agencies, which he calls Education Sense. The agency is based in the south-east of England.

Karl seems the most unlikely person to start a teacher agency. He did not have a positive experience at school when he was young. Karl suffers from dyslexia, which made it difficult for him to progress at school. He was expelled when he was 13, and ran away from home when he was 14.

With no GCSE qualifications to his name, Karl found it difficult to find work. But with funding and support from the Prince's Trust, he managed to get his own business off the ground. Karl decided to specialise in providing special educational needs (SEN) teachers and teaching assistants. He felt that he had been let down when he was at school because his own needs had not been recognised. He was determined to improve things for students who had trouble learning.

Karl needs to recruit teachers regularly to have on his books. He advertises for them in newspapers, but he relies mostly on Education Sense's web pages to attract teachers to the agency.

Once a person has shown an interest in becoming a supply teacher, Karl will ask him or her to complete an **application form**. The form will ask the applicant to give details of their teaching experience and other information, such as whether the person wants full-time or part-time work. If Karl believes that the person applying is suitable, an **interview** will be held. Karl needs to check that the teacher has the right sort of personality and interests to work with SEN children. If it is necessary, Education Sense will provide training in working with special needs students.

The person applying will also be police checked. This means Education Sense will ask the police if there are any reasons why this person should not be allowed to work with children.

Karl believes that it is important to have a good working relationship with the schools that take his supply teachers. He will visit each one personally to find out about the school. Care will then be taken to make sure that the supply teacher that Karl sends to the school matches its needs.

 Take a look at Karl's web page at:
www.education-sense.com

A job interview

Full-time and part-time employees

Education Sense encourages both part-time and full-time teachers to apply to the recruitment agency. Many employees prefer to work part-time. This could be because:

- They have family or other commitments that do not allow them to be away from home for long periods. When part-time work is offered, employers will find it easier to recruit students and mothers with young children.

- Employees might prefer two or three part-time jobs rather than have a full-time one. This can

bring additional security, as if one job ends for some reason; there is another to provide income to the worker. Some people may also like the variety that several part-time jobs bring.

Recent laws have made it illegal to treat part-time employees any differently than their full-time co-workers. So, part-timers have the same job security. They cannot be made redundant before full-time workers are, just because they work part-time. Also, the same wage rate must be given to part-timers as is paid to full-time employees doing the same work.

Full-time employees can bring benefits to businesses:

- Full-timers are more likely to be up to date with what is going on in the business.

- They can become more skilful because they are using their skills more often.

- They know their co-workers better and can fit in more easily as part of a team.

- If the employees have direct contact with customers, then it helps to have full-timers. Customers like to deal with familiar faces.

Summary

- Recruiting staff can be a complicated and time-consuming activity. It can also be expensive in terms of time and effort needed to get the right person for the job.
- It is important that small businesses in particular take care to recruit the right people. If you only employ three people and one is weak that is a large proportion of your staff.
- There are both benefits and disadvantages in employing part-time staff.

Core knowledge

Recruitment

Before an employee is recruited it would make sense to consider if the employee is actually needed. Employing somebody is a long-term commitment. When an employee leaves a business, the business owner could use this opportunity to consider whether the leaver actually needs to be replaced. Or, would it be better to recruit someone with different skills?

A large business might write a detailed job description and a person specification at this point. This way, the managers will have a much clearer idea of the type of person that they are looking for. It is unlikely that a small business will go to this trouble. But the owner of a small business must make sure that he or she recruits a suitable person. A poor choice of employee will have a much bigger impact on a small business than a large one.

It is for this reason that owners might want to promote someone from within the business to fill the vacancy. This is called internal **recruitment**. The owner of the business will know how well the person works. The promotion might even motivate the employee to work even harder. This would only be suitable, however, for recruiting a supervisor or manager. It also means that there will be a vacancy for the promoted person's previous job.

Businesses might choose to recruit from outside the business, which is known as external recruitment. There are different ways that they can attract suitable people:

- *Recruitment agency* These are businesses like Education Sense. They will specialise in providing suitable employees, saving the business the trouble of doing this themselves.

- *Job Centres* These are government agencies that allow job seekers to find suitable work. The centre will also inform businesses of people on their books who might be suitable for the vacancy. Job Centres do not charge businesses for their services.

- *Advertise the vacancy* If a business needs a new employee it is more likely to advertise the job to attract people to apply. Where it advertises will depend upon the business. A small business might advertise in a local newspaper.

A recruitment agency

Selection process

The **selection** process has specific stages:

- *Completing an application form* The application form allows the business to sort out those people who are suitable. Applicants who do not have the required skills or qualifications will be rejected.
- *Short listing* This is when unsuitable candidates are discounted, leaving a smaller, manageable number of people to be interviewed.
- *Interview* This might be a formal meeting with the applicant where the employer asks a series of questions. The employer is trying to determine if the person is capable of doing the job and is motivated. This meeting also gives the applicant a chance to find out about the job and the business.
- *Trial period* Sometimes employees are not taken on permanently until they have successfully completed a trial period. This means they will be watched closely for the first few months. If the work they do is not good enough, they could be asked to leave at the end of the trial period.

And more

The owner of the business might already have a good idea whom he or she wants to fill the vacancy. It could be a person who is working for a competitor. Attracting the employee would save on training as the person already has the skills needed. There is another benefit: a competitor could be losing a key member of staff. Also the former employee might bring along useful information about the competing business. This method of recruitment is sometimes called head hunting or poaching. Not all businesses see poaching as a fair method of recruiting staff.

Sometimes the owner of a small business will ask the people who work in the business if they know anybody suitable for the job vacancy. Recruiting this way is cheaper, as there is no need to pay for an advertisement. There is more chance that the person recommended would fit in to the business if he or she is already known by people employed there. This type of recruitment can also be a good thing as the person who recommended the new employee would not want that employee to do anything to let him or her down.

Have a go!

Group activity

Imagine your school or college needs a new bursar/finance officer, or similar position. As a team, complete the following:

- outline/description of the job;
- list of the skills and qualifications needed;
- newspaper advertisement;
- programme for the day of the interview;
- list of questions to be asked at interview.

Discussion

Discuss in groups whether full-time employees are more likely to be loyal to the business than part-timers.

Quickfire questions

1   What is an application form?
2   What is a employee recruitment agency?
3   What is meant by internal recruitment?
4   Give an advantage of recruiting internally.
5   Describe two methods Education Sense uses to make sure the right type of teacher is recruited.
6   Give two reasons why Education Sense prefers to recruit teachers using its web pages.
7   Produce a list of three questions that Karl Gannon might ask teachers when he interviews them? Explain why you have chosen each of these questions.
8   Give an argument both for and against using a trial period before an employee is taken on permanently.
9   Give a reason why many businesses prefer to get their staff from recruitment agencies.
10 Give an argument both for and against recruiting staff on the recommendation of a current employee.

Hit the spot

> What is meant by (i) recruitment; (ii) selection?

>> Explain two reasons why employers sometimes prefer to appoint part-time staff.

>> Discuss the arguments for and against promoting somebody already working in the business, rather than appointing a person from outside.

Cracking the code

Application form A document filled in by someone wanting to work for a business. The form asks for personal details, employment history and experience.

Interview A chance for the employer and the applicant to meet. It can be formal, with the applicant being asked a series of questions, or just a chat.

Recruitment The process of an employer finding people who might be suitable to employ.

Selection The process of choosing the right person for the job.

Chapter 22
Rewarding staff

Country Estates Garden (CEG) Furniture

CEG Furniture manufactures high quality garden furniture using traditional British timbers of elm and oak. The business is based in the Midlands, but sells its products all around the country. The furniture is targeted at the upper end of the market with prices much higher than customers would expect to pay for lower quality products at garden centres. The business sells through the internet and magazines like *Worcestershire Life*. There is also a display area outside the factory, where customers can inspect the furniture.

CEG employs five woodworkers who produce the furniture using traditional skills. There is also a part-time driver and a part-time secretary. A manager oversees the running of the company. The business is known for its friendly working environment. All but one of the employees have been there for at least ten years.

Each of the woodworkers is paid a **basic wage** of about £320 per week for a 40-hour week. If these workers are asked to work **overtime** because a large order has been received, 'time and a half' is given for hours above eight hours a day. The business's manager, John, is paid a salary of about £30,000 a year. He does not receive any overtime payments, and often works more than ten hours each day.

Besides the wage it pays to its woodworkers, CEG allocates 2 per cent of its profits to share between all employees according to how long they have worked there. Profits last year were £280,000. All employees are allowed to buy the furniture at a big **discount**, but even at the lower price, it is too expensive for them. At Christmas CEG gives each of its employees a luxury hamper.

Did you know...

In 2007, you had to earn £906 per week to be in the top 10 per cent of earners in the UK. If you earned less than £252, you were in the bottom 10 per cent.

Types of reward

CEG rewards its staff in several ways. These rewards can be split into two types: monetary and non-monetary. Most of the monetary rewards come from the wages that are paid each week. The annual **bonus** is another form of monetary reward. Employees, however, will only receive this payment if the business makes a profit, and if they have been there for long enough. Some of the longer-established employees would get a much bigger payment than those who only just qualify for it. This could cause some resentment, particularly if people feel that they have all worked equally hard to make the business profitable.

It is common practice for employers to pay workers at a higher hourly rate when they work longer than their **contracted hours**. Overtime rates vary though from business to business. CEG is quite generous in paying 1.5 times the normal hourly rate. Some businesses pay the lower rate of 'time and a quarter' or 1.25 times the normal hourly rate.

The non-monetary rewards include the Christmas hamper. This could be seen as a fringe benefit for working for CEG. There are other such benefits, however. The discount on the furniture could be viewed as another benefit. It could be argued that, because nobody takes up the offer to buy the furniture, it is not a genuine reward to the staff.

There are aspects of the job that could be seen as being a non-monetary reward. The case study

The Christmas hamper is a non-monetary reward for employees

says that the business is known for its friendly working environment. If CEG employees enjoy this, then in a sense they are being rewarded. Imagine one of the employees being offered an extra £30 per week to go and work for another business that was not as friendly a place. If he decided not to take up the offer, then in a way he has decided that the friendly environment at CEG is worth at least £30 to him.

Summary

- Workers are rewarded in more ways than just wages or salaries
- Rewards can be classed as monetary or non-monetary
- If a person enjoys a job, he or she might be not be prepared to move, even for a higher wage

Core knowledge

Wages and salaries

People often confuse these two terms. They both refer to financial rewards for working for a business, but the methods are different. Wages are usually paid either weekly or fortnightly, while salaries are paid monthly. However, the main difference is that wages are paid for undertaking so many hours work, but salaries are paid for doing a particular job. A manager will be paid a salary for managing a business. He will be expected to put in all the hours necessary to do the job, and not be able to claim overtime payments.

In the case study it says that John, the manager, often worked ten hours each day. Clearly, John felt that the job needed this amount of time to get the work done. The woodworkers on the other hand get paid more if they need to work more than eight hours each day.

Factors affecting the wages/salaries paid

The amount a person is paid, either as a salary or a wage, will depend on many factors. The law says that an employee must be paid at least the national minimum wage. This is considered in more detail in Chapter 24. The owner of a small business would probably look at the wages that are offered for similar jobs in other businesses when deciding on how much to pay his employees. Nevertheless, a worker may be offered a higher wage if he or she has more experience than others on lower wages, or has a particular skill that the business wants.

Fringe benefits are a common way of rewarding staff. Fringe benefits are rewards in addition to a person's normal wages or salaries. These are frequently used to motivate employees. More on this topic can be found in the next chapter.

A limited liability business might decide to offer employees shares in the company. These might be given freely or offered at reduced price. Many people believe that rewarding employees in this way will encourage them to work hard. If the business is successful this way, shareholders will receive a higher dividend. Another fringe benefit is helping the employee save for a pension. If the employee agrees, each week or month an amount of money is taken from his or her wages to put towards the pension. The employer will pay an additional amount to increase the saving (or contribution). Occasionally employers pay all of the pension contributions themselves, which is known as a non-contributory pension.

And more

There are other factors that influence just how much an employee earns. A business might use performance-related pay. This means the wage the employee gets paid depends upon the amount that is produced. At one extreme is **piecework**. With this system of payment an employee is paid so much for each item produced. Someone working in a factory assembling a circuit board may be paid 35p for each board made. If 20 can be made in an hour, the employee would be paid £7. Other performance-related systems might include a bonus payment for reaching a certain target. The problem with performance-related pay is that it is often difficult to measure the performance of a particular employee, especially when people work in teams. Also some jobs do not have any output to measure. How would you measure the output of a police officer, for example?

In the case study for this chapter we looked at how someone might not be willing to move to another job, even if the financial rewards are higher. Many people take more than money into account when they consider the rewards that they receive for doing a job. You will be able to read more about this in the next chapter.

If people enjoy the work that they do, we say they receive job satisfaction. In the example in the case study, the woodworker was not prepared to change jobs, even if he was offered an extra £30 per week. We could argue that the job satisfaction that he receives at CEG is worth £30 to him. If a business can improve the job satisfaction that its employees get, it will find it easy to retain them and still pay them lower wages that they could get elsewhere.

Have a go

Group activity

Working in a group, produce a PowerPoint presentation, or a podcast, explaining the different ways a small business might try to increase the job satisfaction that its employees receive.

Conduct a survey of people to determine the types of fringe benefits that they receive. The results should be presented as a series of graphs with sufficient explanation on a PowerPoint loop.

Quickfire questions

1 What is a fringe benefit?
2 What is piecework?
3 Give an example of a non-monetary reward.
4 Calculate the hourly rate of pay of the CEG woodworkers.
5 What is meant by CEG's customers being at the 'upper end of the market'?
6 Explain the difference between a wage and a salary.
7 What is meant by a non-contributory pension?
8 Explain why some employers allow employees to buy shares in the business at a discounted rate.
9 Explain a problem a business might have using performance-related pay.
10 Explain two possible reasons why one person is paid more than another.

Hit the spot

> What is meant by a non-monetary reward?

>> Explain how a business could benefit by giving its employees non-monetary rewards.

>>> Discuss whether businesses need to offer similar wages as other businesses in order to retain their staff.

Cracking the code

Basic wage The wage paid for working the normal (contracted) hours.

Bonus An additional payment that usually has to be earned in some way or another.

Contracted hours The hours worked as stated in the contract of employment.

Discount A reduction in price.

Overtime Work done in excess of contracted hours.

Piecework A system of pay where someone is paid for how much is produced.

Chapter 23
Motivating employees

IN THE NEWS

Richer Sounds

Richer Sounds is a group of hi-fi stores that can be found around the UK. Julian Richer started the business when he was 19 years old. Julian believes that having a well-motivated staff has played an important part in the success of the business. It has been voted as one of the best places in Britain to work.

Enjoying yourself at work is seen as one way of getting the best out of employees. You need only step into Richer Sounds' head office in south-east London to realise that making work fun is a concept that Richer Sounds takes very seriously. Among the desks and computers you can find a whole army of wacky artworks, including a life-size Elvis. There is no stuffy dress code either. Jeans and t-shirts with shorts in the summer are encouraged to make employees feel comfortable. In a survey at Richer Sounds, 90 per cent of employees find their teams 'fun to work with', and 91 per cent say that they can have a laugh with co-workers.

Communication is seen as important within the organisation. All staff members are encouraged to voice their opinions if they are unhappy with any aspect of their work. There are also opportunities to give feedback at seminars, suggestion meetings and branch dinners. Richer Sounds operates a **suggestion scheme** for employees, with a cash bonus of at least £5 for each idea. This scheme has been remarkably successful, producing on average 20 suggestions a year from each employee.

The boss, Julian, has an open door policy. He is willing to speak to any employee if they have something to say. Salaries are high for the retail industry: a senior sales assistant can expect £18,000. The **perks** are also impressive: the loan of holiday homes in locations such as St Tropez and Venice; free massages, facials and pedicures at Christmas. There is even a take-your-pet-to-work scheme.

Employees at Richer Sounds have fun and are highly motivated

Promotion from within the business is normal. Most of the head office staff have worked on the shop floor. Richer Sounds claims that it is willing to recognise people's potential, and wants to allow them to develop within the business. For example, Lol Lecanu, the company's marketing director, started his career at Richer Sounds as a summer job on the shop floor.

Richer Sounds is also socially responsible, giving one of the highest proportions of pre-tax profits (5 per cent) to charity of any UK company. It is not surprising that 86 per cent of their employees say they are proud to work there.

Richer Sounds operates by these basic rules:

- *Rewards* If you want your staff to give great service, reward them for it.
- *Fun* On top of pay, provide extras that make the job enjoyable.
- *Communication* You can't motivate if you don't communicate.
- *Recognition* The best motivational technique is to say, 'Well done and thank you'.
- *Loyalty* If you want loyalty from people, you must give it to them.

 Take a look at the Richer Sounds website:
www.richersounds.com

Did you know...

The big dispute in motivation theory is whether wages are the most important factor in motivating employees.

There can be no doubt that Julian Richer has a different way of looking at how a business is run. He recognises the importance of having well-motivated employees. But he also knows that there has to be some control over his employees. What he says is: 'Little control and lots of motivation equals anarchy; lots of control and no motivation means repression.'

What managers need to do, according to Julian, is strike a balance between having very keen employees and making sure they are doing what you want them to do. It would be no good, for instance, to have sales staff being overfriendly with customers and bothering them, if they just wanted to browse at the products. Customers might see the sales assistants as being too pushy and be reluctant to come into the shops.

Julian Richer also recognises that it's not just money that motivates people. Many of the staff at Richer Sounds are young and respond well to a fun environment. Rewards can be equally fun and unpredictable. There might be prizes such as an evening's paintballing, hot air ballooning, or a weekend in Prague for the branch with the best sales.

The business wants to feel that its employees are enthusiastic about coming into work each day. Keen employees are more likely to treat customers well, and happy customers are more likely to spend money.

An unusual form of non-monetary reward

Did you know...

Many people give up their spare time to volunteer for unpaid work at charities, hospitals, and helping young people with sports, Duke of Edinburgh awards and organisations like the scouts. They are clearly not motivated by money.

Summary

- Richer Sounds is a business that recognises the important part its employees play in the success of its business
- Staff need to be motivated in order to give their best
- Money is not the only thing that motivates employees

Core knowledge

Over the years, businesses have developed a range of strategies to increase employee motivation. There has also been much research into this topic by universities and other organisations. There is no clear agreement about what is the best way to motivate people. Many people think that what motivates an employee depends upon the type of person and his or her personal circumstances.

Someone who needs money to bring up a family, might be motivated purely by wages. The more this worker is paid, the more enthusiastic he will be to do the work. Employees in their 50s and 60s may be looking for something quite different to motivate them. Money is possibly less important to this group of people. They might work better when they are in teams, enjoying the social side of working life, or like having the status of an important job.

Employees can also be motivated by the 'extras' that an employer provides. These are called fringe benefits and were discussed in the previous chapter.

There are other factors that influence just how happy an employee is. Nobody wants to think that their views are not important or are ignored by their boss. People also like to know what is happening in the business, particularly if there are to be changes. Having good communications between management and employees is usually seen to be a problem for larger organisations. This is because there are often different layers of management and, as a result, more levels for messages to go through before they get to every person. Communications are usually less of a problem within a small business because the employees probably see the manager on a regular basis.

Different employees have different motivations

And more

Work can become boring and monotonous if employees are performing the same task over and over each day. When this happens, employees can become sloppy and mistakes are made. Employers can help reduce the level of boredom by making employees' jobs more interesting, or giving employees the chance to move around from one job to another. For instance, someone who spends his working day cutting up identical pieces of wood may quickly become bored. The job can be made a little more interesting by giving the employee a range of lengths of wood to cut.

A study of motivation many years ago concluded that workers needed to have all their basic requirements satisfied before they can be motivated. These requirements were called **hygiene factors** and included: safe and comfortable working conditions, suitable rest facilities and a decent wage.

Have a go!

Activity

Produce a list of about five factors that could influence the reasons why people work, one of which should be wages. Conduct a survey of adults, asking them what motivates them more in their work. Also ask for their age – consider how this could be done diplomatically. Put your findings into a spreadsheet and graph the results. Try to spot any patterns in the data. Are younger people motivated any differently than older? Is there a difference between genders?

Quickfire questions

1. What type of business is Richer Sounds?
2. Give a way in which a shop assistant's job in a supermarket can be made more interesting.
3. What is an open door management policy?
4. Give two examples of how Julian Richer uses fun to liven up the workplace.
5. What is meant by hygiene factors?
6. Explain why the factors that motivate an 18 year old might be different from those that motivate a middle-aged person.
7. Give two reasons why Richer Sounds offers £5 for each suggestion given by its employees.
8. How are Richer Sounds employees able to get their views across to the management?
9. How does recruiting for managers within a business help with motivation?
10. Explain why Julian Richer believes that motivated staff still need some control.

Hit the spot

> Describe what is meant by motivation.

>> Explain two benefits that a well-motivated workforce can bring to a business.

>>> Discuss whether a pay rise or improved working conditions is likely to have the bigger effect on employees' motivation?

Cracking the code

Hygiene factors The basic needs of an employee, including a reasonable wage.

Loyalty The willingness of an employee to remain at a business. Loyalty can also apply to supporting the business by not being late, taking unnecessary time off and talking positively about it.

Perk Another term to describe a fringe benefit, which is a reward to an employee in addition to his or her wages.

Suggestion scheme A system where employees give ideas to managers about how things can be improved in the business.

Chapter 24
Staff and the law

IN THE NEWS

The King's Head is a country pub and restaurant. Karen Tay, the new manageress, was taking over soon and decided to check that the business was complying with all the necessary **employment laws**. The previous manager, Stan, showed her around the business.

Stan started by saying that the gardener, who had been off ill for a week with a bad cold, was almost 65 years old. Stan explained that his birthday would be an ideal time to get him to retire and get someone younger in to do the work,

Karen also found that the two part-time waitresses were being paid the **minimum wage**, while the full-time waiter was on more than a pound an hour more than them. The previous owner had said that Karen might want to lower the wages of the waiting staff, as customers were generally good tippers, so they received money this way. He explained that he paid the full-time waiter more because he was a good worker and he didn't want to lose him.

Stan explained that he hadn't bothered to adapt any equipment in the pub because no disabled people worked there. He explained that it would be far too expensive to put in a ramp to allow a wheelchair to

Employment laws apply to every workplace

come through the door, so the pub wouldn't be able to take on anyone requiring such access.

When Karen asked whether any of the staff were pregnant, Stan laughed. He suggested that it would be dangerous for a pregnant woman to work in a pub, so she would have no real choice but to leave. Karen thought better about asking about the arrangements for paternity leave.

Employment laws

Clearly the King's Head is a fictitious case study. No business would be allowed to operate this way. Small businesses need to comply with the law as far as their employees are concerned. There are several examples in the case study when employment laws have been broken. The law says that businesses are not allowed to discriminate on the grounds of age, race, gender, sexuality, religion or disability. These laws usually apply no matter how large or how small the business is.

Age discrimination

The Age Discrimination Act came into force on 1 October 2006. It made it illegal for employers to discriminate on the grounds of a person's age. In the act of parliament, age means both old and young, unlike in some countries where it is just the old that are protected. It is illegal to pass over an applicant for employment or training just because of his age. There is no law that a person must leave when he or she reaches normal retirement age. This means it might be difficult to make the gardener retire at age 65 if he wishes to continue to work at the King's Head.

Disability discrimination

On 1 October 2004, the final part of the Disability Discrimination Act came into force. Part III specifies that all service providers, businesses and public sector services must take reasonable action to ensure disabled people can make full use of them. So, the King's Head is breaking the law by not providing suitable access for disabled people.

Is the workplace safe?

Providing access for people with disabilities

Part-time workers

A law passed in 2000 made it illegal to treat part-time workers less favourably than their full-time equivalents. This means that they should receive the same hourly wage as their full-time co-workers. Similarly, they don't have to be the first choice to go, if a business finds that it has too many employees. The two part-time waitresses would have a strong case to be paid the same hourly wages as the full-time waiter. It would seem from the case study that they all do similar work.

Maternity leave/paternity leave

Maternity leave is a right by law to any woman. Women are allowed to take up to one year off work to have a baby. The mother is entitled to return to her previous job and not have to accept a demoted position. A business cannot dismiss a woman just because she is pregnant, or has a family to look after. Paternity leave is an entitlement for fathers of new babies.

An employee cannot be dismissed because she is pregnant

Did you know...

Other forms of discrimination are recognised by some people, but not yet put into laws. These include: adultism – giving preference to adults, such as no-children holidays; lookism – discriminating against someone because a person's appearance; and heightism – favouring tall people.

Summary

- There are many laws that protect employees
- A business is not allowed to discriminate on the grounds of age, race, gender, sexuality, religion or disability

Core knowledge

When the owner of a new business decides to employ somebody, he or she must recognise that there are many laws that need to be considered. The employer cannot pick and choose which laws are obeyed, or think that the law doesn't apply to him or her.

Laws are changing all the time, and it is the responsibility of the employer to keep up to date with them. For instance, at the moment parents who have children under six have the right to apply to work flexibly. This means employers have to look into changing working hours, so mothers and fathers can spend more time with their children. This could be moving from full- to part-time working or changing the hours worked. Parents might, for example, want to be able to take their children to school and pick them up. Employers are required by law to consider these requests seriously. However, employees have no automatic right to demand flexible hours. This may change in the future though, so employees must keep up to date with the law.

It is sometimes said that when laws like this are passed, small businesses will find a way around them. They might argue that it is much easier to make arrangements for maternity leave in a large business with many employees. A key worker in a small business would have a much bigger impact if the business only employed five people. If a business puts undue pressure on an employee to quit, or refuses to employ anyone who might require maternity leave in the future, it would be breaking the law.

Businesses are also required to ensure that the workplace is safe for employees. An organisation called the Health and Safety Executive (HSE) regulates and enforces the rules about safety at work. These are set out in the Health and Safety at Work Act, 1974. This law says that it is the duty of businesses to make sure that employees operate in a safe environment. This is sometimes described as making sure that workers are able to return home as healthy as when they arrive at work.

And more

The need for laws to protect employees' rights can be blamed partly on some myths and prejudices in society. Older workers are sometimes thought of as being slow, forgetful and not willing to learn new skills. Young people, on the other hand, are regarded as lacking communication and interpersonal skills and not having commonsense. Obviously, these are generalisations, but still thought of as being true by a number of people. Some companies are now recognising that there are benefits in employing older workers. This is particularly relevant as there is a growing skills shortage in the UK.

It is for reasons like this that businesses cannot afford to overlook certain people when they are recruiting new employees. By making it difficult for disabled, elderly people and young women, who might become pregnant, to get a job, a business is reducing the number of talented people available to it.

There are a growing number of businesses that actively seek out groups of workers who have been discriminated against. Some of these set employment quotas or targets. This means businesses encourage discriminated groups to apply for jobs with them. This process is sometimes called **positive discrimination**.

Anyone who feels that he or she has been discriminated against in the workplace can take the case to an **Industrial Tribunal**. This is a type of court that deals with employment matters.

Have a go!

Activity

Using ICT facilities, produce a leaflet on employment laws. This can take the form of an outline of the main features of the law, or a series of frequently asked questions (FAQs). The leaflet is intended to provide small businesses with basic information.

Quickfire questions

1 Which employment law was passed in 2004?
2 The Age Discrimination Act protects older workers only. True or false?
3 Describe the rights that a part-time worker has.
4 How long can a woman take for maternity leave?
5 What is paternity leave?
6 What is meant by health and safety regulations?
7 Explain two ways in which an elderly person might be discriminated against in the workplace.
8 Explain two problems that a business might have offering parents flexible working hours.
9 Explain two reasons why a worker might take his employer to an Industrial Tribunal.
10 Explain two ways a restaurant might need to adapt its premises to allow access to disabled people.

Hit the spot

> What is meant by discrimination in employment?

>> If an employer has too many workers, describe a legal way she might decide whom to make redundant.

>>> Discuss whether it is necessary to have laws to protect employees.

Cracking the code

Employment law A series of laws designed to ensure that employees' rights are looked after and to protect them from being exploited by businesses.

Minimum wage The lowest hourly rate that a business can pay employees. The rate for young people is different to the one for adults.

Positive discrimination Being seen to make an effort to recruit or promote people from groups which have been discriminated against.

Industrial Tribunal A court that deals with employment issues, such as discrimination.

Chapter 25
Other legal responsibilities of business

IN THE NEWS

Going to a small claims court

Davies Builders is a small business that specialises in refitting kitchens and bathrooms in the Worcestershire area. **Cash flow is always a problem for a business like Davies. The owner David needs to buy from a supplier the units and appliances that he needs to fit. He knows that he won't be paid until the bathroom or kitchen has been completed to the client's satisfaction. The suppliers will, however, want their money at the end of each month. Like many businesses in this position, Davies Builders' bank account is usually overdrawn until customers' bills are settled.**

David was pleased to receive a new order for a bathroom, which came from the recommendation of a previous customer. The new client was keen to have the job done as quickly as possible. The **quote** of £4500 was accepted. David set about the job, completing it in a week. The customer appeared happy with her bathroom, so David sent out his **invoice** for the amount and waited. After two weeks of hearing nothing, he phoned to remind about the bill and was told the money would be there in a day or two. A week later it still hadn't arrived. He sent a reminder and waited again. Telephone calls went

The small claims court

unanswered. A third letter was sent, but this time it threatened legal action.

During this time, the bathroom supplier was due to be paid the £2000 for the bathroom fittings. David had reached the limit of his overdraft and was struggling to pay his account. He had a good relationship with the supplier that he didn't want to spoil by not paying on time. Though he had never done it before, David realised that he would have to take the customer to the small claims court to recover his money.

 Go to **www.businesslink.gov.uk** and search for information on how to take a customer to the small claims court.

Insurance

Small businesses are required to have proper insurance. Any vehicle the business owns must be insured. Employer's liability insurance is also compulsory by law for anyone operating in the UK and employing staff. This insurance protects the employee against acts of negligence. For instance, if an employee had an accident at work, or a customer was hurt in a shop. Businesses might choose to take out insurance to cover loss of earnings. If there was a fire, for example, this might mean the business cannot operate and loses money. Products insurance can be bought that protects a manufacturer in case there is a fault with the items it makes and a customer is injured. Professionals, such as doctors and lawyers can take out professional indemnity insurance in case mistakes are made and a client decided to sue the business.

Taxes

All small business traders need to keep records of their income and expenditure. Self-employed people need to put in annual tax returns, so the **HM Revenue & Customs** can work out how much tax they need to pay.

VAT (value added tax)

If a small business is registered for VAT purposes, it must charge its customers this tax for any goods that are liable to value added tax. The difference between what the business receives and what it has paid out in VAT on supplies is then sent to the government.

Recovering money through small claims courts

Small claims courts provide an easy, speedy and low-cost way for creditors to recover their money. Unlike the County Court, where it can be expensive because a barrister may be needed, small claims courts are much cheaper. A fee is

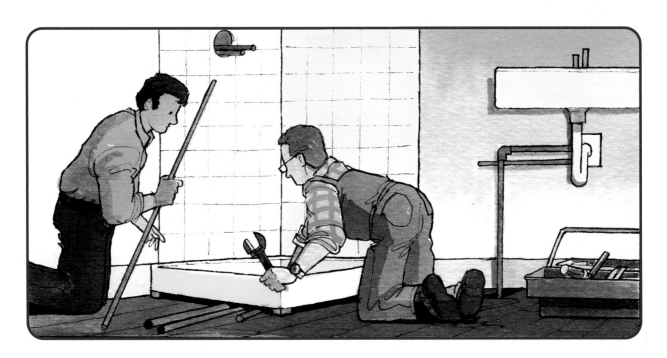

charged by the court, which must be paid upfront. It costs £30 to recover a debt of up to £300. The fee rises to £120 for debts between £1000 and £5000. The maximum that can be claimed in these courts is £5000.

The system works well for small businesses. The cost of the fee for presenting the case at court is added to the amount the debtor owes. So in David's case, if he were successful he would receive £4620 from his customer: £4500 for the bathroom and his £120 court fee.

In this case study, David was suing a customer. He could equally have taken a business to court. When this happens, if the court case is successful, the business that was at fault will get a black mark against its name. This means that the business will have a poor credit history. When the business tries to obtain credit facilities in the future, such as getting a loan to buy a van, banks and other lenders will be reluctant to give it money.

Because of the threat of a poor record, **debtors** will often pay up and not risk contesting in court, even though they may feel that they have a case. There is always the risk that the judgment at a small claims court will go against the person claiming, which does put some people off using the court. An additional risk is that the debtor may not have the money to pay, even if the case goes against him. So, time and effort has gone into preparing for court, the fee paid and in the end no money is forthcoming.

Bad debts can make running a business difficult

Summary

- Businesses have both moral and legal responsibilities to pay their debts
- Small businesses can use small claim courts to recover outstanding debts
- Many cases are settled before they go to court, as businesses do not want a judgment against them affecting their credit record

Core knowledge

Some would argue that bad debts are a way of life for small businesses. Every so often a non-payer will appear and you have to live with it. Many believe that it's simply easier to **write off** the debt than to go to the expense and inconvenience of recovering the money legally. It was to avoid this that the small claims courts were set up. As part of the County Court system, small claims courts can help traders such as David Davies fight back and recover outstanding debts.

Some of the legal issues to do with employing people can be found in Chapter 24. There are other legal issues that a business must address.

And more

Unpaid debts have a crippling effect on small businesses and the problem appears to be getting worse. Unpaid debts increase rapidly when the economy is slowing down because of a **recession**. Businesses have a **liquidity** problem. They do not have the cash to pay their debts so hold back as long as possible. This in turn means that **creditors** find it difficult to pay their own debtors. The overall effect is a downward spiral.

Small businesses will often have a more difficult time than larger companies when the payment of debts is concerned. Large companies are in a stronger position to negotiate delays in payments. A creditor would not want to lose the account of a large buyer, if the business decided to go elsewhere. So, suppliers will often push the small businesses first for payment, knowing that if they do not return, it is not a huge loss.

Recently the law was changed to allow creditors to charge debtors interest on any debts that were not paid by the agreed time. Not all small businesses enforce this law, however. They don't want to upset their customers, so they buy goods elsewhere in the future.

Have a go!

Activity

Imagine David Davies has asked you to help him prepare to take his case to the small claims court. Produce a written statement for him to present to the court.

Web-based activity

Use information from the Citizens' Advice Bureau website **www.adviceguide.org.uk** to produce a flowchart of the different stages that you should go through with small claims before getting to court.

Quickfire questions

1. What is a small claims court?
2. What is the maximum amount that can be recovered in a small claims court?
3. How much fee would someone have to pay at the small claims court fee to recover £2000?
4. What is an annual tax return?
5. By law, what type of insurance must all businesses have?
6. Explain why the number of claims for unpaid invoices increase during a recession.
7. Explain how a dentist might need professional indemnity insurance.
8. Explain why many small claims never actually reach the court hearing.
9. Why do small businesses often choose not to charge interest on outstanding debts?

Hit the spot

➤ Describe a problem a business might face if it did not have proper insurance.

➤➤ Explain why businesses do not always pay their debts.

➤➤➤ Discuss whether a business should always try to recover money it is owed.

Cracking the code

Cash flow The overall effect of cash coming into and out of a business. If more money flows in to the business than out, it is called a positive cash flow.

Creditor Somebody who is owed money by another person or business.

Debtor A person or business that owes money to another.

HM Revenue & Customs The government body that collects taxes.

Invoice Another term for a bill. A formal request for money to be paid.

Liquidity A measure of how easily a business can pay off its immediate debts from cash it has or will receive shortly.

Overdrawn When more money has been spent than was in the bank account, which means the account holder is in debt to the bank.

Quote The amount of money a business is prepared to undertake a job for.

Recession A slowdown in the economy that happens every few years. Businesses do not sell as much, profits fall and workers are made redundant.

Supplier A business that sells materials to another business.

Write off To give up on the chances of recovering a debt.

OPERATIONS MANAGEMENT

IN THE NEWS

Farmhouse Fare

Helen Colley, the founder of Farmhouse Fare, was raised on a farm in rural Lancashire. Helen started a catering business at the age of 18 with £250 that she had borrowed. Over a 20-year period, Helen developed her business so that it became one of the largest outside caterers in Lancashire, specialising in providing food for large events that were often held in marquees.

Farmhouse Fare, a **manufacturer** of traditional puddings, only came about after Helen felt the need to **diversify** away from outside catering. Helen knew that the sticky toffee puddings she made were always popular with diners. She decided that she could sell the puddings during the cold winter when there was no marquee work available. By doing this, she could receive a regular cash flow and keep her full-time staff employed.

The year 2001 was an important one for farms in Britain. The outbreak of foot and mouth disease meant that outdoor catering dried up for Helen. Marqueed events were forbidden for fear of spreading the disease. Helen decided the time was right to make a full-time business based on her puddings.

Helen bought some large-scale containers and a mixer, so she could make larger quantities of puddings than she had before. Initially she sold her puddings through local stores and delicatessens. Her big breakthrough came when Sainsbury's agreed to stock her products. Now most of the major supermarkets buy puddings from her.

When producing the puddings, Helen works to the same basic recipe, but will adapt the style of pudding to meet the needs of the different type of customers that shop at each supermarket. The supermarket buyers give Helen guidance in what type of puddings their customers would enjoy.

As the business grew Helen found that she needed to move to larger premises. She now operates from a purpose-built unit a few miles down the road from her farm. Despite manufacturing the puddings from a **factory**, Helen keeps to the handcrafted nature of the puddings, which come in 14 different flavours. She is always willing to try a new idea for a pudding.

Helen insists on only using natural ingredients and producing the puddings in **batch** size quantities. She chooses not to use mass production methods. The puddings are still made traditionally by hand.

 Take a look at Helen's website at
www.farmhousefare.co.uk

Hand finishing a cake

Methods of production

A large number of small manufacturing businesses make their products using job or batch production. The market for their products is usually not large enough to justify using mass production methods. Very large businesses such as Toyota, Dysons and Nokia use a different type of production. This method of production will be looked at in the next book.

Job production

Job production is when a single item is produced. The whole manufacturing process is completed before another item is made. The product might look the same as all the others, but it is probably unique. For example, when a new kitchen is fitted, the storage units will be standard size but the room itself will be different from other kitchens. The gas and water pipes will need to be adapted to fit and the kitchen storage units arranged to suit the room's shape.

Skilled workers will be required to complete the work. These workers will probably be well motivated as the work is not repetitive and boring. There will be problems for them to think about and solve throughout the whole fitting process. However, skilled labour is more expensive to employ. Also the nature of the work makes it **labour intensive**: this means there will be few opportunities to use equipment to do the work of labour.

Batch production

This is where a manufacturer makes a number, or batch, of products at the same time. Helen Colley uses **batch production** when cooking her puddings. The same equipment can be used to make the different types of puddings. This means there is less factory space required and there is no need to duplicate items of equipment. Farmhouse Fare might produce a batch of 2000 sticky toffee puddings then clean the equipment and make 1500 gingerbread and treacle puddings.

Job production

Did you know...

When products are made in batches the batch number (or lot number) is often stamped on each item. This makes it easier to identify when the product was made. If there is a fault then all the other items in that batch can be checked.

Summary

- Small businesses usually use job or batch production
- Job production is suitable for making products that are unique
- Job production can be labour intensive
- Batch production involves making a number of identical items at once
- The work can be more repetitive for employees with batch production

Core knowledge

When a business is set up that will manufacture a product an important decision has to be made. Should the product be made one at a time, each being completed before the next is started? Or should several products be made together, in batches?

Sometimes there is no real choice. An artist who paints pictures for a living is unlikely to paint the same picture many times over. It would be unusual for an artist to paint the same sky on 30 pictures, followed by the same tree on each picture, and so on. The artist is more likely to paint one picture then start another. In this case job production would be used. A customer would not be impressed if she thought there were 29 similar pictures to the one that she had just bought.

A factory that produced pine furniture is more likely to use batch production methods. Rather than making just one chest of drawers at a time, the manufacturer will find it more economical to make, say, ten together. Ten lots of wood could be cut and used to make the frame. When these have been completed the wood for the drawers would be cut and assembled. When all ten chests of drawers had been made, they could all be varnished.

And more

Batch production can be a far more efficient way to make the puddings. Less skilful labour is needed, which is less expensive. There is also some opportunity to have employees specialise in a particular process. Someone could concentrate on the mixing of ingredients, while someone else looks after the baking process. The advantage of this is that workers become better at doing their own particular jobs.

Batch production may also require more equipment and machinery than job production. For example, a different tool might be needed for each stage of batch production to drill holes into metal. A worker making the product using job production would probably use the same drill, but just change the bit each time a different size hole was needed. More storage space is also required to keep the stock needed for making larger quantities of goods.

Another problem with batch production is that the work can become repetitive. A solution to this problem though would be to move employees between different jobs. This is known as job rotation.

Have a go!

Activity

Find a range of products that have a batch or lot number stamped on them. Produce a poster to explain what batch numbers are.

Group activity

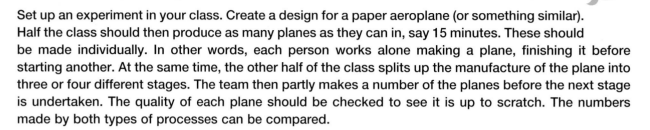

Set up an experiment in your class. Create a design for a paper aeroplane (or something similar). Half the class should then produce as many planes as they can in, say 15 minutes. These should be made individually. In other words, each person works alone making a plane, finishing it before starting another. At the same time, the other half of the class splits up the manufacture of the plane into three or four different stages. The team then partly makes a number of the planes before the next stage is undertaken. The quality of each plane should be checked to see it is up to scratch. The numbers made by both types of processes can be compared.

Quickfire questions

1   What is meant by job production?
2   What is meant by batch production?
3   Why would a new pedestrian bridge across a road probably be made using job production?
4   Why do businesses put batch numbers on their products?
5   How can job rotation help make their work more interesting for employees?
6   Why would it be very expensive for Farmhouse Fare to make the puddings individually?
7   Why are batch numbers placed on products?
8   Why is batch production able to use less skilled workers than job production?
9   Describe how a florist making bouquets might use batch production.
10 Describe how Farmhouse Fare's puddings might be changed to suit the needs of different supermarkets.

Hit the spot

> Explain the differences between job and batch production.
>> Give two advantages to a business of using batch rather than job production.
>>> Discuss the reasons why a business might choose not to use batch production.

Cracking the code

Batch production Making products a number at a time, rather than individually.

Diversify Operating in more than one market to reduce the risk to the business if one declines.

Factory A place where products are made.

Job production The process of completing one product before starting on another.

Labour intensive A process of making goods where many people are needed compared with the amount of machinery used.

Manufacturer A business that makes goods, rather than offers a service.

Chapter 27
Providing a service

IN THE NEWS

SportStars

James Taylor was given a £1000 cheque for his twenty-first birthday. The gift was meant to allow him to buy an around the world plane ticket. Instead, James used the money to start a business.

James' experiences as a sports coach in America after he had finished university persuaded him that there was a market for similar coaching in this country. James recognised that many children were not as active as they should be and childhood obesity was becoming a serious problem.

With his £1000 funding James bought some sporting equipment and started SportStars, his children's coaching venture. He managed to convince a small team of coaches to work for no pay until the business got established.

At the time SportStars was being planned, a law was introduced that allowed teachers 10 per cent of their working time away from the classroom to plan lessons and mark books. James realised that head teachers had to cover absent teachers and what better way than by providing sports coaching for the children? SportStars, therefore, targeted primary schools to find customers.

Appointments were set up with head teachers, where James explained the advantages of using SportStars. The coaches were cheaper to hire than supply teachers and the sporting activities fitted in well with the national project to improve children's

health. SportStars also made sure that every child covered the requirements of the national curriculum.

A month of free trials led to five initial paid contracts. Word of mouth spread, the **contracts** grew in number and so did the SportStars product range. James introduced holiday courses where a venue was hired out for 11 weeks of the year and the kids came along for five hours every day.

At present James employs 15 full-time, 20 part-time, and up to 60 temporary coaches during the school holidays. Current **turnover** is around £1.2 million, and the company has offices in Cardiff, Bristol and Swansea, with plans to roll the service out across the UK, and even overseas.

 Take a look at the Sportstars website at
www.sport-stars.co.uk

Did you know...

In 2008, financial and business services accounted for about one in five jobs in the UK, compared with about one in ten in 1981.

Service industries

James provides a service to schools. In return for a payment, he will provide a sports coach who will train the pupils. At the end of the lesson, the pupils should be better at sport and the school will feel that it has done something to make the children healthier. Neither the school nor the pupils will actually own something physical at the end of the day, as they would if they had bought a product from a business. This is what we mean by a service: something provided to a consumer at a point in time. The same would apply if you took a taxi ride, had a driving lesson, made a call on your mobile phone or had your hair cut at a hairdresser. These are all examples of services. Service industries sell directly to the customer or client and not to another business, which sells it on to the customer. Services are used up at the point they are delivered. They cannot be transferred to somebody else.

Many small businesses provide services

Did you know...

Some people believe that we now have a fourth type of industry: quaternary, which includes areas such as scientific research and intellectual property.

Summary

- James Taylor providing sports teachers to schools is an example of a service
- When a service is provided, nothing physical is given to the customer
- People pay for services because it often saves them having to do the work themselves

Core knowledge

Service industries are becoming increasingly important in the UK economy. Britain produces far fewer physical goods than it used to in the past. Let's take making cars as an example. Thirty years ago there were several UK car manufacturers producing hundreds of thousands of cars each year. Today, very few cars are made in the UK. Most of the cars on British roads have been built abroad and imported into this country. So Britain relies more on providing services as an industry. These services are sold both in Britain and abroad.

It was often thought that manufacturing industries were somehow better than service industries. This could be because something physical is made with manufacturing, which is not the case with services. Most people now recognise that a high proportion of wealth produced in services is a sign of an advanced economy.

A service industry

Even manufacturers, however, have to provide a service. More on this can be found in Chapter 29.

The main types of services

- *Financial* These include the services provided by banks and insurance companies. Banks will lend money and receive a rate of interest in return. Insurance companies will insure against unforeseen events, such as a car being damaged in an accident. People who want insurance pay a fee (called a premium) for this service. Many financial services are sold to people abroad.

- *Retailing* This is another way of saying 'shopping'. The retailer will sell products made by manufacturers to customers. It is a service as it saves consumers having to go to manufacturers to buy the goods that they want. The retailer does this for their customers and has the goods available in their shops.

- *Defence* We all want to feel protected and safe. The police and armed services, such as the army, provide us with the service of protection.

- *Education* Having an educated workforce is important if we are to grow as an economy. An education allows young people to become more capable of doing a wider range of jobs. Schools, colleges and universities provide the service of education. But there are many businesses that support education. SportStars is an example of such a business.

- *Health* Healthy people enjoy life better and live longer. There are many businesses that are involved in the health industry. Care homes for the elderly, medicine and drug manufacturers, doctors and dentists are just some of the ways the health service is provided.

- *Leisure* As people get better off they have more opportunity to enjoy their leisure time. Industries have grown up to provide leisure services to people. These include hotels, sporting facilities, eating out and travel.

And more

Sometimes services are called tertiary industries. Tertiary actually means third. Primary (or first) industries are those that obtain raw materials from the earth. Primary industries would, therefore, cover areas like mining, quarrying, forestry, farming and fishing. Secondary industries are the manufacturing industries – those that make products from the raw materials obtained from primary industries. Examples of secondary industries would be construction (building houses and factories), manufacturing washing machines and other domestic appliances, and furniture making.

As economies develop, the proportion of primary, secondary and tertiary industries tend to change. Primary and secondary become less important and services, or tertiary, industries grow. Changes in technology can explain some of this change. Factories, for example, have machinery that replaces the number of workers needed. Information technology has made it easier to develop service industries. As just one example, computer technology has allowed banks to transfer money and manage people's accounts anywhere in the world. Britain can also buy raw materials and manufactured goods more cheaply abroad than they can be produced in the UK.

Many people still worry that Britain relies so much on service industries. They believe that the move from secondary to tertiary (which is sometimes called **deindustrialisation**) means we depend too much on foreign countries producing goods for us. They also worry that if the economy is not doing very well, people cut back first on luxury items like staying in hotels and other leisure activities. This means that services are hit particularly badly when the economy is down turning.

Have a go!

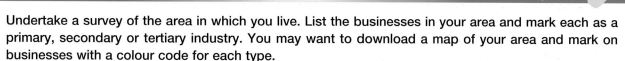

Activity

Undertake a survey of the area in which you live. List the businesses in your area and mark each as a primary, secondary or tertiary industry. You may want to download a map of your area and mark on businesses with a colour code for each type.

Web-based activity

Go to the National Statistics website **www.statistics.gov.uk/glance**. Use this site to research the number of people who work in different types of industries.

Quickfire questions

1 Who started SportsStars?
2 Describe the service that SportStars provides to schools.
3 Give two examples of services that banks can provide to customers.
4 Which of these is not a service: a haircut; car insurance; replacement windows?
5 Explain why having security guards at a shopping centre is an example of a service.
6 Which service industry employed one person in five in 2008?
7 Explain two reasons why there are less people employed manufacturing goods.
8 Give two reasons why some people worry about the amount of service industries in the UK.
9 Explain how advances in ICT have helped financial services become more important.
10 Explain why it is important that Britain sells some of its services abroad.

Hit the spot

> Describe what is meant by a service.
>> Describe the range of services provided by a leisure centre.
>>> Discuss whether all services are badly affected by the economy slowing down.

Cracking the code

Contract A legal agreement between a business supplying a service and the customer.
Deindustrialisation The movement away from manufacturing goods to providing services.
Turnover The money coming into a business from the goods and services it sells.

IN THE NEWS

Streetcar

Andrew Valentine and Brett Akker got the idea for their different type of car rental business during a visit to America. After considering many options, the two university friends, came across the American Zipcars. The idea was simple: instead of having to go to the expense of buying and running a car, urban dwellers could hire a pay-as-you-go car just when they needed one. They could collect it from a range of parking sites, returning it when they had finished their journey. Calling their rental business Streetcar, the business's fleet of hire cars was originally based in London.

The attraction of pay-as-you-go car rental is that it is more convenient to customers. The cars are available 24 hours a day. The cars can be opened and the engine started with a **smart card** and number that is punched into the car's specially designed keypad. Membership of the scheme is £25 and there is an hourly rental fee to be paid. The cars are targeted at those who live in cities who only need a car occasionally for short periods. It is estimated that there are more than 1 million of these people in London alone.

In the beginning the entrepreneurs had just six cars in their fleet. This has now expanded to 125. The business is hoping to expand to other UK cities. The success of the scheme depends totally on the use of **ICT**.

After trawling the streets to find suitable premises to locate the cars, the founders have now established nearly 80 sites where users can access their vehicles. Valentine and Akker tracked down an overseas manufacturer who could cheaply produce the technology needed to allow secure use of the cars to genuine customers.

Streetcars used many aspects of ICT within the business. Including:

- Membership details are stored using smart card technology.
- Driving licence details are confirmed with the DVLA using telephone conference calling.
- Customers book a car online.
- Email and text messages are sent with details and confirmation.
- The car is opened with a smart card.
- Communication system in each car links to Streetcar base – allows mileage and costs to be debited from user's account.

 Find out more about Streetcar at **www.streetcar.co.uk**.

The advantages of ICT

The idea of hiring a car for short periods would be impossible without modern technology. Technology allows Streetcars to deal with its customers without ever meeting them personally. This would be unthinkable with a traditional car hire business, which would want to check the drivers' details before allowing them to rent a vehicle.

The use of ICT allows Streetcar to run with minimum operating costs. Once the technology has been bought, the business needs very few staff to keep it running. Technology that was unavailable just a few years ago now allows businesses to operate in quite different ways. Having a flexible system with minimum staffing means that customers can hire a car or van for as little as half an hour at a low hire charge.

Since starting the business, its owners have expanded beyond the London area. Streetcars can be found in Brighton, Southampton, Guildford, Kent and Cambridge. The scheme is particularly attractive in those towns and cities with heavy traffic congestion. It is estimated that for every Streetcar vehicle, six others are taken off the road, as they are no longer needed.

Smart card technology

Summary

- Without modern technology it would be impossible to operate a business like Streetcar
- Modern technology has allowed Streetcar to reduce the cost to the customer of hiring a car

Core knowledge

A computer is a standard feature of even the smallest business these days. Many do not go to the lengths that Streetcar goes to when using ICT but without ICT Streetcar would not be able to operate. Most businesses take advantage of the benefits that ICT offers and the main uses of ICT within a small business are explored below.

Record keeping

Businesses need to keep details of their customers and suppliers. Having these on a computer **database** means that they can be updated easily. Finding a phone number or contact name is much easier on a database than searching through a filing cabinet of records. Also it is easy to make a copy, so the records are less likely to get lost or destroyed.

Computers are essential in business today

Producing documents

Word processing has revolutionised the writing of business letters and memos. A business can store a series of standard letters on the computer to save having to type out similar documents over and over. The file with the required letter in can be opened and just the name and addressed changed. If many letters need to be sent, then a mail merge can be performed. This involves using details from a database to produce personalised letters.

Emails and the internet

Emails allow a business to send a message cheaply and quickly. Documents including photographs, maps, web pages and letters can be attached to messages. Small businesses can use the internet to advertise its products. The smallest business's website can be seen all over the world. The internet can also be used for market research purposes by keeping an eye on what the business's competitors are doing.

Other aspects of technology

Satellite navigation systems make it easier for deliveries to be made. This saves the business money and even shows the distance travelled so accurate delivery charges can be made. Online money transfers, such as PayPal, allow customers to pay for goods securely without waiting for the bank to clear the payment.

EPOS means Electronic Point of Sale. This is the system that allows readers to scan a barcode to record the product being sold and its price. The system allows the information from the barcode to be read quickly. EPOS systems can keep track of goods leaving the business so new stock can be ordered. While barcodes are found frequently in retailing, they can also be used to check the stock of a business and on parcels to show the address and postcode instantly.

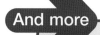
And more

Most businesses want to be efficient. In simple terms this means getting the most from the available resources to the business. A business becomes more efficient when it produces more output from the same amount of inputs, or the same output from less inputs.

Information technology has done much to increase the efficiency of businesses. Modern computer-controlled machines have reduced the level of skills employees need. This is sometimes called deskilling. In manufacturing, the work no longer needs someone who has served a long apprenticeship, as the machinery is mainly controlled by a computer. At one time a small business would have had a secretary to type letters. This service is no longer needed as word processing software allows documents of all sorts to be produced quickly and efficiently even by people who are not trained typists.

ICT can be expensive in the short run. The business needs to pay for the hardware (computers, printers, etc.) and for training staff. In the long run, however, this investment will probably pay for itself in terms of lower costs.

Have a go!

Web-based activities

Go to the Streetcar website and another car hire company. Compare the prices charged by each company.

Produce a web page showing the benefits of Streetcar to the occasional car user, living in London.

Quickfire questions

1 What makes Streetcar different from other car hire businesses?
2 How does Streetcar know how many miles each customer has driven?
3 How does Streetcar use smart card technology?
4 Give a reason why so many of Streetcar's vehicles are mainly based in London.
5 Why would a traditional car hire company find it difficult to hire vehicles for just 30 minutes?
6 What is a standard letter?
7 Give two uses of the internet to small businesses.
8 Describe how a used car dealer might use a database of his customers.
9 Explain how EPOS can help a supermarket avoid running out of a product.
10 A customer leaves her name and address when she buys a new computer. Explain two ways the retailer might use this information.

Hit the spot

> Describe two ways a small business might use ICT to reduce its costs.

>> Explain two ways in which ICT has changed the way that people work.

>>> Discuss whether it is appropriate for businesses to send spam emails and SMS messages to customers.

Cracking the code

Database A store of electronic information, such as customers' names and addresses.

ICT Information and communication technology.

Smart cards Pocket-size cards with a computer chip that contains information.

Chapter 29
The importance of customer service

IN THE NEWS

Tours4.com

Tours4 is a sports tour and group travel operator that was set up in 2005. The small business started by organising travel, accommodation and sporting fixtures for UK teams that wanted to play abroad.

Twenty-four-year-old Daniel Smith and his business partner Sam Jennings met when they were working as language teachers in French schools. Both were keen sportsmen and had organised football and rugby tours from the UK to play with French teams. The feedback they received from the players was very good, so the pair considered turning to tour organising as a career.

The Manchester and Kent-based business has diversified and in addition now organises stag and hen celebrations, often to major European locations. Many of the sporting tours last for 4–7 days, but an increasing number of events are for shorter periods of time. Tours4 offers shorter, often single day, visits to theatres, comedy clubs, ice rinks and paintballing venues. Tours4 is also moving into the school market, with events such as skiing holidays.

Daniel and Sam did a lot of **market research** before starting Tours4. They were particularly concerned to get the pricing right, and to check the level of service that they offered to customers was

Satisfied customers

appropriate. To achieve this, they contacted players and managers of sports teams at schools, clubs and universities throughout the UK to ask for their opinions.

Young people pay between £50 and £1000 for a sports tour, depending on where it is and the duration of the tour. In return they expect a smooth event, coaches on time, accommodation booked and an opportunity to relax and enjoy themselves. Accommodation does not have to be 5-star standard. Young people tend not to want the tour to be over-organised, with guides telling them what to do.

Take a look at **www.tours4.com**.

Customer satisfaction

Tours4 is often used to save sports teams having to organise their own trips. Sports teams are prepared to rely on Tours4's expertise in organising this type of event. It is even possible that the tours will be cheaper, as Tours4 will probably get **discounts** the clubs would not receive when organising the tour themselves.

What most of Tours4 customers want is a guide, someone who can speak the language. They also want the reassurance of someone on a phone in the UK in case there is a problem.

Different customers have different needs

A school sports tour will be looking for different levels of service than group of young people on a stag or hen night, or university students going paintballing. The school taking the tour will need to reassure parents that the trip is safe and well organised. It is for this reason that Daniel and Sam are prepared to visit schools to talk about the arrangements with parents.

Most of Tours4 clients are young people, quite often students. Tours4 need to make sure that the services that they offer these people suits their needs. What the young people are looking for is a good time, with plenty of fun activities. They will not be too worried about the state of the accommodation; there will be no need for 5-star hotels and the students will be happy to share rooms to keep costs down.

If Tours4 is successful in providing good customer service, then the level of customer satisfaction will be high. Customer satisfaction means people feel that they have had a good experience on the tour. The service was at a standard customers were expecting, or even better than this. Customers also feel that they have had good value for money.

Customer satisfaction is important to a business like Tours4. The business relies on word of mouth advertising. If a group had a good tour with them, they would tell others. This would encourage other teams to use the service. A poor trip would, of course, have the opposite effect. Tours4 also wants to get its customers to use its services again. Having a good experience will stop teams going to other operators when they book their next tour.

Did you know...

It is said that two-thirds of customers do not feel valued by those serving them.

Summary

- A successful business needs to offer a good service to its customers
- If customers are satisfied with the service they receive, they are more likely to return and to tell their friends
- **Customer satisfaction** comes from making the customers feel special, giving them what they want and offering value for money

Core knowledge

A good business would want to know how satisfied its customers are with the service that was provided. Often, businesses will ask customers for feedback, so they can find out how successful they have been. Market research can also provide businesses with ideas of how the service can be improved; so future customers are more likely to be satisfied.

There are several ways in which businesses can help improve the level of customer satisfaction:

Customer service This means giving personal attention to make the customers feel important. Customers are most likely to appreciate the goods and services that they buy if they are made to feel special. This occurs when they feel that the goods and services that they buy have been specially produced for them.

Quality of service This does not necessarily mean the best quality. Tours4's customers would not expect expensive hotels, for example. But the service should be at least as good as the customer expects.

After sales service Nobody wants to feel that they have been forgotten about when the bill has been paid. Businesses can following up with after sales support. This may be something as simple as a questionnaire or a phone call, asking if everything went well. Manufacturers could provide maintenance and updating. A computer software business, for example, might want to provide updates to packages when they are available.

Excellent customer service

And more

Some businesses go as far as to measure the level of customer satisfaction. This can be achieved with survey techniques and questionnaires. A major problem with customer surveys, however, is that the response rate can be very low. This can produce distorted results, as people who have had a poor experience are far more likely to respond to the survey. The questionnaires also must be straightforward and not too lengthy. A long, complicated form would put people off completing it.

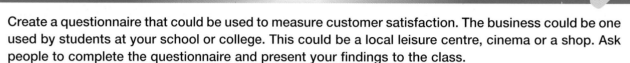

Have a go!

Activity

Create a questionnaire that could be used to measure customer satisfaction. The business could be one used by students at your school or college. This could be a local leisure centre, cinema or a shop. Ask people to complete the questionnaire and present your findings to the class.

Web-based activity

Go on to the Tours4 website. Produce a flyer that could be sent to schools advertising the business. Stress the level of service that the business offers when arranging trips for schools.

Quickfire questions

1   What type of business is Tours4?
2   Who are Tours4's main customers?
3   Describe two ways Tours4 offers a good service to its customers.
4   Give two reasons why schools might choose to use Tours4, rather than organising a skiing trip themselves.
5   Describe a way in which market research can help a business improve its service.
6   Give an advantage and a disadvantage of a business relying on word of mouth advertising.
7   Explain what after-sales service a painter and decorator might offer his customers.
8   What benefits could an improvement in service bring to a business?
9   Use the Tours4 case study to help explain what is meant by an appropriate standard of quality.
10 Discuss how a school offers a service to the parents of students.

Hit the spot

> What is meant by customer satisfaction?

>> Explain two ways in which a business could improve the level of its customers' satisfaction.

>>> Discuss whether a business can accurately measure the amount of satisfaction its customers get.

Cracking the code

Customer satisfaction A measure of how pleased a customer is with a service or good.

Discount Reduction in price often given to regular or large spending customers.

Market research Investigating potential customers or competitors. Looking at issues such as what customers want and the price they are prepared to pay.

Chapter 30
Protecting the consumer

Trading Standards

Unfortunately not all businesses operate in a fair and honest manner. Throughout history there have been many examples of businesses that have tried to cheat customers in one way or another. This could be something as simple as selling underweight items. An unscrupulous trader might have adjusted his scales so they weigh his products heavier than should be the case. There are other ways in which customers can be cheated. The trader might describe the product unfairly, saying things about it that simply aren't true.

To overcome these sorts of problems, various governments over the years have set up organisations to monitor business and protect the **consumer**. One of these government organisations is **Trading Standards**. One issue that Trading Standards is particularly concerned about these days is the growth in counterfeit goods.

Counterfeit goods are illegally copied items that are passed off for sale as the genuine article. These copied goods are normally an inferior product, but rely on the selling power of the brand. The main items that are counterfeited are:

- designer labelled clothing, sportswear, perfume, watches and equipment;
- CD and DVD copies of popular films and chart-topping music;
- computer software, especially games and business programs;
- artistic works, such as paintings, pottery and models.

Counterfeit goods may be sold at car boot sales or markets

Trading Standards departments take very seriously the production, distribution and sale of counterfeit products. The organisation has many of the powers of police in entering premises, seizing illegal goods and arresting those involved with counterfeiting.

There are many reasons for taking such a tough approach. Many brands are Trade Marks ™ or protected by copyright ©. Using these brands without permission is illegal. Unsuspecting customers might buy the copies in good faith. But when things go wrong with the product they find there is no after-sales support or guarantees provided. As the products are usually made from inferior materials, the items could even be dangerous to use.

 Take a look at the Trading Standards website:
www.tradingstandards.gov.uk

Consumer legislation

The laws on counterfeited goods are just one of the ways in which consumers are protected. Over the years there has been other legislation.

Sale of Goods Act

One of the most powerful laws is the Sale of Goods Act. This states that goods sold must be:

- 'Fit for purpose' – which means the product should do what it is meant to do. A jacket that is described as machine washable must be able to go through the washing machine without being damaged.

- 'Satisfactory quality' – this means that there should not be any faults with the product. A pair of jeans with stitching that was coming away would not be of satisfactory quality. However, if the fault were pointed out before the sale took place, then the customer must accept that the product is seconds quality.

Trade Descriptions Act

Another law protecting consumers is the Trade Descriptions Act. This controls how goods can be promoted in advertising or on packaging. To describe a car as having had only one previous owner, when there had been three, would be breaking the law.

Food and toy safety

These are special laws that apply to particular products. The government feels that both toy and food production deserve special attention. Environmental Health officers have the power to check conditions in places that prepare food and to close these places down if they do not meet certain standards. Similarly, quality and safety are important when manufacturing toys. There are rules about materials that are used in toys. Toys have to pass certain tests to prove that they are safe when young children play with them.

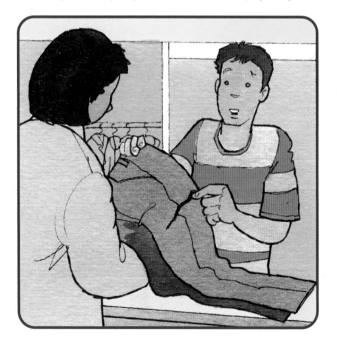

Quality and safety are very important

Did you know...

It is estimated that in Britain more than £10 billion is lost through the illegal sale of counterfeit goods.

Summary

- There are a range of laws that protect consumers from being cheated by businesses
- There are laws that ensure that goods and services sold meet certain basic standards
- Sellers must describe their goods and services accurately

Core knowledge

Customers do not want to feel that they have been cheated in some way by a business. Most of us take reasonable care to look after our own interests. We won't return to a business whose service or product we are not happy with. Many of us will complain if we do not get the service that we expect from a business.

When you pay for a service you are entitled to certain standards. For instance, imagine you are having your car serviced. The job should be done to a proper standard of workmanship. You should expect the car not to break down the day after the service. If your car developed a fault not long after you had bought it with a guarantee or warranty, it is not unreasonable to expect it to be repaired promptly. If you have to have a repair to the car and had not agreed a price beforehand, the price charged should be reasonable.

And more

You might find it strange that some people believe that not only is consumer protection unnecessary, but it is actually bad for consumers. Some of their arguments are:

- Producers of branded goods charge high prices, so they are beyond the reach of many consumers. Counterfeiting these branded goods makes them less attractive to consumers who were willing to pay high prices. So in order to sell their goods the brand producers have to lower their prices, allowing more people to be able to afford them.

- Operating consumer protection laws costs a great deal of money. Trading Standard officers need to be paid, just as one example. To fund this spending the government will increase taxes that people have to pay.

- A need for consumer protection suggests that consumers are unable to look after their own interests. If consumers are cheated, they will not go back to the business that cheated them. The business would get a bad reputation, losing custom and eventually closing. The rule of letting customers look after their own interests is very old. It is given the Latin name, *caveat emptor*, which means 'Let the buyer beware'.

But there are other issues as well. It is not unusual for unscrupulous traders to copy safety marks on to clothing to make them more attractive to consumers. Children's clothing might be marked as flame resistant when it is not.

As goods become more technologically advanced, it's not always easy to spot faults in a product. If you are buying a new bike that is meant to have an aluminium frame, carbon forks and aerodynamic spokes in the wheels, can you be sure you are getting just that, or inferior materials?

Have a go!

Activities

Produce a quiz based on *Who Wants to be a Millionaire?* The questions should all be about consumer protection.

Research the British Standards Institute (BSI). Produce a PowerPoint presentation on the work of this organisation.

Web-based activity

Go on to the Trading Standards website **www.tradingstandards.gov.uk** and produce a leaflet on consumers' rights when buying goods.

Quickfire questions

1 What are counterfeited goods?
2 What is the function of the Trading Standards?
3 A shop sells a radio alarm clock. Use this to explain the meaning of fit for purpose.
4 Draw three examples of trademarks that you have seen.
5 Explain how a vacuum cleaner might be seen as not being of satisfactory quality.
6 Give two reasons why trading standards officers might close down a restaurant.
7 Give two ways in which a manufacture of mobile phones might break the Trade Descriptions Act.
8 Explain why the producers of branded goods are keen to stop counterfeit copies being made.
9 Explain two possible reasons why toys are a particular concern for trading standards.
10 Explain why some people do not believe that consumer protection laws are needed.

Hit the spot

> What is meant by consumer protection?

>> Explain how stopping counterfeit goods being sold can help the consumer.

>>> Discuss the arguments both for and against having consumer protections laws.

Cracking the code

Consumer Someone who buys goods and services.

Trading Standards A government organisation that looks after consumers to stop them from being cheated.

BUSINESS ORGANISATION

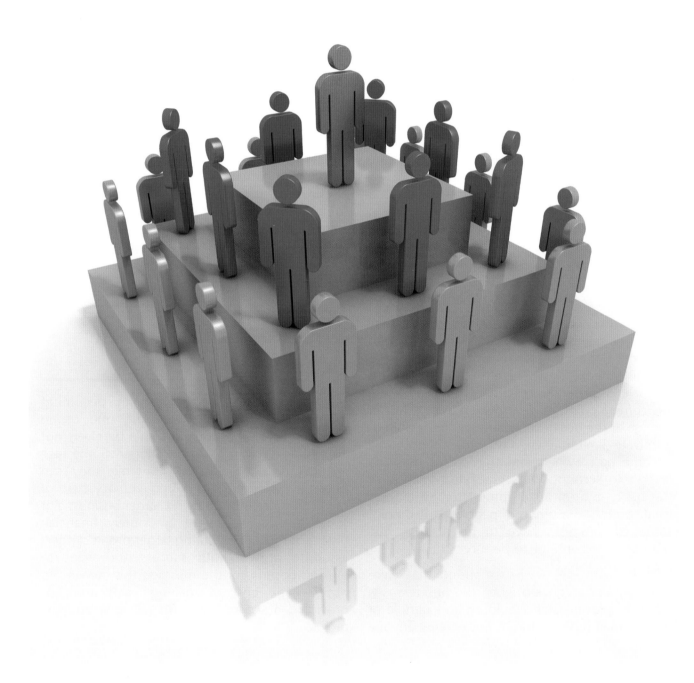

Chapter 31
Introduction to business organisation

In the first part of this book we concentrated on how small businesses operate. We looked at the legal side of business, how funds could be raised and other aspects such as marketing and dealing with staff. As businesses grow, we notice a change in the ownership. With a small organisation, the owner – the entrepreneur – tends to both own and manage the business. But as a business gets bigger, the owners are less likely to play a part in running their company.

Many owners of small businesses see what they have created as their baby. Often faced with challenges, the entrepreneur works long hours to establish the business. There is pride in the birth of the enterprise and relief at its survival. There will come a point, however, when things start to change. If the business becomes a partnership or a private limited company, other people will become part owners and their views must be taken into account. We see a shift in control of the business from a sole proprietor, who takes total control, to a group of people. At this point some compromises have to be made if the business is to continue to be successful.

With growth, we see issues arising that were probably not a concern when the business was small. Employing staff would be an example of this. A small business might not employ anyone but the entrepreneur and his or her immediate family. As a business grows, others will need to be taken on, which brings with it concerns. Employment laws are strict and it is not as easy to 'let staff go' as some people think. Employees' wages are also a cost of the business that need to be paid each week or month, even if the money coming in is low.

Should a business grow?

Many businesses see benefits in becoming bigger. Growth might even be one of an organisation's objectives. But let's be clear, not all businesses want to grow bigger. Some face restrictions that limit just how big they can become. However, it is a frequent objective of many entrepreneurs to own a larger business. For some the reason might be purely financial: bigger businesses can bring larger profits. Others associate growth with success and want to expand because of the message this conveys to others. The cost of making each item, or providing a service, can also fall as a business grows.

The market for a product can increase through clever marketing and changes in consumers' attitudes and preferences. But a point may be reached when a business will have to look to overseas markets if the home market has become saturated. Selling abroad brings with it a range of challenges for a business to overcome.

Do we 'go public'?

If a growing private limited company wishes to raise capital from selling shares, it will eventually have to accept that it cannot rely on obtaining this finance from existing shareholders. It is at this point that it must decide whether to 'go public'. While the process of becoming a public limited company is relatively straightforward, particularly when businesses can pay experts to complete the process for them, becoming a public limited company is not something that a business should enter into lightly. Businesses like the idea of being able to sell shares to the general public, but becoming a public limited company is not without its downside.

What about aims and objectives?

The aims and objectives of a small business are unlikely to be something that the owner stops to think about on a daily basis. What the owner wants from the business is probably the thing that drives him or her on each day. But the objectives of the business are probably so deep rooted in the owner's mind that decisions are almost instinctively made to realise these objectives. As many small businesses have the objective of reaching a certain profit, each decision is based on the business moving closer to that goal.

Large businesses also have aims and objectives, which set out the reason for the business's very existence. These are often published so that everyone who has an interest in the business, often called its stakeholders, is aware of them. Unfortunately, things never remain constant in business and if a business is to survive, it might need to review its objectives to see whether a change needs to be made. A company might have the objective of obtaining a stated profit one year. However, if a new competitor enters the market, this objective might become unachievable. The business might decide that the objective of maintaining a certain market share would now be more appropriate. If a business is to survive, it will need to be flexible with its objectives to take into account changing circumstances.

We might also want to question how sincere some companies' objectives are. Many businesses like to give the impression that they are ethical concerns. If competitors have taken this stance, a business may have no real choice but to follow suit. As a result, many large businesses have objectives that include social and environmental targets. While this might appear praiseworthy, is this perhaps a form of marketing rather than proof of a social conscience?

Where should the business be located?

For the sake of convenience, entrepreneurs tend to set up their businesses close to where they live. If nothing else, it is a way of keeping costs down. It is likely that the most important consideration for a small business is where its customers are. As the business expands there will be other factors that need to be kept in mind. Availability of raw materials and the costs of transport are just two of these things. A cost saving of 10p per item might be insignificant to a small business dealing with 500 items a month. But to a large business that produces half a million of these items monthly, it is equivalent to saving £50,000 a month. So, larger companies are more sensitive to cost savings than small businesses.

Chapter 32
Expanding as a business

IN THE NEWS

Cadbury plc

Cadbury, the well-known chocolate maker, has expanded as a business in several different ways. The company started back in 1824 when John Cadbury set up a tea and coffee shop in Bull Street in Birmingham. John introduced drinking chocolate and cocoa as drinks, which became popular with the people of Birmingham.

The business flourished over the next 50 years. Cadbury used its **retained profits** to pay to expand its business. In 1879, the business made a major decision and left the polluted centre of Birmingham and set up a factory, and later a workers' village, at Bournville. Cadbury always had the welfare of its employees at heart and wanted a healthier environment in which the workers could live and work. Bournville is four miles to the south of Birmingham and at the time was in the countryside and a pleasant place to live.

A major change to Cadbury came about in 1969 when the business merged with the soft drinks giant, Schweppes. The **merger** allowed both Cadbury and Schweppes to save money by sharing a management team. Other savings were made, for example sharing delivery lorries and a distribution network. The merger also allowed Cadbury to **diversify**. There followed a period when Cadbury Schweppes expanded by taking over other confectionery

manufacturers. Some familiar names joined the Cadbury Schweppes stable of brands, including Dr Pepper, Bassett's, Trebor and Orangina.

Cadbury does not always manufacture the products that bear its name. Biscuits bearing the Cadbury brand, such as Cadbury Fingers, are produced under licence by another company. Ice cream based on Cadbury products, like 99 Flake, is made under licence by another business.

In May 2008, Cadbury Schweppes **demerged**. This means the business was broken down into two separate companies. Cadbury continued with confectionery products and the drinks side of the business became Dr Pepper Snapple Inc.

 Take a look at the Cadbury website at **www.cadbury.com**

Cadbury is a good example of an expanding business, as it has grown in several different ways.

Organic

Organic growth refers to the usually slow method of expanding by increasing output and sales. A business might decide to open a new shop or factory, take on more employees and produce more items for sale. Alternatively the organic growth might come about by using existing equipment and labour more productively, so the business does not actually grow physically bigger but more is produced. When this happens we say efficiency has been improved because more has been produced with the same **inputs**.

If a business has the objective of expanding rapidly, it's unlikely that organic growth would be the best strategy to achieve this. One of the other methods outlined below would be more suitable.

Mergers

Cadbury increased its size greatly when it merged with Schweppes in 1969. The two businesses manufactured different products, so were not in direct competition with each other. By merging, though, they were able to reduce their costs by sharing some of their resources. This avoided unnecessary duplication and helped make the profits of the Cadbury Schweppes company greater than the profits of the two separate businesses. When two businesses merge, it is not unusual for some employees and managers to be made **redundant**.

Takeovers

If a business wishes to expand quickly, it may decide to **take over** a competitor. This method of expansion not only allows a business to grow quickly; it has the extra benefit of removing a competitor from the market. Takeovers are sometimes called **acquisitions**, especially when the business being taken over is a private limited company. Taking over a public limited company (plc) involves buying enough shares in the business to take control of it. You will be looking more at **public limited companies**, or plcs, in the next chapter. If Cadbury were to buy half the shares in another confectionery business, it would be able to outvote the other shareholders. Cadbury could then vote for the new business to become part of the Cadbury group of businesses. Alternatively, Cadbury could persuade the board of directors that it would be in the shareholders' interests to be taken over. If the directors were convinced, they could recommend the takeover to the other shareholders.

Independent Newspapers needed this new building as the business grew

Franchising/licensing

If a business has a strong brand, as Cadbury has, it may allow, or license, other businesses to trade using its **brand name**. Cadbury does not actually make the cakes and ice cream that carry its name. Instead, other businesses make these products and in return for trading with the powerful Cadbury brand, they pay a **royalty**. While this is not technically expanding the amount that Cadbury produces, it provides a source of finance to the company.

Summary

- Businesses often want to expand as a way of increasing profits or achieving other objectives
- There are several ways in which a business can expand
- Many businesses expand organically, but if a faster growth rate is required, other methods might be used
- Growing as a business may bring in more profits, but there are risks associated with expansion

Did you know...

The world's biggest chocolate shop can be found at Cadbury World.

Core knowledge

Expanding their businesses is often seen as an attractive prospect to business owners. In simple terms the owners may think: if a business grows to twice its original size, it will make twice the profits. Unfortunately, the relationship between size and profits will probably not be as neat as the last sentence suggests. If conditions are wrong, a business might actually lose money if it grows, especially if it tries to grow too quickly. When this happens, we sometimes say the business has **overstretched** itself.

Overstretching can happen because a business owner has borrowed money to buy new equipment, machinery and premises and increased the business's costs as a result. The interest on the loan has to be paid off monthly, but it may take some time before new customers are found.

There are other reasons why owners want to expand their business, besides hoping to see an increase in profits. Business owners might want more control of the market than they currently have. Being the major business in an industry gives that company more scope to put up its prices, without losing customers to its competitors.

Expanding can also be a way of reducing the risks that a business faces. This is particularly the case when the expansion comes about by diversifying. Producing several products that are sold in different markets can spread risk: so, if one market fails, you have other products in other markets to fall back on.

Business owners might want to grow bigger because there is a good investment opportunity available to them. The owners might have discovered a gap in the market or a chance to increase sales. For instance, there has been an increase in the number of people keeping chickens and other poultry in their back gardens. This is because consumers are less willing to buy eggs from caged birds. A manufacturer of chicken coops or houses might decide to expand the business to be able to sell more while demand is high.

Many small businesses decide to grow organically. In order to be able to do this, a business needs finance to pay for new factories and other factors of production. There also have to be additional employees available. The market for the product or service must be large enough for consumers to be willing to buy the additional output of the business. If there is a limited demand for the product, or if there are many competitors, organic growth may be a problem. Of course, the demand for a product or service can be stimulated by price cuts, through effective advertising and by increasing the product range. If Cadbury were to simply make more products, there is no guarantee that they would be sold.

Many businesses use franchising as a way of expanding. Of course, for this to succeed, the business must have a good product that is respected by customers. The attraction of franchising is that the person who buys the franchise bears many of the risks. The franchisee puts money into the business, so the franchisor does not have to find the funding. If the business fails, it is the franchisee who suffers and not the franchisor. The franchisor is also paid a royalty payment for the privilege of letting another business use its brand.

Did you know...

Many of Cadbury's product brands have been around for a long time. Cadbury Dairy Milk, for example, was first produced in 1905, with Milk Tray starting in 1915 and Roses in 1938.

And more

When a business expands, there will be an effect on profit. Hopefully, the growth will result in more profits being made, but this might not be the case. Shareholders might have mixed views on their business expanding because of the risks involved.

The expansion will require funding, which will have an impact on shareholders. The funding could come from:

- **retained profits** – this will mean less money going to the shareholders. The shareholders might, however, be willing to sacrifice some money today to gain even more in the future;

- **bank loan/mortgage** – this source of finance would need to be serviced. This simply means interest will have to be paid on the amount borrowed, which will be an extra cost to the business;

- **selling more shares** – shareholders might be happy with this method to pay for the expansion, as they are not losing out directly. However, new shareholders mean the existing shareholders have less say in how the business is run. It will also mean that future profits have to be shared between a greater number of people.

How might shareholders react to business growth? Shareholders, like all people, will have different views on the matter. Some might be happy to take the risk for the reward of more dividends in the future; others might be more cautious and oppose growth, fearing it could lose rather than gain money. These shareholders could believe it would be difficult to attract new customers or new employees to produce the extra goods or services. They might worry about raising the money to fund the expansion, or about new shareholders joining the organisation.

Occasionally a large organisation might decide to split into two separate businesses. This is known as a demerger. The company might think it is becoming too large to function properly and it would be more profitable to operate as two independent concerns. Sometimes the split is forced by the government. This is usually because it is thought that the single large business has too much power in the market and customers are suffering through high prices and a lack of competition.

Sometimes a business will grow by producing more of the same product. This is known as horizontal growth. If Cadbury merged with another chocolate maker, this would be horizontal growth, or integration. Vertical growth refers to moving further up and down the production process. Cadbury buying a cocoa plantation in West Africa would be an example of vertical growth backwards. This is because cocoa is a raw material in chocolate making. If Cadbury decided to open up Cadbury shops to sell its products, this would be vertical growth forwards.

A benefit to a business of becoming larger is its costs per item can go down. We call this effect 'economies of scale'. But businesses can become so big that costs actually start to rise faster than the amount of extra goods being produced. This is the opposite of economies of scale and is called 'diseconomies of scale'. The whole topic of economies of scale will be dealt with later in this book.

Have a go!

Group activity

As a group, identify as many reasons as possible why a business might choose not to expand. Outline your reasons in a series of PowerPoint slides. Give your ideas as a presentation to the rest of the class.

Imagine you have an established business with a recognised brand name – you can choose a suitable product or service for this. Produce an A4-sized leaflet on the benefits of another business franchising your brand.

Discussion

Discuss how a business might recognise that it has grown so large it would be beneficial to demerge.

Quickfire questions

1 In which city did John Cadbury set up his tea and coffee shop?
2 What is the name of the Cadbury village?
3 Which company did Cadbury merge with in 1969?
4 What percentage of shares must a business buy in another company to have control of it?
5 What is a franchise royalty payment?
6 What is meant by diversifying?
7 What do we call it when a business has grown too quickly and is losing profits as a result?
8 Give two reasons why a business might not choose to grow bigger.
9 Explain what is meant by economies and diseconomies of scale.
10 Give an advantage to a business of expanding by vertical growth backwards.

Hit the spot

> Give two reasons why businesses want to expand.

>> Explain two factors that limit how fast a business can grow.

>>> Discuss whether the bigger a business is, the more profits it will earn.

Cracking the code

Retained profit That part of its profit used by a company to put back into the business, rather than be given to its shareholders.

Merger Two businesses joining together to save on their costs or reduce competition.

Diversify Produce a range of goods or services, which spreads the risk of the business failing.

Demerger Breaking up a business into two or more separate parts, each run independently.

Organic growth Growing by increasing turnover and sales.

Inputs The resources or factors of production that a business uses to produce its products.

Redundant When resources, such as members of the labour force, are no longer needed.

Takeover Taking control of another business by buying more than half of its shares.

Acquisition A business that has been taken over or bought by another company.

Public limited company A business that is allowed to sell its shares to anyone who wants to buy them.

Brand name A well-known company or product that consumers trust.

Royalty The fee paid to a business for using its brand name.

Overstretched When a business tries to grow too quickly, which can result in profits falling.

Chapter 33
Choosing the right legal structure

Center Parcs

Center Parcs (UK) is a business that specialises in providing short-break holidays. The company owns four holiday villages around the UK, each set within a forest. The idea of forest holiday villages was developed by Dutch entrepreneur Piet Derkson, and the first Center Parcs village was opened in Holland in 1967. The business moved into the UK market in 1987, when the Sherwood Forest village was opened. Each village is based upon a large indoor swimming pool. There are many other leisure and sporting activities that the guests can enjoy, but these have an additional charge.

The chalet-style accommodation is self-catering, with guests able to cook for themselves, but there are several restaurants around the village for those who prefer to eat out. The main target market for Center Parcs holidays is families with higher-than-average incomes. The holiday company is also trying to attract business customers who use the facilities for conferences or team building.

It is very expensive for Center Parcs to build a holiday village. The company has to buy or lease the land and adapt it so that accommodation units can be built but without losing the attractiveness of the forest. There is also the cost of the domed swimming pool and other buildings and equipment. Center Parcs is in the process of building a new village at Warren Wood in Bedfordshire, scheduled to open in 2010. This new village will be smaller than the previous four villages, but it is estimated that it will cost about £160 million to complete the project.

Center Parcs' ownership has changed several times over recent years. The business was owned by Scottish and Newcastle (S&N) until 2001 when it was sold to allow S&N to concentrate on its core brewing business. In 2003 the owner of Center Parcs, Mid Ocean, sold the business once again to an organisation called Arbor. Center Parcs was then floated on the London Stock Exchange's Alternative Investment Market (**AIM**). This means Center Parcs was allowed to sell shares to the public, but without having to obey many of the regulations that the **Stock Exchange** imposes.

Center Parcs became a full public limited company (**plc**) in 2005. As a plc, Center Parcs did not have to limit its shareholders to those directly connected with the business – it was able to sell shares to the general public on the stock exchange. However, in 2006 the business was sold to the Blackstone Group of companies. The holiday business was brought back once again as a private limited company, with the support of its large parent company.

 Take a look at the Center Parcs website at
www.centerparcs.com

Center Parcs has experienced many different types of legal ownership, particularly since 2001. The company had made the decision to expand organically by building another holiday village in Bedfordshire. The estimated £160 million it needed would have been very difficult to fund from existing shareholders. But as a private limited company it was not allowed to sell shares to anyone outside the organisation.

By becoming a public limited company (plc), Center Parcs would be permitted to sell its shares on the Stock Exchange to the general public. This would allow outside investors to put money into the business and more easily raise the large amounts of money needed.

Becoming a plc is neither a very expensive nor a complicated operation for a private limited business. It involves producing a number of documents and showing that the business is reliable. Many businesses, however, choose to use the services of a bank or an expert in these matters to guide them through the application. Once plc status has been achieved, the company is listed on the Stock Exchange and can begin to sell shares to anybody prepared to pay the going rate for them. We say that the business is now a quoted or listed company.

In the first part of this book, you will have read about what we mean by limited liability. You might remember that when the owners of small businesses want to expand, they will need to attract investors to put money into the business. These shareholders are technically owners of the business and are responsible for its debts. They probably have very little to do with the day-to-day running of the business, so feel that they should not be expected to have to sell their houses and other property to pay the company's debts. Limited liability grew from the need of investors to be protected from the creditors of the businesses in which they had bought shares.

If a private limited company wishes to raise additional capital it is not allowed to sell its shares to just anybody – only existing shareholders are allowed to put extra money into the business.

Did you know...

Sometimes people confuse a public limited business with the public sector. The two are quite different: the public sector is the businesses owned by the government, but plcs are owned by their shareholders.

Summary

- Private limited businesses that wish to raise large amounts of capital might choose to do this by becoming a public limited company (plc)
- There are disadvantages in becoming a plc and sometimes businesses return to being private limited companies

Core knowledge

Many private limited businesses are happy to remain as Ltd businesses. Becoming a public limited company may be a way to raise large amounts of capital, but being a plc can bring with it drawbacks for its owners.

It would be unreasonable to expect investors to part with their money unless they were confident that the business was stable and not likely to become bankrupt in the near future. To ensure that anyone thinking about buying shares is informed about the business, plc businesses must publish their **annual accounts** and send copies to anyone who requests them. To save the time and expense of this, most plcs publish their accounts on their websites.

This legal requirement to publish accounts does mean that competitors know exactly how well the business is doing. It provides them with information about the business's efficiency and whether new products, markets or advertising campaigns have been profitable. Many plc businesses would like to keep this type of information secret, but they are not permitted to do so.

As any person, or organisation, is allowed to buy shares in a plc, this means that competitors can buy the shares as well. Why should a competitor want to buy shares in another business? There is more than one reason for this. It may be simply a sort of insurance policy. If a business manages to attract other business's customers, then owning part of the successful company can provide some compensation to the one losing out. The loss in profits can be offset by the dividend payment from the thriving business.

Another reason could be the competitor is trying to take over the company in which it is buying shares. Once enough shares have been bought, the purchasing business can outvote other shareholders and take over the company. The company can then determine how the taken-over business operates, or even whether it closes down.

Buying and selling shares

The owners of some private limited companies are reluctant to go public for another reason. Some believe that public shareholders are more interested in earning quick profits rather than watching the business develop over a long period. This is a short-term view of buying shares – looking for a quick profit.

Shareholders are entitled to a share of their businesses' profits. This payment is called a **dividend**. Often businesses pay their dividends twice a year. Most of this money is paid when the accounts have been published and, quite often, some money is given to shareholders halfway through the year. This second dividend is often called an interim payment.

Not all profits are given to shareholders. After the profits have been calculated and all of the business's costs and tax liabilities have been paid, the company must decide what proportion of the profits to put back into the business. This money is needed to finance any expansion plans the company might have. The funds that are kept back are called retained profits. What is left is given out to the shareholders and is called distributed profits.

Did you know...

Many people incorrectly believe that when a business's share price fall, the business loses money. If the share price falls, the shareholder loses out, not the business.

Did you know...

Price rises and falls can be shown using index numbers, such as the FT 100SE, sometimes called the Footsie. This index measures the cost of buying shares in the top 100 businesses in the UK. The latest form of the Footsie began on 3 January 1984 when it was given the value 1000. When it reached 2000, shares, on average, had doubled in price.

And more

Businesses sell more than one type of share.

- *Preference shares*. The owners of preference shares have the right to be paid their dividends before other shareholders. They are usually paid a fixed amount each year for each share that they own. Because they are paid first there is less risk involved. As long as the business earns enough profit to pay its preference shareholders, they will be paid in full. Some preference shares are even cumulative. This means that if, for any reason, the business does not make enough profit to pay its preference shareholders, the shortfall will be made up the following year. This helps to reduce even further the risk of holding shares.

- *Ordinary shares*. Ordinary shares, as their name suggests, have no special rights or privileges. Ordinary shareholders have no guarantee that they will receive a dividend each year. Even if the business in which they hold shares earns a profit, it might decide to retain this profit, rather than distribute it to shareholders. Ordinary shareholders will receive what is left of the distributed profits after the preference shareholders have been paid.

The annual general meeting

- *Debentures.* Debentures are not really shares as the debenture holder does not receive a voting right. They are long-term loans to a business in exchange for a rate of interest, which will be the same each year. Some companies do not even pay this fixed rate of return. Sporting clubs occasionally fund some of the cost of their stadiums by selling debentures that guarantee a seat, rather than a rate of return. Examples include the All England Tennis and Croquet Club (Wimbledon), the Emirates Stadium (home of Arsenal Football Club), Lord's Cricket Ground, the Millennium Stadium and Wembley Stadium.

Most shareholders are happy to have nothing to do with the operations of the businesses in which they hold shares. As long as the business is paying a dividend which compares well with other similar companies, shareholders will often leave the business to get on with it.

Very few shareholders go to a company's annual general meeting (AGM). Many companies will interpret poor attendance at the AGM as shareholders being happy with the business so they have not bothered to go along. If a business is having problems, far more shareholders will attend, but still only a small percentage of all shareholders will be there.

Did you know...

The price a business's share trades for in the Stock Exchange changes many times during an average working day. If investors are confident that the business will make profits in the future, they will want to buy the shares, pushing up their price.

Have a go!

Group activity

Have a share-buying competition within your class. Working in small groups, decide how you would invest £100,000 in public limited company shares. Agree the rules that you will play to – for example, if there is a maximum number of companies, how often you can trade (sell or buy shares), and when the competition ends.

Each group should put their shares on a spreadsheet and use it to calculate the valuation. This should be repeated as share prices change. The winning team will be the group that has the highest share valuation at the end of the competition.

Discussion

Discuss ways by which Center Parcs might encourage business users to use its facilities.

Web-based activity

Produce a graph of how the value of the Footsie changes over the next two or three days. Try to explain any large changes by looking at news stories that could have influenced the price of shares.

Quickfire questions

1 What type of holidays do Center Parcs provide?
2 Who does Center Parcs target as its customers?
3 What is the estimated cost of building a new Center Parcs village?
4 Which company currently owns Center Parcs?
5 Where is the proposed site for the next Center Parcs village?
6 What is an AGM?
7 Give one difference between private and public limited companies.
8 Explain two differences between preference and ordinary shareholders.
9 Give two things that a company's shareholder might do if he/she thought the business was not making enough profit.
10 What does the Footsie measure?

Hit the spot

➤   What is meant by a public limited company (plc)?

➤➤   Explain an advantage of a business becoming a plc.

➤➤➤ Discuss whether going public is the best way for a business to raise large amounts of capital.

Cracking the code

AIM Alternative Investments Market. This is a group of businesses that sell shares to the public on the Stock Exchange. There are fewer regulations to obey with this type of listing.

Plc A public limited company. A business allowed to sell its shares to the general public.

Stock Exchange A place where shares can be bought and sold.

Annual accounts Financial details of a business, published each year.

Dividend The share of the profits that goes to each shareholder.

Chapter 34
Business aims and objectives

IN THE NEWS

In November 2008, Vodafone was voted the top company in a new set of awards that has been running for just five years. The award is called the Accountability Rating and measures how responsible companies are in the way they do business. In particular, it looks at how they have a positive impact on the societies and environments in which they operate.

Vodafone, the mobile network operator, is the largest telecommunications company in the world,

with an annual turnover of over £5 billion. As can be seen from the award, it is achieving one of its aims, which is linked to **corporate social responsibility (CSR)**. This is a measure of how well the business treats the communities and environments in which it works. The importance that Vodafone gives to CSR can be seen from the way it is included in its aims in both its mission statement and its vision statement. One way in which the business reduces its impact on the environment is by encouraging the recycling and re-use of mobile phones. In the UK there is one mobile phone for every man, woman and child in the population. Many of these are no longer used, so could be re-used in poorer countries or broken down and their parts recycled. Between 65% and 80% of a mobile can be recycled and re-used. When this includes some of the plastics, the total can be raised to 90%.

Vodafone is in partnership with Global Cool Foundation UK, a registered charity, Solar Aid, and The Million Superheroes Campaign. Each has a target linked to CSR. The Global Cool Foundation aims to reduce CO_2 emissions by 1 million tonnes; Solar Aid works to provide solar devices in sunny but poor African countries; and Superheroes wants to persuade 1 million people in the UK to sign up to become a Superhero and reduce their carbon emissions. The company sees CSR as central to its aims and produces a yearly CSR report to say how it has hit targets and what new targets it will set.

Go to **www.vodafone.com/start/ responsibility.html** and read about the areas in which Vodafone is trying to be responsible. Rate them in order of which you think is most important.

Changing aims

As a business grows, its aims and objectives are likely to change. You have already learned about how a business may start with aims such as survival, breaking even or making a modest profit. Once it has achieved these aims, it may then want to think about setting itself new aims, targets that may be harder to reach or take longer to achieve.

Why grow?

Some businesses never grow – because they serve a small market (like a local newsagent), for instance, or provide a specialist service. Others aim to grow to increase their share of the market, so that they can compete more effectively, perhaps take market share from rivals and also protect themselves from competitors.

As a business grows it may find that its home market is no longer big enough for it and so will look for ways to expand elsewhere. It can either expand through **diversification** – that is, moving into markets for other products or into other markets, physically separated from its current market. If it diversifies, it may do this in markets that are similar to the ones it is in (for example, National Express, the bus company, moving into operating as a train company) or it may move into completely new markets (for example, Whitbread, the brewers, moving into the fast-food market with Pizza Hut and the health market with David Lloyd Health Clubs).

Market dominance

Often a business which decides to compete in a particular market may be aiming to become the leading or **dominant business** in that market. This may give it many advantages over its competitors. It may become the preferred business of suppliers, or of retailers who see market size as a good indicator of success (or of ability to pay). It may become the leading brand and therefore the best known business in its particular market. It may be in a position to put pressure on suppliers to keep prices low, or to prevent other businesses from competing in the market. If, for example, every town has a major supermarket (such as Tesco), then it becomes increasingly difficult for other supermarkets to compete and almost impossible for smaller retail outlets to grow into the same market.

Overseas expansion

If a business moves into overseas markets, it will face new competition, language barriers, different laws and regulations, different transport and location problems and the need to employ local staff. Each of these areas will need to be addressed with new aims and objectives, and new policies to make sure that the business is competing effectively, efficiently and legally.

Ethics

Growing businesses, such as Vodafone, will also have to take into account ethical and environmental considerations. '**Ethics**' and being 'ethical' means 'doing the right thing'. In business terms it means not harming the places or communities where it works and not taking advantage of poorer countries or markets. Vodafone does this as part of its corporate social policy. The business must also consider the environment. This means aiming to do as little harm to the environment as possible. One part of this is to reduce its **carbon footprint**. The carbon footprint is the total amount of carbon dioxide (CO_2) and other greenhouse gases (gases that harm the environment) that are produced over the lifetime of a product (or by an organisation). For a mobile phone this includes the raw materials, the energy used in manufacture, transport, storage, marketing and the eventual disposal of the phone.

It is in the interests of businesses to consider these as they are important to consumers and other stakeholders. A business that looks after the environment and has a low carbon footprint is one that is likely to be more attractive because it is being more responsible.

The disposal of an old phone contributes to its carbon footprint

Did you know...

Businesses can also grow by moving into different sectors of the market, which they have not targeted previously. For example, Wilkinson, the high street shop, decided to encourage students to shop there by targeting them through their universities. This was a part of the market that did not previously shop at the store, but which was encouraged to do so.

Summary

- As a business grows, its aims and objectives are likely to change
- Businesses can grow in different ways, e.g. into new markets or new locations
- Aims for a growing business could include increased market share or market domination
- Businesses will need new aims if they expand overseas
- Two key aims for modern businesses are to be ethical and environmentally responsible

Core knowledge

All businesses have aims and objectives. Often these are written down in the 'mission statement' or 'vision' of the business. The longer-term objectives are usually broken down into smaller, shorter-term targets, or aims. As a business grows, it will have to consider wider aims than those that it had when it was smaller. Aims and objectives will alter not only as the business grows but also according to how the business has decided to grow. The increased size of a growing business will immediately give it more responsibilities and these will need to be reflected in its aims. Examples include:

- if it begins to operate in overseas markets, it will need to take account of local laws and regulations, customs and holidays, and matters of transport and communication;
- if it has a larger or more diverse workforce, it will need to take into account differences in culture, working conditions and wage rates, and the need to treat all of its employees equally, no matter where they are working;
- if it gains new groups of stakeholders, it will need to take into account their interests. In particular, it will gain new customers whose loyalty it will need to work on, new communities in which it works and possibly new investors concerned with profits and returns.

One of the most important considerations for many businesses, but especially growing ones, has become environmental and ethical considerations. Customers, suppliers, shareholders, governments and other stakeholders want to see that a business is being responsible in many different ways. Businesses are expected to treat all of their workers equally, no matter where in the world they work. They are also expected to be as good to the environment as possible, for instance, looking for green sources of energy or better ways to dispose of waste. Many also provide for the communities where they work by paying for services such as education or health care.

And more

The main aim of almost all businesses is to make a profit. Some social enterprises (like charities or co-operatives) may aim to maximise the good that they do, but even with these types of organisation it is important to make sure that costs are lower than revenues. Other businesses claim many aims and objectives. Some commentators would say that, looking at the early – and basic – aims of a small business, and comparing these with the aims and objectives of a growing business, there are not any that are not directly linked to profit.

In its early days a business may look to survive or break even – it can do this only if it makes enough money to buy stock, market its products and pay the wages of its staff (including the owner). In the longer run, aims such as corporate social and environmental responsibility, increased market share and international expansion may all be considered as ways to make more profit. If a business is a significant player in a market, it can compete more effectively, take a greater market share, introduce new product lines and target new customers – all of which could be profitable. If its customers are happy, then they will return to buy more products and recommend the business to friends, so good customer service becomes a key part of profitability. If the business is good to the communities and people where it works, it is likely to be more efficient and therefore more profitable. It may therefore be true to say that if a business hits its aims of efficiency, environmental responsibility and growth, it is also likely to increase profit.

Have a go!

Group activity

Visit **www.direct.gov.uk/actonCO$_2$** where you can calculate your carbon footprint. Compare this with other members of your group. Find out how you could reduce your footprint and calculate how much carbon you could save for your whole group.

Discussion

Find out what the 'mission statement' or 'vision statement' is for your school or college. Discuss whether or not you agree with it and how you would alter it. If your school or college does not have a statement, then agree the details of one for it.

Web-based activity

Visit a selection of 5–10 websites of leading companies and list their aims and objectives. Group them into similar types of aims (e.g. efficiency, profitability, returns to investors, corporate responsibility, innovation). See which are the most common aims and say why you think this is so.

Quickfire questions

1   List the likely aims of a start-up business.
2   List the likely aims of a growing business.
3   What is meant by 'diversification'?
4   What is market dominance?
5   Give two possible new responsibilities of a growing business.
6   List two possible advantages of moving into overseas markets.
7   List two possible disadvantages of moving into overseas markets.
8   Explain what is meant by 'ethics'.
9   Why is an ethical approach important to some businesses?
10 What is a carbon footprint?

Hit the spot

> Give two reasons why a business may decide that it does not want to grow.

>> Explain what is meant by a market leader or dominant business in a market. Explain why a business would want to be in this position.

>>> Is it true to say that all aims and objectives are linked to profits? Explain how you have come to your conclusion.

Cracking the code

Carbon footprint The amount of greenhouse gases or CO_2 released during the life of a product or related to a particular activity.

Corporate social responsibility (CSR) A measure of how well the business treats the communities and environments in which it works.

Diversification When a business moves into markets for other products or into other markets.

Dominant business or market leader The leading business in a particular market because it has the largest share of the market.

Ethics The idea of 'doing the right thing' and not harming the places or communities where a business is located.

Chapter 35
Business location

IN THE NEWS

Aston Science Park is a specialist location for science- and technology-based industries. It was founded by Birmingham City Council, Lloyds Bank and Aston University in 1982 and is recognised worldwide as a leading science park. It is home to a number of businesses that can benefit from the research facilities of Birmingham's Aston University, which shares the site with them. The businesses can work in partnership with the University, making use of its expertise and research facilities. In 2008, this led to science park business Arden Photonics and Aston University winning a major award for a development that will help to make fibre optic cables more efficient.

The University runs what it calls a 'Knowledge Transfer Initiative', in which it works with businesses in order to share and transfer knowledge between the business and research sectors. Aston represents the research part of this link, while the Science Park attracts the right sort of 'cutting edge' businesses to take advantage of such research. Representatives of both the University and the businesses have praised the location and the partnership. Dr Kate Sugden, Senior Lecturer of the Photonics Research Group at Aston University, commented: 'Aston University has a well deserved reputation for its highly successful knowledge transfer activities with regional companies and we're pleased that this award will raise our profile still further.'

Arden Photonics itself, Aston University and other businesses located on Aston Science Park were pleased with the award, which they said would raise the profile of the Park still further and enhance its reputation. Everyone was looking forward to working together in the future at what is seen as a prestigious and successful location.

 Visit **www.astonsciencepark. co.uk/about-us.html** to see the main types of companies that are located at the science park. Using this information, define what you think is the purpose of a science park.

Type of business

Location is an important factor for many businesses, but just how important depends on the type of business and the goods or services that it produces. A business needs to look at two major elements.

The first are the **factors of production** that it needs to produce its good or service. A manufacturer may need to be close to raw material supplies, or to a reliable power source. A wholesaler may need to be close to a good distribution network such as a railway or motorway system. Power, transport and other vital services are called '**infrastructure**'.

The second is its market. A retailer may need to be close to its market, but will also need to be close to transport so that goods can be delivered. For some businesses, therefore, geographical location is important – for example, raw material extraction can only take place where the raw materials are located. For other businesses, geographical location may be of little or no importance. An internet selling operation needs an internet connection and to send products out from warehouses or distribution centres, but may be located almost anywhere in the world. Businesses selling a service need to be close to customers if this is a personal service (like haircutting) but may be located anywhere if it is information or advice related or similar. For example, the actual location of an online bank, insurance company or tax adviser is of no importance to the quality or availability of the service.

International businesses will need transport links

Key questions

A business seeking a location must therefore be able to answer the following questions:

- What space do I need?
- What facilities (such as IT and storage) do I need?
- What transport links do I need?
- What labour, including specialists or specialisms, do I need?
- How close to my customers do I need to be?
- How much am I willing to pay?

International expansion

Businesses might also grow by expanding internationally or even globally. Sometimes this means that they will have to establish a physical presence in a different country. Overseas locations can bring their own advantages and disadvantages. The main decision regarding location will be whether to **export** from the current location or to set up a new base in the overseas country or countries in which the business is operating. Each has possible benefits and drawbacks, so the choice is a crucial one.

If the business is a manufacturing company, it may make sense to continue to produce where there are established raw material supplies, existing machinery and trained labour. However, if costs are lower in the new country, it could make sense to establish the business there. This also cuts out the costs of transporting the products. The disadvantage of such a move could be that the new country has different laws or regulations, or charges more in taxation. There could also be language difficulties. Businesses also have to decide whether it is best to put their own people into the new country or employ locals. Their own people will be trained and experienced but may not speak the language or know the customs of the country. New people will need to be trained and this could prove costly.

Businesses can also decide on a 'middle way' which is to use **agents** in the new country.

These have the advantage of local knowledge and language skills and do not need a lot of training from the business. The disadvantage is that they are not actually employees of the business, so may not always be working in its best interests.

Did you know...

Not only does the UK government provide assistance for businesses to locate in the UK, but the European Union provides assistance for businesses to locate in various poorer parts of Europe.

Summary

- Location may be an important factor for a business
- How important will depend on the type of business
- All businesses will locate with the intention of keeping costs down
- Generally, businesses need to be close to raw materials or close to their markets
- Businesses have to ask key questions about cost and availability of resources before choosing a location
- International expansion brings a whole new set of location decisions

Core knowledge

When a business first starts, a correct choice of location is often central to its success. A small business may need to be convenient to its customers. Later, the growing business will look at location in terms of keeping costs as low as possible while increasing revenues. Costs can be kept low by locating either near the market or near the raw materials, depending on the product being sold. Costs can also be kept down by being near infrastructure and by taking advantage of government grants. Revenue can be increased by being able to sell at convenient locations. Some locations will attract customers because there are other businesses of the same type at that location. For example, a computer or electrical

An overseas call centre

goods shop will attract more custom if it is on a retail estate with similar shops. Customers will be attracted to a group of shops so that they have a choice. Costs may be reduced by locating certain operations where they are cheapest. This could mean setting up a central storage or distribution depot, for example, or locating some services overseas. Many call centres are now located in India, as this is cheaper than paying similarly qualified staff in the UK.

There are also historical factors that affect the location of a business. If an area has a tradition of, for example, shoe manufacture (Leicester) or fine textiles for suits (Huddersfield), then other businesses, producing similar products, will be drawn to the same area. Even though the original reasons for such a location may have vanished, there will be other factors – such as the availability of trained labour – that still attract businesses.

Businesses may also receive help from national or local government in the form of grants or lower rents or rates to encourage them to certain areas. These may be, for example, areas of high unemployment or where there has been a decline in traditional industries.

Did you know...

For some businesses, a single location factor is of great importance. Textile mills, for example, had to be located near fast-flowing rivers both to provide power and to clean textiles.

And more

Different businesses may be pulled or pushed towards a particular type of geographical location. For example, a manufacturing business may be pulled in a different direction to a retail business. Some businesses are drawn more towards locations near their markets. These are often **bulk decreasing industries**. If a product loses weight, size or bulk during the manufacturing process, then it makes sense to do most of the work – such as manufacturing, refining and processing – as near to the raw material source as possible. The business can then reduce costs by being able to transport the product when it is less bulky. So the best place for refining oil is on the coast, where the oil is landed, or even on an oil rig. (This is also a dangerous process so should take place away from centres of population.) Some businesses, meanwhile, operate in what are called **bulk increasing industries**. It is much easier and cheaper to transport wood to as near to the customer as possible before manufacturing furniture, which may be delicate and is certainly more bulky. The journey to the retailer is thus relatively short.

Businesses can take advantage of international locations to help keep costs down. For example, a business that has production and sales bases in a number of countries may be able to take advantage of local labour rates, or health and safety regulations. It may also be able to choose to pay its taxes in the country that has the lowest levels of taxation. Sometimes this is seen as unfair and, in recent years, there have been many controversies. These often involve the use of cheap (even child) labour and unsafe working conditions where businesses have been accused of taking advantage of poorer or less developed countries.

Did you know...

Some businesses need to be located where they will do least harm if something goes wrong. Nuclear power plants, for example, are located away from major centres of population.

Have a go!

Group activity

Find out the difference between a greenfield site and a brownfield site. What are the advantages and disadvantages for businesses and local communities of locating on either?

Discussion

Some businesses have been accused of using their international locations to take advantage of local laws and taxes. See what information you can research about any recent cases and discuss your findings. Discuss whether this will change any of your shopping habits or brand loyalties.

Web-based activity

Use the internet to investigate a local retail park or shopping centre and list all of the shops there. See how many of them are selling similar goods. Explain why you think this is so.

Quickfire questions

1   Name the factors of production.
2   What is meant by 'infrastructure'?
3   Name two services that have to be close to the customer.
4   Name two services that can be geographically distant from the customer.
5   Give one way in which a growing business can use location to keep costs low.
6   Give one way in which a growing business can keep costs low.
7   Give one way in which a growing business can increase revenue.
8   Give two possible problems with overseas locations.
9   Give one advantage and one disadvantage of using an agent.
10 What is the difference between bulk increasing and bulk decreasing industries?

Hit the spot

➤   Give two reasons why a business might need to locate near to its market.

➤➤   Explain why a business might decide to keep production in the UK and export goods rather than set up a plant overseas.

➤➤➤ An expanding business must ask key questions about its location. Which of these questions is the most important? Explain why you think so.

Cracking the code

Agents Anyone in business acting on behalf of another person, business or organisation.

Bulk decreasing industries Where the manufacturing or processing process makes goods smaller, or easier to transport.

Bulk increasing industries Where the manufacturing or processing process makes goods bigger, or harder to transport.

Export When goods or services are sent out of one country to another (the receiving country imports them).

Factors of production The inputs needed by a business in order to produce – land, labour and capital.

Infrastructure The availability of services that help businesses: a good infrastructure provides sources of power, transport and communications.

ADVANCED MARKETING

Marketing mix

This section uses marketing ideas – in particular the marketing mix of product, price, promotion and place – and looks at how each (and combinations of each) might change as a business grows. The marketing mix is the balance of its four elements as used by a business. These are the product itself (product could be either a good or a service), place (where the good or service is available, or methods by which a business can get it to the customer), price, which must be competitive (i.e. within the customer's range for such a product) and promotion – telling people about the product.

Each element of 'the mix' is important in its own right – but more so when combined with the others, like mixing paint on a palette

Balance

It is the balance of the marketing mix that is more important than any of the individual elements. Without products to sell, there is no point in setting a price. A competitive price – i.e. one where consumers will consider the product is worth buying – is necessary to attract customers. Promotion is necessary to tell customers of the existence of products and to persuade them to buy. Place includes both where the products are sold (everywhere from online to market stalls) and how the products are distributed to consumers. Distribution and location are important to create somewhere where buyers and sellers can come together to complete the sale. This means that there must be a place where customers can come to buy, or the business must be prepared to distribute products to an appropriate place.

A marketing mix is not fixed for any particular period of time. It has to be fluid, something that has to keep changing as circumstances change. Businesses are constantly adapting their marketing mix to try to improve their performance. Sometimes this is in response to competitor actions, sometimes in response to changes in the market. Businesses that grow will do so as a result of changing their marketing mix and gaining the benefits from these changes. A new product line, a price reduction, a successful promotion, a new distribution strategy (such as opening up internet sales) can all lead to growth. Businesses can also grow by moving into new markets, sometimes linked to the ones in which they currently operate, sometimes in completely new directions.

The role of market research

Businesses will, of course, use market research to find out about the possible changes in their market (or to find out how best they can bring about change in their market). They will gather information on who currently buys the product, who might be persuaded to buy it in the future, what competitors are doing, how the market is changing and how they might take advantage of those changes. They can look at how markets are divided (or 'segmented') and how they can turn this to their advantage. No sensible business would embark on a growth strategy without good market research information to back them up.

Growth

It is worth, here, taking a brief look at what is meant by growth in relation to markets and how it might happen. As business size can be measured in several different ways, so businesses can grow in several different ways. Size may be measured through number of employees, value of assets, stock market valuation, size of sales revenue or share of market. You need to investigate the type of business and type of market before you can say whether a business is small, medium or large – and whether or not it has grown. For example, an engineering firm is likely to have a lot of assets by way of machinery and factories, but may employ few people. (The use of robots and automated systems in

manufacturing may mean that large engineering companies inevitably have high-value assets but few employees.) A service-based industry (such as a postal delivery or courier service), meanwhile, may have many employees but little in the way of tangible assets. You should also be sure, if using market share as a guide to growth, that it is the business that has grown rather than the market that has shrunk. A 20% share of £1 million market is £200,000. If the market shrinks to £500,000 but market share rises to 25%, the share is now worth £125,000. Has the business grown or not? Looking just at market share, the business would appear to have grown – comparing it with changes in the market, you can see that this is not the case.

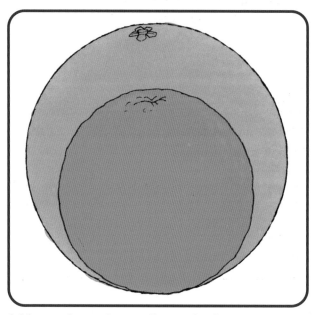

A bigger share of a smaller market?

Where does growth take place?

Internal growth is a direct result of changes to the marketing mix – for example, an increase in sales, the use of new technology in its production processes that allow the business to expand its product range, or by using promotion to tap into bigger market shares. External growth is when a business grows by joining up with other businesses. Sometimes this is when two businesses merge. Sometimes it is when one business takes over another.

SMEs

SMEs are a group of businesses that the government particularly targets for help as they are seen as the backbone of an enterprise economy and the most likely to grow in the future. SME stands for small and medium-sized enterprises. Many are very small so-called micro businesses, with fewer than ten employees, but the definition includes businesses employing up to 249 people.

Staying small

Of course, not every business wants to grow. A business that has just started may be more concerned with ensuring its survival, and may be happy to provide a local service or supply specialist products to small markets. In some cases, the type of business is such that there is little opportunity to expand – local services like window cleaning or gardening are likely to stay local rather than seek to establish national chains.

A small, local business

Chapter 37
The marketing mix: product

Mobile phones – and the ringtones that owners download to go with them – may now be considered a **mature market in the UK**. The mobile phone market in the UK would find it difficult to expand its basic service through increased ownership of mobile phones. As long ago as 2003, it was reported (by telephone regulator Oftel) that over 90% of 15–34 year olds in the UK owned at least one mobile phone and that ownership even in the youngest category – the 7–10 age group – was at 25% and rising rapidly.

Monstermob is a growing business that has done well out of this increase. It is a content provider based in Lancashire, with one of its biggest lines being mobile phone ringtone downloads. Every phone has, of course, at least one ringtone, but most have several. Some have even entered the music charts they have been so popular. (Crazy Frog, for example, earned over $28 million for the firm that released it and even had its own album!) Some are seasonal (especially Christmas jingles), while others, like current pop songs, are temporary. In other parts of the world, expansion through increased ownership is still feasible (although all but the poorest countries are rapidly catching up), so Monstermob needs to find a way of extending the product life cycle for the ringtones it produces.

One way to do this would be to provide more content, but, of course, this is expensive. Another is to find different markets in which to sell existing content. Monstermob decided that the best way to extend the life of its product was to sell ringtones into those markets where phone ownership is on the increase, but ringtones and other content have not yet become popular. To do so, it bought up providers in Malaysia, China and the Philippines, along with Russian content provider Mobicon. The biggest of these markets are China and Russia. Russia has widespread ownership of mobile phones, but people use them for calls and texts rather than entertainment, while the Chinese market is estimated to be some six years behind the European one. Monstermob's acquisitions have allowed it to extend the life cycle by introducing the product to completely new markets.

@ Looking at the figures for 2007/8 at **www.csu.nisra.gov.uk/Mobile_ phone_ownership_by_sex_and_ age_Trend.htm**, which section of the market would you suggest a mobile phone company could target? Suggest the sort of campaign that might attract this sector or age group.

Did you know...

Different aspects of a product will be important in different markets: for example, reliability would be essential to mechanical and engineering items, durability (the ability to last) to those products that will see heavy use, performance to technological items and good design to areas like clothes and furnishings.

Growth

The **product** is often said to be the most important part of the **marketing mix**. Without the product, there is no need for promotion, no price to set and no location or distribution needed. Businesses may grow by increasing the sales of a product, or by expanding into new products. Monstermob has, in the past, grown through first providing ringtones, then a range of ringtones, and then by targeting markets where demand is set to grow (and also where competitors are not yet strong).

Changes in demand

Demand for a product is not static but will be changing all the time. Changes are caused by changes in taste or fashion, new products coming on to the market, changes in price and changes in income and spending patterns. As a business gains market share or becomes more profitable, it may feel that it can bring new products into its range. Monstermob is still developing products such as different novelty ringtones and better quality ones. For example, early ringtones were 'two tone', later ones (as mobile phone technology has improved) now have full music quality. Sometimes a business may feel that it needs to broaden the range available, sometimes to balance what may seem a one-sided product mix. Any business which has a narrow product range is vulnerable to changes in demand, so needs to either develop new products or target new markets.

How being bigger helps

A larger business is able to support a wider product portfolio so is better able to compete. It can support the introduction of new lines with the profits from existing ones. It may also be able to gain **economies of scale** – discounts from buying, selling or transporting in larger amounts. Such gains (or at least part of them) may then be passed on to customers in the form of lower prices.

Product life cycle

The demand for a product – the number of people who wish to buy it and think the price is reasonable – will alter over time. Often this is due to the natural '**product life cycle**'. A product, once launched, passes through various stages – growth, maturity, market saturation and finally decline (see the figure below). Different product life cycles are possible and businesses have to try to take advantage of them as best they can. They can be exceedingly long or very short. A long life cycle might mean a product that grows slowly but steadily, but provides a good income over a number of years. Some products will still be selling hundreds of years after their launch – tobacco has been around since the 16th century but only recently have sales started to decline. If businesses predict a short life cycle, they need to reap as much from it in a short time period as possible. A novelty seasonal item (such as a Christmas Number 1 chart hit) will find sales vanishing on December 26th.

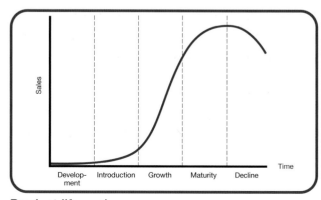

Product life cycle

Changing marketing mixes

At each stage of the life cycle, the business can use different marketing mixes to support sales. At the launch or growth stage, promotional prices may be used and there may be heavy spending on advertising. Once the product reaches maturity and competitors enter the market, there may be additions to the product or variations on it. Prices may also have to fall in response to competition.

Extending the life cycle

A product can benefit from additions, alterations or modifications that extend the life cycle. Methods that a business might use to extend the product life cycle include:

- cosmetic changes – changing packaging or the look of a product;
- real changes – introducing new versions of the product;
- technological change – making more advanced versions of the product, with more technological features;
- finding new uses for a product;
- extra promotional activities;
- adding to the product range.

Each method has to be carefully considered by the business, as any product development could have an impact on other lines. All the time, the business needs to make sure that it is supporting its various products in a balanced way. Sometimes a business just has to realise that the life cycle is at an end and let the product die. Once the iPod was launched, for example, this spelled the end for personal CD players.

Summary

- Product is just one part of the marketing mix, but an important part
- Growing businesses may need a bigger product range or a greater variety of products
- Products follow a product life cycle
- At each stage of the life cycle, other parts of the marketing mix may be changed to support the product
- Product life cycles follow the same stages, but can range from very long to very short
- There are various ways to extend product life cycles

Core knowledge

As the business grows it may feel that it should not rely on a single product but look at variations of the product, or at other product lines. The three main routes for expansion using products are expanded product range, product differentiation and diversification. Each will lead to a different product portfolio for the business. This is a reminder of what each of those terms means:

- *Product range*: this refers to the different lines that a business sells, such as a car manufacturer selling a range of cars. Look at any make of car and you will know that there is a range of models. At one end will be the small family saloon, at the other a luxury version. In between you will find hatchbacks, two- or four-door models and, of course, a huge range of colours.

- *Product mix*: this refers to the variety of products for sale. For example, Rolls-Royce Motors has a fairly narrow mix, concentrating on the luxury car market. Ford, meanwhile, has a wide mix, including cars at all levels, vans and commercial vehicles.

- *Diversification*: this is the process of expanding into product areas where the business did not previously have a presence. The Virgin group of companies shows how the business has diversified from its original product base (a record shop) into travel, leisure, banking, communications and other areas.

Monstermob has a single range of products and a very narrow mix. However, this is not a problem if it can enter growing markets where demand for ringtones is only just starting to grow.

And more

Products – goods or services – are provided to target all types of market. In each case, there are certain aspects of the product that are particularly important. Growing businesses need to concentrate on these aspects in relation to the markets that are their targets. One important aspect may be a strong brand. In some cases having a branded product may be important to a market – genuine car parts may be better than substitutes that may or may not do the job. In other cases a brand makes little difference. Does the brand of salt bought matter, for example?

Products provide tangible and intangible benefits at a number of levels. Tangible benefits are the 'real' benefits to owning or using a product. The tangible benefit from listening to an iPod is the enjoyment of the music. Intangible benefits are those that come with the product but are not part of its function. The intangible benefit of owning an iPod is the impression that you are a person with style. Benefits come at three levels. If you buy a laptop, for example, the core reason may be to do school or college work, so the core product is the one that has word-processing and spreadsheet programs. Maybe you also want it for games, so this

What is the *real* reason for buying a particular laptop?

would form part of the core. The secondary reason for buying that particular product will be a combination of design appeal, packaging, brand and other product features such as reputation and quality – the 'actual product' or 'tangible benefits'. At yet another level, the third or 'tertiary' reason might be linked to the product's availability and to guarantees of quality and customer support – this is called the 'augmented product' and is linked to the intangible benefits. Sometimes the augmented product is more important (the guarantees and service agreements on cars, for example), sometimes the core product (basic foodstuffs), sometimes secondary reasons like design (designer clothes are meant to make you look good, not necessarily keep you warm or comfortable, the core benefit of clothing).

Did you know...

A strong product identity is often linked to a strong brand name or image. If a business has a strong brand, it can transfer this to other products. A good example is the Virgin brand, which has been spread across many different businesses from travel and leisure to mobile phones and banking, or top sports brands like Nike, that have moved into branded bathroom products.

Have a go!

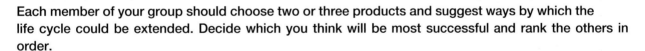

Group activity

Each member of your group should choose two or three products and suggest ways by which the life cycle could be extended. Decide which you think will be most successful and rank the others in order.

Discussion

Many people say that it is a waste to have so many different product types and ranges. For example, what is the point of having different coloured cars, or different fashions for clothes? It would be a lot more efficient to have things all the same. Discuss whether or not you agree with this point of view.

Web-based activity

Read the article at **www.guardian.co.uk/media/2006/jul/11/newmedia.citynews**. How do you think that this news will affect Monstermob in the long term? What strategy would you suggest the company adopts in order to recover?

Quickfire questions

1 What is meant by 'product'?
2 What is a 'product life cycle'?
3 Give three factors that cause changes in the demand for products.
4 What is 'diversification'?
5 What is meant by 'product portfolio'?
6 What are the stages of the product life cycle?
7 What is a narrow product range? What problems might this cause for the business?
8 What is the difference between a tangible and intangible benefit from a product?
9 Suggest two reasons why a strong brand may be important for a product.
10 Suggest three ways to extend a product life cycle.

Hit the spot

> Give two reasons why a business might change its marketing mix.

>> Explain why a business might need to broaden and balance its product range.

>> Which part of the life cycle do you think is most important to a growing business? Explain why you think so.

Cracking the code

Diversification Expanding into product areas or markets where the business did not previously have a presence.

Economies of scale Discounts from buying, selling or transporting in larger amounts.

Marketing mix The balance of product, price, promotion and place.

Mature market The point when most people who are likely to buy the product have bought it.

Product The good or service offered for sale by the business.

Product life cycle The various stages of sales through which a product passes, from launch to eventual decline.

Product mix The variety of products for sale.

Product range The different lines that a business sells.

Chapter 38
The marketing mix: price

IN THE NEWS

The Apple iPhone 3G, with built-in GPS* and Wi-Fi, itself a development from an earlier version, hit the market in 2008. By October of the same year, Blackberry had announced the launch of its latest 'smart' phone, the Blackberry Storm, also with 3G, built-in GPS and mobile broadband capability. As well as competing in the mobile phone and PDA** market, phones such as these could spell the death of separate satellite navigation devices (satnavs).

Satnavs are a good example of the type of pricing that can be used for new products. In November 2005, the most popular types were priced at around £350 – a price that 'skimmed' the market – attracting those who wanted to be first with the new technology. Even though there were several competing systems, this was a technological novelty so prices were not driven down.

Retailers maintained the price for as long as they could, as demand grew up to Christmas – and then, the **skimming** phase over, dropped it dramatically so that, by January 2006, you could pick up a Navman (a popular brand) for less than £200. Competition in the market such as that from the iPhone and the Storm is likely to drive prices down even further. Separate sales may also fall as car manufacturers decide that the satnav is the latest device that should be 'built in' to new cars. At the moment, the popularity of the portable ones is demonstrated by the

fact that these are now the item most often stolen from a vehicle, but built-in ones will be much more secure.

Satnav manufacturers have managed to use a number of pricing strategies to keep sales of their product going, but may, in the end, have to accept that there is no longer a market for a portable satnav device.

* Global Positioning System
** Personal Digital Assistant, also known as a palm-top device

Go to **www.vodafone.co.uk/Storm** and **www.apple.com/uk/iphone** to find out about the Blackberry Storm and the iPhone 3G. What sort of pricing strategies are being used to sell each product?

What is it worth?

How much would you pay for a satellite navigation system for a car? If you were buying one as a gift for an older brother or sister, or a parent, what would you be willing to pay? In other words, how much do you think a satnav is worth? If your answer is £200 to £250, then you would probably have bought one in 2006. If it is £40 to £50, then you might have considered buying one for Christmas 2008. This shows the range of prices that you will be looking at and hoping that a retailer agrees with your estimate.

When these devices first came on the market a few years ago, they were priced at a high level. If you were buying for Christmas 2005, for example, you could not expect to buy one for less than £350. This was a price intended to 'skim' or 'cream' the market. As a new, high-technology product, satnavs could be priced at a high price in order to make the most of the market. Even with a number of competing manufacturers, the price stayed high, especially in the run-up to Christmas, when the highest volume sales were made. With new technology products, there is often a group of consumers which sees them as a 'must have'. They are therefore willing to pay a high price. In January 2006, the price dropped to a more realistic £200 and has continued to fall.

By the start of 2009 models were available priced at around £50 and the satnav was no longer considered a luxury item. Many new car models now have them built in and they are likely to become a standard feature, like central locking, electric windows and airbags – all luxuries in their day. Also, GPS devices that operate in the same way are now being installed in mobile phones and PDAs.

Pricing strategies for growth

Businesses use a number of strategies to increase **market share** or to gain a foothold in new markets. These include:

- **loss leaders** – a business deliberately prices a product at a loss (a price that does not cover cost). This will attract customers to the business. Other strategies can then be used to try to develop customer loyalty to keep their custom;

- **skimming** – the product is sold at an initial high price to those customers ready to pay for it. These products are usually luxury items and often 'cutting-edge' technology. Examples include flat-screen TVs, DVD players, Blu-Ray players and satnavs. Once the initial surge in demand has gone, prices are dropped. In some cases, the products barely survive beyond the introductory phase as newer technology is brought out;

Satnav units had high prices at first

- **premium pricing** – this is when prices are set at a high level to try to emphasise the quality of the product – designer clothes, for example;

- **penetration price** – price is set below competitor prices so that a business can gain a share in a market. In some industries, customers are reluctant to change to competitors. (In the UK, people are very unlikely to change banks, for example.) Often penetration prices are short term and last only as long as the business needs to gain a place in the target market.

How being bigger helps

A larger business is able to make short-term losses on, for example, loss leaders or new products that it is introducing. It can also afford to charge promotional prices on certain lines, paid for by the profit it is making on others.

Did you know...

Although there are many different types of pricing, they can almost all be called 'competitive' pricing. This is because, in any market where there are businesses competing to sell rival products, the price range of products of similar quality is likely to be fairly narrow.

Summary

- Price has to be set within a reasonable range – the amounts people are willing to pay
- This will change according to the product and its stage in the life cycle
- The most important type of pricing is still cost-plus, as costs must be covered
- Businesses can use special pricing strategies to help them grow
- Larger businesses can afford to make short-term losses on products, so are better able to use different pricing strategies

Core knowledge

Most prices are, to some degree, consumer-led and need to be in a particular price range before purchase is even considered. A diamond ring priced at £2.50 would find few takers – consumers would be convinced that it was not worth it. One priced at £25,000 would be out of the price range of most consumers. A ring in the price range of £250 to £2,500 is much more likely to fall within most people's idea of what such a ring should cost.

The most important form of pricing is cost-plus pricing, as this is intended to deliver a profit to the business. You will remember that this is where the business tries to set a price that will cover its costs and allow it to make a profit. To do this it needs to add up all the costs to make a product and then add a mark-up – an extra amount that represents the profit on each product.

Businesses can use different pricing strategies in order to grow. Most pricing strategies may be considered as either short-term promotional prices or different types of competitive pricing that are used at different stages of the product life cycle (see Chapter 37).

There are a number of factors that influence pricing strategy decisions, such as the type of market in which the business operates and the amount of competition in the market. Some markets have high start-up costs or need special machinery or technology. Smaller businesses might therefore find it difficult to enter such markets. Oil and power companies are a good example. Other markets may be highly competitive and easy to enter (certain types of high-street shops, for instance) but also, of course, much easier to exit.

And more

In some markets, the business may have little or no say in the price that it can charge for a product. In a market with many competing businesses all facing similar costs, if any one business tries to raise prices, it is likely to lose a lot of its custom. Customers faced with a lower priced competitor will switch to it in order to save money (providing quality is seen as being equal). In such competitive markets, cost structures usually mean that businesses do not have the option of lowering prices, except in the short term to try to gain market share. Businesses therefore have to accept the market price and are called price takers. They can still compete – but through other elements of the marketing mix rather than price. If there is a leading business in a competitive market, it may decide to use predator or **destroyer pricing**. This is where a business undercuts competitors with the intention of driving them out of business. Sometimes this backfires – the winner is the one that can stand the losses in revenue the longest.

Not all markets, however, have many equal-sized businesses in competition. In some markets there is one dominant business and a number of smaller rivals. In this case, the dominant business may be a price leader or what is called a '**price maker**'. This means that whatever price it charges, all other businesses are forced to follow suit. For example, Brazil produces so much of the world's coffee that it decides on the world price. It can force prices up by restricting supply or down by releasing more of the commodity on to the market. Other businesses in the market have no choice but to accept this price and are called **price takers**.

Brazil's coffee industry is a 'price maker'

Did you know...

Sometimes businesses can charge different prices for the same product because they are selling it in different markets. This works as long as the different markets can be kept separate. Different train fares for different times of the day, or bought in advance or on the day, or online or in person, are all examples.

Have a go!

Group activity

In your group, decide on a commercial TV channel for each of you to watch for one evening. Make a record of each product that is advertised and the pricing strategy that you think is being used. Put these all together and decide which are the most commonly used strategies and why.

Discussion

Businesses with a larger market share may be able to price smaller competitors out of business. These businesses would say that they were more efficient, so the customer is getting a better deal. Customers, however, may think they are being denied choice. What do you think?

Web-based activity

Find 8–10 new products that are currently being launched. 'I Want One of Those' at **www.iwantoneofthose.com** could be a good place to start. Now look at the prices that are being charged for each of them. Draw up a table to show which price strategies you think are being used.

Quickfire questions

1 Name one pricing strategy that could be used for an expensive product.
2 Name one pricing strategy that could be used to enter a market.
3 Name one pricing strategy more likely to be available to a larger business than a small one.
4 Outline what is meant by a 'price range'.
5 Outline what is meant by 'cost-plus' pricing.
6 What sort of products in general are launched with prices that skim the market?
7 What is a loss leader? Why is it used?
8 What is a premium price? Why is it used?
9 What is a penetration price? Why is it used?
10 Outline how market dominance is linked to price.

Hit the spot

> Outline three possible factors that might influence pricing strategy decisions.

> Explain the difference between a 'price maker' and a 'price taker'.

> What is competitive pricing? Explain, with reasons, whether it is true to say that most prices may be defined as competitive.

Cracking the code

Destroyer pricing Where a business charges a low price to drive rivals out of business.

Loss leaders Products priced at a low price that does not cover cost to attract customers to the business.

Market share The slice of a market that each business has – usually measured as a percentage.

Penetration price Price set below those of competitors so that a business can gain a share in a market.

Premium pricing When prices are set at a high level to try to emphasise the quality of the product.

Price maker When one business dominates a market, it can dictate price.

Price takers Businesses in a competitive market, or small businesses in a market dominated by a price maker.

Skimming An initial high price, aimed to 'skim the cream' off the market.

Chapter 39
The marketing mix: promotion

IN THE NEWS

It is not just businesses that want to grow. Sometimes governments encourage business growth by providing the framework and facilities for businesses. Sponsorship, product endorsements and the use of famous names and brands can be key factors in the success of a product or project.

In the case of Dubai Sports City, the product is the first purpose-built sports city in the world. The promoters were keen to attract businesses, suppliers and customers, so have made use of some of the biggest names in sport to promote their $2 billion investment. The investors have gone for top-name sponsorship – Manchester United will host the football academy, with their own branded Manchester United Soccer School, and football (along with rugby and athletics) will take place in a new 60,000-seat stadium. The football academy is being established with the help of United's commercial partner, Nike. Top international golfer Ernie Els has designed the championship golf course, The Dunes, which is at the centre of a residential development. The golf academy will be run by another top player, Butch Harmon, while former international tennis star David Lloyd will lend his name to the tennis academy and Rodney Marsh, Test cricketer and former director of the England and Wales Cricket Board National Academy, will run the world's first global cricket academy.

Of course, it is not just a sports city but a community, including schools, hospitals, leisure opportunities, residences and shops. At the heart of it there will be a sports-themed retail mall of around 1.2 million square feet. The big names will help to draw in retailers, leisure providers and the public, allowing businesses already based in Dubai to grow on the back of this promotion, or encourage new businesses to establish. While sponsorship and product endorsements are 'below-the-line', this does not stop them being just as powerful as the 'above-the-line' spending.

The first stage of the complex opened in 2007 and it is due for completion in 2010.

@ You can see a promotional video for Dubai Sports City at **www.youtube.com/ watch?v=0cOavxxiMxo**. List the key business messages that the promotion is trying to put across.

Purpose of promotion

Dubai knows that its use of famous names and leading brands will attract businesses to its development. These, in turn, will attract customers using their own **promotional strategies**. Promotion serves two main purposes: to inform the customer of the existence of a product and to persuade them to buy it. Promotion can therefore be a major tool in helping a business to grow. It will be used not only to help boost sales but also to increase market share.

Did you know...

Promotion may be to the consumer, but may also be directly to the trade to encourage suppliers to push products through the distribution system (see Chapter 40). Such promotion is often at specialist trade fairs and exhibitions aimed at businesses.

How being bigger helps

As a business grows it is likely to have a bigger budget for advertising and promotional activities. It may also be able to concentrate on particular products if it has a wider product portfolio (see Chapter 37) and target promotion on those products that are likely to be more profitable.

Promotion is used to help a business grow by encouraging more sales and a bigger market share. All promotional activities come with a cost – advertising, promotional prices and all **above-the-line** activities come at a price. Businesses must carefully budget and be aware of whether promotion is being effective not just in terms of sales but in terms of what it is costing to gain those sales.

Above and below

Any promotional activity (such as advertising) that is paid for directly is called 'above-the-line'

promotional expenditure. Other methods of promotion are called **'below-the-line'** expenditure. Much below-the-line promotion is public relations (PR). PR is used to bring a product or brand to the attention of the public without using direct advertising. It includes areas such as celebrity endorsement of products, sponsorship and creating 'news' items around products. It is, for example, worth paying a 'celebrity' to open a new facility, providing there is plenty of publicity to go with the event. Sponsorship is also used to link a product to its positive benefits, e.g. performance oils and motor racing, and sometimes just to keep a name in the public eye, for example, the Emirates Stadium, the Carling Cup. PR agencies will arrange newsworthy 'photo opportunities', interviews and other publicity, such as book signings or product placement in films or magazines. **Corporate hospitality** is another PR growth area. A business will buy tickets for a sporting or other event and use them to 'reward' clients to encourage loyalty and repeat business.

A growing business will use sales promotion and special promotional prices. Short-term price cuts such as sale prices, competitions and 'added-value' promotions (money off, Buy One Get One Free, etc.) are all used to boost sales, market share and customer loyalty.

The Carling Cup

Advertising

Advertising – above-the-line – spending tends to be expensive, but can also be effective. The more effective it is, the more it will cost. TV advertising reaches millions and is therefore very expensive. However, businesses can cut down costs by trying to target particular groups. Direct marketing targets likely customers through mailshots or, increasingly, by using new technology. E-mails, texts and automated phone calls are all popular now.

Influence of markets

The choice of promotional method will be influenced by the nature of the product and the market in which it is being sold. For example, a specialist product will target advertising at its specialist market. Some products are so specialist (and often so expensive) that they are usually sold through agents advertising in specialist publications or on websites. Examples include industrial machinery, plant and equipment.

Businesses may also respond to competitor promotions with promotions of their own. Often a successful campaign by one business in a market will be followed by a counter-campaign by another, intent on gaining back its market share.

Summary

- Promotion has two main purposes – information and persuasion
- Growing businesses will have the opportunity for larger promotional budgets
- Bigger businesses must still make sure that promotion is effective
- Promotion is either paid for directly (above-the-line) or is indirect (below-the-line)
- The choice of promotion is linked to the type of product and type and size of market
- Direct marketing can cut down promotional costs and reach specific target groups

Core knowledge

Promotion needs to tell customers and potential customers about the existence and benefits of a product. The main way to achieve this is through advertising, with its aim summed up by the acronym **AIDA**. Advertising should attract Attention, create Interest, develop Desire and lead to Action. It should highlight the positive features of a product that will attract customers – price, performance, variety, etc. – depending on the product and market. Promotion should highlight the USP (unique selling point) – this is the single aspect that makes this product better than any of the competition.

Good timing is vital. The business needs to make sure that products are available to coincide with promotion, to cope with increased demand. If they are not and there are shortages, this could make the advertising counter-productive. There are key 'moments' when certain advertising is most effective. For instance, it is immediately after Christmas, in the dark days of January, that people are persuaded to cheer themselves up by booking a summer holiday, whereas before Christmas toys and games will be advertised much more heavily (and prices will stay high).

The media mix chosen to promote a product must be linked closely to the target market, the budget for promotion and the product itself.

Promotion is all about passing on a message (about a product) to a customer through the appropriate media. Media just means the way in which the message is carried. Advertising media include broadcast media, such as television and cinema advertisements – these are expensive to make and broadcast but highly effective, reaching a wide audience. Radio advertisements are much cheaper to make and to broadcast, but surprisingly effective. Print media (catalogues, leaflets, magazines, newspapers) can be colourful and contain additional detailed information. They can also encourage instant customer response through reply or order forms. Posters and billboards are also classed as print media. A national poster campaign can be highly effective, but will also be expensive.

Did you know...

A successful brand is worth its weight in gold. The message of a good brand can achieve all the parts of AIDA on its own. A brand image can attract attention, is heavily linked to the image of the business or product, is desirable and will encourage people to buy products with that brand instead of other products.

And more

Advertising media become more expensive as they become more effective. So TV advertising or national poster campaigns are the most expensive of all. Some advertising can be fairly precisely targeted using particular broadcast times, particular TV and radio programmes, specialist magazines and journals and even postcode areas. Other promotions, such as poster advertising, will just aim to reach as many people as possible and hit the target market in this way. Businesses need to try to choose the right media to ensure that the message is being delivered to the correct market segment. Delivering a powerful and persuasive message, but to the wrong market segment, is a waste of time and promotional budget. Promotional budgets have to be carefully spent to achieve a balance between three different aims: coverage, penetration and cost.

- Coverage refers to the number of people reached – poster advertisements have very high coverage but reach many more than the intended target market.
- Penetration refers to how much of a particular market the promotion reaches. For example, a print advertisement in a popular specialist magazine (such as one linked to a sport or hobby) is likely to have high penetration of that market. If you are going to advertise football boots, advertise them in a football magazine, not a gardening one! Advertising costs for print media are linked to circulation, with figures and costs published each year in *BRAD* (*British Rate and Data*). There are hundreds of specialist publications that can be targeted.
- Cost must include two elements – the making or design and the distribution or broadcast costs. Most expensive is TV advertising, both to make and to broadcast. At the opposite end of the scale, leaflets can be cheap to produce and distribute, but still be highly effective in reaching a target market.

Did you know...

Product placement can extend to some very high-cost items. In some action movies, cars and even helicopters may be provided for free by the manufacturer. The resulting publicity from a successful film would have cost much, much more to buy.

Have a go!

Group activity

In your group, decide on a commercial TV channel for each of you to watch for one evening. Make a record of each product that is advertised and note the group at which you think it is targeted. Suggest how each advertisement could be rewritten to target a different group.

Discussion

Advertising, whether by TV, radio, poster, magazine or even point-of-sale, is all a waste of resources that could be better used on making more products. Advertising contributes nothing to business but does cost a lot of money. Do you think this is true? Should all advertising be banned?

Web-based activity

@

Visit **www.brandchannel.com/brandcameo_films.asp** where you can see which brands have been featured in recent movies. Choose three of these and explain for each what it is you think the product manufacturers were hoping to gain from that particular film.

Quickfire questions

1 Give the two reasons for promotion.
2 What is 'above-the-line' promotion?
3 What is 'below-the-line' promotion?
4 Give an example of 'below-the-line' promotion.
5 What is meant by 'corporate hospitality'?
6 Give an example of a short-term sales promotion.
7 Give an example of how a business could target particular groups through promotions.
8 What does AIDA stand for?
9 What is a USP?
10 Give two reasons why some media are more expensive than others.

Hit the spot

> Describe how the growth of a business might help it in terms of promotion.

>> Explain why a promotional campaign in a particular market is often followed by another campaign in the same market.

>>> Outline three of the promotional strategies being used by Dubai Sports City. Explain which you think will be most effective and why.

Cracking the code

Above-the-line Promotional activity, such as advertising, that is paid for directly.

Aida Used as a reminder that advertising should attract Attention, create Interest, develop Desire and lead to Action

Below-the-line Promotional activity that is not directly paid-for advertising expenditure.

Corporate hospitality When a business provides 'gifts' for its clients as a reward for their loyalty. These can include free bars, tickets to events and seats at shows and concerts.

Promotional strategies The various 'mixes' of different promotions used by businesses.

Chapter 40
The marketing mix: place

IN THE NEWS

The 2008 Christmas charts were dominated by two versions of Leonard Cohen's ballad 'Hallelujah', with over half a million downloads. X Factor winner Alexandra Burke hit number one, selling 576,000 copies on CD and via downloads. Jeff Buckley's version, which fans claim is better than Burke's, reached number two – remarkably, on download sales alone. The charts have become vital to the music industry, but it was not until 1952 that enough recorded music was sold in order to make a chart possible. The very first number 1 (Al Martino's 'Here in My Heart') was in November of that year. Since then, popular music has had a habit of reinventing itself to take advantage of the latest technology. First, single records, then EPs and LPs (Extended Play records and Long Playing albums), tapes and cassettes. Later CDs were used for better-quality digital sound.

More recently, recorded music has found a whole new way of being distributed. Traditionally, sounds were recorded on disk or some other form of hard media, sent into shops, bought and played on home systems. Now, all that has changed and the physical distribution of recorded music is no longer the main way by which music is distributed. The medium of choice for playing music is now a portable digital player, or even a mobile phone – 60% of digital tracks are downloaded to computer devices, 40% to mobile phones. The means of buying music, led by iTunes but with many more websites following, is by internet download. There are now more than 500 legitimate digital music services worldwide, offering over 6 million tracks, with single-track downloads rapidly approaching 2 billion a year. (Around 20 times the amount bought have been swapped via illegal file-sharing sites.)

Once downloads were counted in the charts alongside physical sales, they were always bound to increase. Just after Christmas 2005, an important milestone was reached with the download of over 1 million digital tracks in a single week and by the end of 2008, downloads accounted for more than 15% of record companies' revenue, up from 0% in 2004, and in America, the main digital market, over 30%. In the same period, CD sales fell by around 10%. Chairman of IFPI (the International Federation of the Phonographic Industry) John Kennedy commented: 'A new wave of digital commerce, from mobile to broadband, is rolling out across the world. It is generating billions of dollars and being driven to a large extent by music' (*IFPI Annual Digital Music Report,* January 2006).

@ You will find the report 'Internet shopping – an OFT (Office of Fair Trading) market study' at **www.oft.gov.uk/ shared_oft/reports/consumer_ protection/oft921.pdf**
In the summary of the report there are four bullet points that outline some of the problems of online trade. Suggest possible solutions for each.

Internet sales

How do you buy your music? Is it 'physical' – through a high-street outlet or traditional record store – or is it digital – via a legal music site? It is not just music, however, that is taking advantage of low-cost distribution. The value of all goods sold over the internet continues to increase at a rapid rate. The most recent UK government figures are for 2005, when there was £21 billion worth of sales made by over 20 million UK adults, over half of whom spent over £500. These UK Office for National Statistics figures also state that at least 62,000 UK businesses were selling online. Online spending increased by 76% between 2006 and 2007, in figures taken from www.sitemakers.co.uk that put spending at £53.3 billion.

The most popular purchases are travel and holidays, with electricals, clothing and groceries rapidly catching up. The spread of high-speed broadband, and its improved reliability, has been one of the major factors in the increase in online shopping. The size of a business does not affect the ability of that business to put up a website and take orders, but will affect the number of product lines it can reliably offer for sale and may also affect its ability to deliver an effective service.

According to the OFT, people shop online because they find it convenient, it increases choice and helps them find lower prices. Retailers sell online to reach more customers, to sell 24/7 and to compete with rivals.

Did you know...

Major retail outlets that offered internet sales early have built up a strong customer base. Tesco, the grocery chain, is the fourth largest UK internet retailer behind Amazon, Dell and Argos. Amazon is an internet-only retailer, with huge warehouses and a sophisticated distribution system, Dell decided as early as 1996 to offer an online service, to cut out the 'middle man' and pass the savings on to the customer, while Argos found it easy to transfer its catalogue-based experience onto the web.

Different channels of distribution

Place is not just the place where you can buy the product but how the product is delivered to the consumer. As you learned in Section 1, different **distribution channels** are used depending on the product (does it need to get there quickly, safely?) and the market (size and location). Traditional **long-chain distribution** passes from the manufacturer through wholesaler to retail outlets. Each 'link' is called an **intermediary**. Businesses can either push products out to intermediaries or rely on consumer demand pulling the products through the distribution chain. To push products down the chain, a business can offer incentives to intermediaries. This applies to any business in the chain pushing to the next one, a wholesaler to a retailer, for example. Pull strategy involves using promotion to increase customer demand.

Wholesalers and retailers then have to order more products to meet demand.

The shortest distribution chain is directly to the consumer. Businesses can look for sales through direct approaches such as e-mail and telephone sales and a small number of products may still be sold door-to-door. There is also still a fairly large market for mail-order goods, via catalogues, although this is rapidly being replaced with internet sales.

Why customers choose

Customers choose retail outlets according to a number of factors which include:

- convenience – the act of buying a product needs to be easy; this includes ease of ordering, having different methods of payment available and home delivery if necessary;

- cost – if the cost of distribution, or to get to a retail outlet, outweighs the benefit from the product, then the customer will not buy. Amazon would sell a lot fewer books if people had to go to a shop rather than order online;

- reliability – customers want to know that products will be available when they want, at the stated prices;

- value added – this includes areas like low-cost credit, after-sales service and competitive pricing.

A high street site could also be high cost

Why businesses choose

The key factors when a business is choosing 'place' include:

- cost – expensive sites or networks have to 'earn their keep' in sales;

- available distribution channels – if there are competing channels from which to choose, this can keep costs down;

- margins – lower costs and higher revenues lead to greater profit margins.

Summary

- Place refers to both where a product is bought and how it gets there – distribution
- It is an important part of the marketing mix
- The correct 'place' depends on the type of product and the market that it is in
- Distribution is changing as new channels, such as the internet, become available
- This means channels can be shortened, even to the shortest distribution channel – direct from producer to consumer
- Customers' choice of 'place' is influenced by convenience, cost, reliability and value added
- Businesses' choice of 'place' is influenced by cost, distribution channels and margins

Core knowledge

The distribution of a product refers both to the place where it may be bought and to the means by which it is delivered to that place. The traditional places for retail transactions are shops; other outlets and methods have also been developed as businesses seek better ways to compete. A growing business will have the choice of more distribution channels and will be able to carry a greater variety of stock. Shops range from department store to small convenience stores, including multiple chains selling goods or services such as WH Smith selling books and stationery or KwikFit selling car services. Other outlets include vending machines, catalogues and direct sales.

Many small retailers survive by offering a specialist or personalised service (e.g. haircutting) or value added in other ways, such as convenience or personal service. Much retail trade now takes place via mail order or the internet. This, too, has revolutionised retailing, so that many shops have felt that they need an internet presence alongside their high-street one. These are called 'bricks and clicks' retailers, while increasingly many have done away with (or never had) the 'bricks' element. In some cases, such as with expensive items like industrial machinery or houses, sales are direct or through an agent, although even here online elements are possible.

Consumers will choose outlets according to convenience, cost, reliability and value added, producers according to cost, distribution channels and the profit margins they can earn (see Chapter 40). Being the leading or largest business in a market is important. Smaller outlets that have room to stock only a limited amount of a product will prefer to stock the market leading product and other products may be 'frozen out'.

And more

Place is just one part of the marketing mix, but an important one, that needs a whole range of specialised transport and storage services. Distribution is the way in which the product travels from the producer to the consumer (sometimes via an outlet, but not always). The business branch that deals with transport, delivery and the management of the entire supply chain from producer to consumer is called logistics. The channel of distribution chosen and amount and type of storage necessary depend on a number of factors. Some products must be delivered fresh; some are bulky and expensive to store; some require refrigeration, or security, or other special treatment.

Traditional 'long-channel' distribution passes along a chain from producer to manufacturer via wholesaler and retailer to the final consumer. Any channel which succeeds in cutting out one or more of these stages is called short-channel distribution and, in general, is cheaper than long-channel distribution. Typically, the shorter the distribution channel, the lower the costs involved. So, for example, Amazon's postal deliveries of books and DVDs and Dell's direct delivery to customers is cheaper than using intermediaries. Intermediaries are the 'middle men' (or women) who provide a service to the people before and after them in the chain of distribution. The major intermediaries are:

● wholesalers, who provide storage (including special storage such as refrigerated or secure units) and 'break bulk'. This means that they buy in large amounts ('bulk', e.g. by the lorry load) and sell on in smaller amounts (e.g. by the case);

● merchants, who buy goods at a price with the intention of selling them on at a higher price; and

● agents, who buy and sell products on behalf of both customers and businesses (such as estate agents selling houses for owners).

Did you know...

Many businesses prefer to have their own stock and distribution systems and have developed their own warehouses and logistics to ensure that they have what they want when they need it. In a number of cases, this has given them such market power that they can pressurise producers for lower prices.

Did you know...

Stockless distribution is a version of the 'just-in-time' production method. Stock is timed to arrive at a retail outlet exactly when it is needed in a continuous cycle of sales and re-stocking. This means lower costs. It also means that fresh produce really is fresh.

Transport is just one part of 'place' – distributing product

Have a go!

Group activity

Carry out a survey in your group to find out how much is now bought online rather than at shops. Each person should write down the last ten things that they bought and say whether it was online or at a retail outlet. What sort of patterns emerge? What sort of reasons can people give for using one method or another?

Discussion

The growth of chains has been blamed for making all high streets look the same, while the growth of some retail giants (supermarkets in particular) has been blamed for the decline of small local shops and specialists. Others say that chains and supermarkets bring more reliability and lower prices. What do you think?

Web-based activity

Go to **www.bbc.co.uk/radio1/chart/singles.shtml** and look at the official charts, then go to **www.bbc.co.uk/radio1/chart/downloads.shtml** for the downloads chart. Are they the same or different? Explain why you think this is so. (You should refer to different parts of the market.)

Quickfire questions

1 Outline the two parts to 'place' in the marketing mix.
2 What are the most popular online purchases?
3 Outline the stages in long-chain distribution.
4 What is the shortest possible chain of distribution?
5 Name three traditional places for retail transactions.
6 What is meant by 'logistics'?
7 Suggest three ways by which products can be sold directly.
8 Suggest two areas where a retailer could add value for a consumer.
9 Suggest two ways by which a retailer can make the act of purchasing more convenient.
10 Give the two factors that affect the profit margins of a business.

Hit the spot

›   Give two reasons why internet sales have increased so rapidly.

›› Explain the difference between 'push' and 'pull' strategies in the distribution chain.

››› Explain the reasons why both consumers and retailers are keen to trade online. Which do you think is the most important reason for each and why?

Cracking the code

Distribution channels **The ways by which products reach the final consumer.**

Intermediary **Any person or organisation that provides a 'link', such as agents, wholesalers, retailers.**

Long-chain distribution **When a product passes through every intermediary from manufacturer to consumer.**

FINANCE FOR A LARGE BUSINESS

Chapter 41
Introduction to finance for a large business

The finance function is central to all businesses, large and small. Businesses need finance with which to start up, with which to buy stock, premises, equipment, marketing and advertising materials. This must not only be found – from sources as varied as private investors, venture capitalists, pension funds, banks, governments, property, local authorities, etc. – but also managed. Someone has to be in charge of knowing what money is flowing into the business and what is leaving it, and at what rate. While a small business may have its finance managed by its owner, or may employ a specialist accounting firm, in many larger businesses financial management will be carried out by a separate department within the business. The people in the finance or accounting department will be responsible for managing flows of money and for ensuring that all other parts of the business receive sufficient funds as and when they need them. They will also keep accurate records of such flows and be able to provide these to stakeholders and external bodies which have a right to see them, for example, shareholders and the tax authorities.

Although some sources are available to both large and small businesses, in general large businesses have different ways of raising finance to small businesses. They might have profits made from past transactions that they can re-invest in the business, they might be able to issue shares on the stock exchange, or sell more shares to existing shareholders, they might be able to sell equipment, buildings, factories, transport – even processes and brand names – that they no longer need. They can also use those things that they own – assets – as security for further loans.

You need a good head for figures to keep track of all this

Chapter 37
The marketing mix: product

Mobile phones – and the ringtones that owners download to go with them – may now be considered a **mature market** in the UK. The mobile phone market in the UK would find it difficult to expand its basic service through increased ownership of mobile phones. As long ago as 2003, it was reported (by telephone regulator Oftel) that over 90% of 15–34 year olds in the UK owned at least one mobile phone and that ownership even in the youngest category – the 7–10 age group – was at 25% and rising rapidly.

Monstermob is a growing business that has done well out of this increase. It is a content provider based in Lancashire, with one of its biggest lines being mobile phone ringtone downloads. Every phone has, of course, at least one ringtone, but most have several. Some have even entered the music charts they have been so popular. (Crazy Frog, for example, earned over $28 million for the firm that released it and even had its own album!) Some are seasonal (especially Christmas jingles), while others, like current pop songs, are temporary. In other parts of the world, expansion through increased ownership is still feasible (although all but the poorest countries are rapidly catching up), so Monstermob needs to find a way of extending the product life cycle for the ringtones it produces.

One way to do this would be to provide more content, but, of course, this is expensive. Another is to find different markets in which to sell existing content. Monstermob decided that the best way to extend the life of its product was to sell ringtones into those markets where phone ownership is on the increase, but ringtones and other content have not yet

become popular. To do so, it bought up providers in Malaysia, China and the Philippines, along with Russian content provider Mobicon. The biggest of these markets are China and Russia. Russia has widespread ownership of mobile phones, but people use them for calls and texts rather than entertainment, while the Chinese market is estimated to be some six years behind the European one. Monstermob's acquisitions have allowed it to extend the life cycle by introducing the product to completely new markets.

@ Looking at the figures for 2007/8 at **www.csu.nisra.gov.uk/Mobile_ phone_ownership_by_sex_and_ age_Trend.htm**, which section of the market would you suggest a mobile phone company could target? Suggest the sort of campaign that might attract this sector or age group.

Did you know...

Different aspects of a product will be important in different markets: for example, reliability would be essential to mechanical and engineering items, durability (the ability to last) to those products that will see heavy use, performance to technological items and good design to areas like clothes and furnishings.

Growth

The **product** is often said to be the most important part of the **marketing mix**. Without the product, there is no need for promotion, no price to set and no location or distribution needed. Businesses may grow by increasing the sales of a product, or by expanding into new products. Monstermob has, in the past, grown through first providing ringtones, then a range of ringtones, and then by targeting markets where demand is set to grow (and also where competitors are not yet strong).

Changes in demand

Demand for a product is not static but will be changing all the time. Changes are caused by changes in taste or fashion, new products coming on to the market, changes in price and changes in income and spending patterns. As a business gains market share or becomes more profitable, it may feel that it can bring new products into its range. Monstermob is still developing products such as different novelty ringtones and better quality ones. For example, early ringtones were 'two tone', later ones (as mobile phone technology has improved) now have full music quality. Sometimes a business may feel that it needs to broaden the range available, sometimes to balance what may seem a one-sided product mix. Any business which has a narrow product range is vulnerable to changes in demand, so needs to either develop new products or target new markets.

How being bigger helps

A larger business is able to support a wider product portfolio so is better able to compete. It can support the introduction of new lines with the profits from existing ones. It may also be able to gain **economies of scale** – discounts from buying, selling or transporting in larger amounts. Such gains (or at least part of them) may then be passed on to customers in the form of lower prices.

Product life cycle

The demand for a product – the number of people who wish to buy it and think the price is reasonable – will alter over time. Often this is due to the natural '**product life cycle**'. A product, once launched, passes through various stages – growth, maturity, market saturation and finally decline (see the figure below). Different product life cycles are possible and businesses have to try to take advantage of them as best they can. They can be exceedingly long or very short. A long life cycle might mean a product that grows slowly but steadily, but provides a good income over a number of years. Some products will still be selling hundreds of years after their launch – tobacco has been around since the 16th century but only recently have sales started to decline. If businesses predict a short life cycle, they need to reap as much from it in a short time period as possible. A novelty seasonal item (such as a Christmas Number 1 chart hit) will find sales vanishing on December 26th.

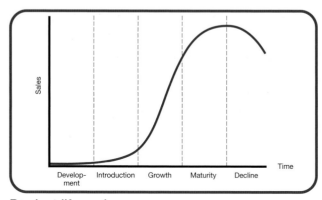

Product life cycle

Financial records

The financial records of the business are kept in its yearly accounts. For small businesses, these are for the benefit of the owners and may also be used by the tax authorities to work out how much tax is owed. Larger businesses have a wider range of people to whom their accounts might be important. Public limited companies, in particular, have a legal duty to publish their annual accounts and to make them available to the general public as well as their own shareholders and the tax authorities. People with an interest in the performance of the business (stakeholders) can then use these accounts to assess how well the business is performing. A large business may produce monthly, weekly or even day-to-day accounts and may also produce separate sets of accounts for different parts of the business. These may be divided up geographically or by product, so that the business can see the costs (and contribution to profits) of different parts of the business.

Cost accounting

A key part of the management of finance is cost accounting. These are the detailed records of costs kept by the business to help it keep track of its expenditure. Cost accounting is complicated by there being so many different types of cost. It is up to the financial managers in the business to decide how each cost is defined. For example, costs may be:

● *direct or indirect*. Direct costs are those that are paid as a result of the production of a good or service. They will therefore include raw materials, components and parts and labour. These are also called variable costs, as they vary with production. Indirect costs are those that are not directly linked to production but which are essential to it, such as heating and lighting, power, rent, rates and even part of the costs of labour (such as management costs). These are also called fixed costs as they do not change as production changes;

● *set-up or running costs*. Some costs have to be paid only once, when the business is

established – others have to be paid to keep the business going.

Types of accountant

The accountants that create and use the accounts of a business are divided into two groups – management accounting and financial accounting. Financial accountants are those who create the formal accounts of the business to show how it has performed over a certain time period, usually the previous year. These are prepared in order to comply with legal requirements and can allow the business to review its progress against previous years or against competitors in the same time period.

The 1985 Companies Act requires large companies to publish a balance sheet, a profit and loss account and a cash flow statement. Essentially, these are accounts that look at, and record, the past performance of a business. They show the importance of profit and loss accounts, the balance sheet and records of cash flows into and out of the business. By contrast, management accounts are drawn up for internal use. Management accounting is the production of accounts and figures that forecast the future performance of the business and which can

Figures can be used to make forecasts

therefore be used to make predictions and to manage the business. This type of account includes cash flow forecasts (the *forecast* looks to the future, the *statement* looks to the past).

The main types of account

You will need to understand the main types of account and some of the key tools that are available to accountants and managers to judge how well a business is doing. The accounts that are most important are the profit and loss account and the balance sheet. From these two sets of figures, a business can work out its gross and net profit and see how well it is performing in its market. It can also measure how profitable it is and how efficient it is by using ratios – these will show it, for instance, which products are most profitable and which resources are being used most efficiently. This will enable the business to plan production, marketing and other activities in the next time period.

Two important factors for a business are therefore the accuracy and thoroughness of financial figures and records and the ability to interpret these figures in order to make decisions.

Changes

It is also worth remembering that this part of business, like all other parts, is constantly changing. To make accounts clearer, plcs are being asked to use different terms for some parts of their accounts and smaller businesses will have to follow suit. Keep a look out for these new terms, which may, for a while, appear alongside the current ones.

Chapter 42
Sources of finance for a large business

In the autumn of 2008, many large businesses found themselves under pressure due to falling order books as growth in the economy slowed. Some big businesses, in particular banks and other financial institutions, found themselves in deep trouble and short of funds. They therefore took a traditional route to raising funds and asked shareholders for more money. Halifax Bank of Scotland (HBOS) asked its investors for a further £4 billion. Raising funds in this way is called a 'rights' issue. This is because existing shareholders are given the right to buy the new shares. The issue was announced on 29 April 2008, with the new shares priced at 275p – almost half the price of its shares at the time, which stood at 500p. But a lack of confidence in the bank led shareholders to take up few of the shares on offer. Just 124 million shares – less than 9% of the number on offer – were bought, leaving the underwriters (businesses that had promised to buy the few shares they thought would remain) with 1,375 billion shares, or almost £3.8 billion worth.

In the week before the offer, shares in HBOS had fallen to as low as 225p. This meant that it was cheaper for investors to buy existing shares in the market than the new issue – if they were persuaded to buy at all! Although the price rose to 282p, this was too late to persuade investors to change their minds.

Usually such a 'cash call' (as this is known) would be successful and a good way for a large business to raise additional finance. In this case,

however, confidence in the banking system – and the fall in the share price of HBOS – left it to fail. Money was still raised – but not as much as had been hoped – and most of the shares stayed in the hands of the merchant banks that were the underwriters for the issue, rather than with small investors. The two investment banks that were the underwriters tried to sell some of the shares in the market, but were still left with over 1 billion shares each.

Go to **www.guardian.co.uk/ business/2008/jul/22/ hbosbusiness.banking1** where you can read about the rights issue. Links from this page will take you to other examples of rights issues and frequently asked questions about rights.

More sources of finance

Some sources of finance are from within the business. These are called internal sources. Some, called external sources, are from outside the business.

External sources

- *Share capital*. A business which changes its ownership from, for example, a partnership or private limited company to a public limited company does so in order to raise finance via the stock exchange. It offers shares for sale to investors. This is called '**floating**' a company. After it has been floated, or if it needs to raise more money, it can issue new shares. These can be offered for sale to everyone or just to its existing shareholders. If a business decides to issue extra shares in order to raise more money, investors run the risk of losing their money if things do not go well. For the business, it means that there are more people or organisations with an interest in the business, so existing owners and directors could lose some of their power.

- ***Venture capital***. Some entrepreneurs are happy to take a risk on a new business so will provide investment. They are likely to want a share in the running of the business and certainly a share in its profits, should it make any. Such investments are generally in higher-risk businesses such as, for example, those developing new technology. However, the benefit to the entrepreneur is that they are also businesses that have a chance of making high profits. For the business, the advantage may come in having the expertise of the entrepreneur and his or her business connections, and that such investments are

not loans, so do not carry interest. The downside is that current owners will have to lose some control over the business and share their profits.

- *Loans*. Banks and other financial institutions may agree to lend money to a business. They will want to be sure that the money will be repaid. Often this means that they ask for some sort of **security**. This could, for example, be the assets of the business (buildings, factories, vehicles, processes, brands, etc.). In other cases they may want a say in the management of the business. The government also provides a loan-guarantee scheme through the Department of Trade and Industry. Loans may be short, medium or long term and have fixed or variable interest rates. Obtaining the right loan might give a business security and flexibility, but loans can also be costly in terms of interest payments. Banks can also decide that a risk is too great and demand that the loan is returned. This could cause the business to fail.

- *Leasing*. A business can 'rent' assets (such as machinery or vehicles) through a leasing arrangement. It pays a fixed amount per year to hire the assets so gains the use of them without having to pay for the capital.

Internal sources

- ***Retained profits***. An important source of finance for a large business may be its own profits. Profits may be either shared among the shareholders or kept by the business. Profits that are shared are called distributed profits. They are usually shared in the form of a dividend. This means that the profit is divided by the number of shares and each share receives an equal part of it. That kept by the business is called undistributed or retained profit. The main advantage for the business is that this money is not borrowed, so no interest is paid. The main disadvantage may be in shareholders not receiving high dividends.

- *Selling unwanted assets.* If a business has an **asset** (something it owns) that it no longer needs, then it can sell it. Some businesses may move into different markets and no longer need certain assets. For example, a food producer that decided to stop selling frozen food and concentrate on fresh food would no longer need refrigerators and other freezing plant and equipment.

Plant may be sold off if no longer needed

Did you know...

Short-term finance is generally defined as borrowing from a few days up to three years and includes overdrafts, loans, trade credit and hire purchase. Medium-term finance is from three to ten years. Long-term finance is ten years plus and includes term loans and mortgages.

Summary

- When a business grows it may need more sources of finance than a small business
- It will also have access to more sources of finance
- Sources may be internal (from within the business) or external (from outside the business)
- Finance has to be of the appropriate size, risk and time period for the business
- The type of business is therefore important when choosing the type of finance

Core knowledge

Small businesses, you will remember from Section 2: Starting a Business, have limited sources of finance. Most often, the owners use their personal funds to finance the business. Should the business be a success and grow, however, it can then think about other sources of finance. Sources of finance for a large business may be external or internal. Internal finance comes from within the business. The main sources of internal finance for a large business are retained profit and the sale of assets. Retained profit is estimated to provide up to two thirds of the finance of large businesses. But owners' funds also form a key part of the finance of larger businesses. With a limited company, in particular a public limited company, the owners will be the shareholders. To become a public limited company, the business must sell shares on the stock exchange. Once it has done so, it has the option of raising more money from existing shareholders. As the business grows, it is also likely to have much more in the way of assets that can therefore be used as security against loans.

The performance of the business and the size to which it has grown will also be major factors that affect both how the business obtains finance and, perhaps more significantly, the cost of the finance. If a business is seen to be doing well, can report increased sales, bigger markets and better profits, then the value of its shares will increase. This does not raise any more money for the company as the shares have already been sold into the market. It does, however, raise the value of the company, so that lending to it may be more attractive, and gives it the confidence to issue new shares. The cost of a loan may also be lowered by a larger business. If a loan is particularly large or the business is particularly strong, lenders may agree to lower rates of interest or other specialist terms.

And more

Each method of raising funds may have advantages and disadvantages as explained, but will also be more or less suitable depending on the situation. Different businesses, in different situations, will find that one method is more suitable than another. Key factors include the size of the finance, the time period over which it is needed or can be paid back and the cost of the finance.

Some businesses have a very broad asset base – in other words, they need a lot of assets in order to operate. A steel manufacturer, for example, needs plant, equipment, factories and stocks of raw materials so is likely to have many assets that can be used to raise money. Other businesses may have few assets. A business like eBay, for example, is run on the internet and needs little more than office space. It would have to find other ways to raise finance if it wished to expand, as it has no assets to sell or to provide as security.

Sometimes finance can be raised through other flexible and imaginative routes. A common one of these is 'sale and leaseback'. This is where the business still needs the asset but wants to raise money from it. Supermarket giant Tesco, for example, has sold a number of its sites and then leased them back. This means that it no longer owns the asset but still has use of it. The advantage of this is that it raises finance without borrowing. The disadvantage is that the business runs the risk of losing the use of the asset altogether. The business could also mortgage property that it owns (this means raising money with the property as security), again running the risk of losing the asset.

Some Tesco sites were sold and leased back

Did you know...

Underwriters are people who take on risks – often they work for insurance companies. They are called underwriters because, in the old days, as each investor took on a share of a risk, she or he wrote his or her name under the other risk-takers.

Have a go!

Group activity

Use the link **www.guardian.co.uk/business/2008/jul/22/hbosbusiness. banking1** to find out all you can about rights issues. Put together an information leaflet or web page to explain rights issues to someone who has no idea what they are. Remember, you will have to explain all the technical terms that you use as well!

Discussion

Once a business has shareholders, it is possible for the owners to lose some degree of control over the business. Do you think that this is a good or bad thing to happen? What extra benefits do you think that shareholders bring and what problems might they introduce?

Web-based activity

@

Visit **www.bbc.co.uk/celebdaq/** and you can take part in a game that simulates the movement of stocks and shares by letting you buy shares in celebrities rather than companies. Once you sign up you have £10,000 to spend on 'shares' in celebrities, whose price goes up and down (as with real shares) according to their performance. The aim is to make money from dividend payments and from buying and selling shares and the game mirrors how a real stock market works.

Quickfire questions

1 What is a rights issue?
2 What is an underwriter?
3 Why are underwriters called underwriters?
4 Outline the difference between internal and external sources of finance.
5 Give one reason why a larger business has more choice of finance than a smaller one.
6 What does it mean to 'float' a business?
7 What is venture capital?
8 Who sets the main interest rate, to which all others are linked?
9 Which government department provides business loan guarantees?
10 What is the most important source of internal finance?

Hit the spot

> Give two sources of external finance.

>> Explain what is meant by security and why it is important to some lenders.

>>> Judge which you think is the best form of external finance and explain why you think so.

Cracking the code

Asset Something which a business owns.

Floating a company When the company offers shares for sale to the public, via a stock exchange.

Retained profits The profits of the company not distributed in dividends but kept to invest in the business.

Rights issue When existing shareholders are given the right to buy new shares in a business.

Security Property or other assets offered as backing for a loan.

Venture capital Money put up by an entrepreneur willing to take a risk on a new business.

Chapter 43
Profit and loss accounts

IN THE NEWS

Unlike most top football clubs, Arsenal FC is a public limited company. This means that its accounts are published and anyone can see how well it is doing. Arsenal is owned by Arsenal Holdings plc, with the major shareholders being Danny Fiszman, a Swiss-resident diamond dealer with 24.1%, Russian residents Alisher Usmanov and Farhad Moshiri with 24.0%, Lady Nina Bracewell-Smith with 15.9%, US resident Stan Kroenke with 12.4%, and UK-based Richard Carr with 4.3%. The club has two major trading arms – football and property – and is one of the few Premiership clubs that makes a profit, posting £36.7 million profit in the financial year ending 2008. (Chelsea lost £76 million in the same period, Manchester United £58 million and Liverpool £22 million.)

The profit and loss account lets all shareholders – major and minor ones – and all those stakeholders interested in the fortunes of the club (on and off the pitch) know how well it is doing. In the year ended 31 May 2008, Arsenal's revenue was up £23 million on the previous period to £223 million, due to factors such as increased income from selling broadcasting and TV rights and, of course, match-day income from supporters, season ticket holders and corporate clients, which was up to £94.6 million.

The property part of the business is responsible for redeveloping the Highbury site now the club has moved to its new ground at the Emirates Stadium. This did not do as well as expected, although 65 apartments released at the end of July 2008 have raised £18.7 million. The poor performance of the property sector – caused by factors beyond the control of the business – was offset by the higher

revenues at the Emirates Stadium since the move. Even though wage costs also went up – by almost a quarter to more than £100 million – the group still managed to make a profit.

A spokesman for Arsenal Holdings plc said that the business had benefited from increased revenue from the new Premier League TV deals and the first Emirates Cup Tournament, which was held in the normally football-free summer months and attracted 110,000 supporters to see Arsenal, Inter Milan, Paris Saint Germain and Valencia compete. Arsenal has also launched its own television channel. Peter Hill-Wood, non-executive chairman, stated in the annual accounts that the figures 'clearly confirm the strength of the Group's financial position following the move to the Emirates Stadium'.

@ By putting 'arsenal holdings plc' into a search engine, you will find a list of sites that describe the company, what it is worth, how it trades, who its directors are and so forth. Within a group of four or five, choose one of these sites each and compare them in terms of the detail they provide. Decide which your group thinks is best and why.

Profit and loss account

The **profit and loss account** shows the operational side of the business and whether it is succeeding. It may therefore be divided (as is the case with Arsenal) into different areas. In this way, owners and other stakeholders can see which part of the business is profitable and which

less so. However, in published accounts, the business may not wish to give away this information, so can just publish the global figures. Although the whole thing is generally referred to as the profit and loss account, it actually consists of three parts, only one of which is profit and loss. These three parts are the trading account, the profit and loss account and the appropriation account.

Did you know...

Even the 'quality' of profit may be judged. Profit from continuing good sales of a product (such as Arsenal continuing to perform well in the Premiership) is considered better quality profit than, for example, one-off sales (such as of flats in its property trading arm).

The trading account

The **trading account** shows what products or services have been sold by the business in a specified time period. It shows the income of the business, i.e. what it has earned. For the most part this will be revenue from sales, but some businesses will also have other sources of income. Examples could be interest on investments or loans that have been made, rent from properties or income from patents or licences (another business could pay to use a particular process, for

example). For goods and services sold there are associated costs. These are called the '**cost of sales**' and include items such as raw materials and components. Taking the total cost of sales from total revenue gives the **gross profit**.

This part of the account could look like this: £10,000 worth of **sales revenue** (also called **turnover**). Cost of sales then takes into account that some stock existed at the start of the period (£4000), other stock has been bought (£3000) and some materials have yet to be used (closing stock of £2000).

The trading account

Sales revenue		10000
Minus Cost of sales	opening stock 4000 plus purchases 3000 minus closing stock 2000	5000
Gross profit		5000

The profit and loss account

The middle part of the account is called the profit and loss account. This shows gross profit minus expenses. Gross profit (the final figure on the trading account) is the starting point for this.

Gross profit is the amount that you have made before expenses are taken into account. **Net profit** is the amount after expenses are taken off. Expenses include wages, cost of premises, power, equipment, etc. This part of the account might look like this:

Profit and loss account

Gross profit		5000
Minus Expenses	Rent 500 Wages 500 Transport 200 Power 400 Fuel 200 Equipment 200	2000
Net profit		3000

Did you know...

Many businesses have failed because they have not been able to tell the difference between profit and cash flow. Often a business may think it is doing well because it has full order books and lots of sales, but at the same time its costs may be rising by more than the increase in revenue. This is why it is so important to keep accounts.

The appropriation account

The **appropriation account** shows where the net profit has gone. The starting point for this is net profit (the final figure from the profit and loss account). This account shows what happens to net profit. Some of it goes in taxes, some may be paid to shareholders as dividends, some, as you learned in the previous chapter, may be kept to help finance the business in the future. This is called **retained profit**.

Using the account

The profit and loss account is of use to various groups of stakeholders. It can be used to compare how successful the business was in this trading period compared with the previous one and to see whether it has met its objectives (e.g. Arsenal knows that both revenue and costs have increased, but so has profit). It also helps managers to plan for the future – how can revenue be increased, for example, or costs reduced? In addition, it can help in raising loans from banks, other lenders and investors by showing where costs and revenues arise.

Appropriation account

Net profit		3000
Minus Taxation	1000	
Post-tax profit		2000
Minus Dividends	500	
Retained profit		1500

Summary

- The profit and loss account is used to show the operational side of the business over a set time period
- It can be divided into three parts. These are:
  - the trading account, which shows what the business has earned from sales along with the cost of these sales (cost of sales)
  - the profit and loss account, which shows the effect of expenses on the gross profit figure
  - the appropriation account, which shows how any net profit has been distributed
- The account is useful to various stakeholder groups who can use the figures to assess the performance of the business against similar businesses and in previous time periods

Core knowledge

The profit and loss account is just one of the sets of financial figures that are used by larger businesses. It shows the income of the business from trading and from other activities. For most businesses, the biggest slice of income comes from sales. The number of products sold times the price of those products is the sales revenue. For such sales to take place, however, there must be some associated costs. You may have a mini-enterprise and sell a service such as car washing. In order to sell the service, you would need sponges, wash leathers and detergent. These are the cost of sales. For many businesses, these are the raw materials or components that are used to make the product.

There are also other expenses – for your mini-enterprise, these could be your time and effort, the cost of renting a space on a garage forecourt or the cost of advertising your service. For a large business, expenses include wages, power and equipment costs. What is left is net profit. This is then subject to taxation (it is the income of the business) and what is left can then be distributed to owners or retained for further investment in the business.

In our example, you may want to keep the money for yourself or set up a second site and use the money for this. In a larger business, the same choice – distribute the money to investors or plough it back into the business – is faced. The profit and loss account is an important tool for the stakeholders of the business when assessing the performance of a business. They can see how well sales are doing, which are the most important costs and whether they are rising or falling. Managers and owners can use the figures to make decisions about expansion, prices, costs and the distribution of profits.

And more

Profitability is often the main consideration for stakeholders. A profitable company usually means that the value of shares (and therefore of shareholder holdings) increases, and also gives shareholders the possibility of dividends. Suppliers and other creditors will want to be able to supply with confidence, and profitability is a good indicator of whether or not they will be paid. Taxation authorities such as the Inland Revenue in the UK will be keen to know about company profit so that they can tax the income of the business. Potential investors and lenders, such as entrepreneurs, venture capitalists and banks, will use the account to assess possible risk and reward in the future. It is often, therefore, a useful tool when a business is seeking extra finance from lenders. The main disadvantage of the profit and loss account, however, is that it is always looking backwards at what has happened previously. This means that stakeholders are using past performance in order to judge the likely future performance of a business and this may not always be accurate.

There is also the question of what profit means to a large business. Even in our simplified account above, there are four types of profit. Gross profit is the figure with just cost of sales taken out, net profit (also sometimes termed operating profit) also takes account of expenses and overheads (or fixed costs), while the most important figure for many stakeholders is net profit after taxation, as this shows exactly what is available for distribution to investors, or to provide extra investment for the business to fuel future efficiency (perhaps through new technology or processes) which would improve profitability, or for growth or expansion. If profit is ploughed back into the business, rather than being distributed, it is then termed retained profit.

Did you know...

As this book was being printed, new accounting terms and standards were being introduced to comply with international rules. Exam boards will, for a time, use both, with the new terms in brackets after the old terms. (See Appendix.)

Have a go!

Group activity

List all the different types of profit that you can think of in your group. Each person in the group should then take the role of one stakeholder group and say why the profit and loss account is of particular importance to that group.

Discussion

The law requires companies to produce profit and loss accounts to certain standards and at regular intervals. Why do you think that such accounts have to be made public? Do you think that it is fair that company income should be revealed to everyone in this way?

Web-based activity

Look at the other clubs in the football Premiership and find out which are publicly quoted. Look at the profit and loss accounts for each (go to the 'corporate' or 'investors' part of the website) and decide which is the most profitable. Make sure you follow the rules for making comparisons. If you are not interested in football, you could compare businesses in another sector, fashion for example, or technology.

Quickfire questions

1   What is a public limited company?
2   What is meant by 'sales revenue'?
3   Name three other sources of income, besides sales revenue.
4   Define gross profit.
5   Define net profit.
6   Name the three parts of the profit and loss account.
7   Explain what happens to retained profit.
8   Outline the usual items included in cost of sales.
9   Explain what is meant by 'dividends'.
10 Give one major limitation to the usefulness of profit and loss accounts.

Hit the spot

➤   Draw up an imaginary profit and loss account for a company of your choice. Label each part and add definitions.

➤➤ Give three stakeholder groups for whom profit is important and say why.

➤➤➤ Explain how you can be sure that you are comparing like with like when looking at different businesses and why this is important.

Cracking the code

Appropriation account This shows where the net profit has been distributed.

Cost of sales The cost of items such as raw materials and components used to make goods or provide services.

Gross profit Sales revenue minus cost of sales.

Net profit The amount after expenses are taken off gross profit.

Profit and loss account The account that shows the operational side of the business.

Retained profit Profit that is kept to help finance the business in the future.

Sales revenue Product sold times price.

Trading account The part of the profit and loss account that shows the income of the business, i.e. what it has earned.

Turnover Another way of saying 'sales revenue'.

Chapter 44
Balance sheets

During the late summer and early autumn of 2008, as stock markets fell and unemployment began to rise, a number of financial institutions found themselves under pressure. All banks and building societies that accept deposits rely on the confidence of those who have trusted money to them. If that confidence ever slips, this causes what is called a 'run' on the bank, which may force it to call in loans in order to keep depositors happy.

Northern Rock became one of the first major victims of the 2008 financial crisis when customers began to demand their deposits back. Eventually the building society turned bank could no longer rely on the confidence of its depositors and the government had to launch a rescue attempt. In effect, the Chancellor of the Exchequer, Alistair Darling, nationalised the bank – taking it into public ownership – so that the government could provide the guarantees of safety and security that depositors needed. It emerged that part of the lack of confidence in Northern Rock was due to its balance sheet not being as transparent and accurate as everyone had thought. Northern Rock had lent money, in mortgages, to people who were at high risk of defaulting. These mortgages were liabilities and should have appeared on the balance sheet. Had they done so, they would have shown how much risk was being carried by the bank. However, Northern Rock kept some of its riskiest liabilities – those most likely to default – in a special way that meant it could keep them out of the public eye.

Many of these liabilities were kept 'off balance sheet' by being turned into what were called 'special investment vehicles'. Northern Rock kept these liabilities in a separate business called 'Granite' and registered in the offshore tax haven of Jersey. Although this was perfectly acceptable under accounting rules at the time, many people have seen it as a way of not declaring the true state of assets and liabilities that a balance sheet should show. The Prime Minister, Gordon Brown, promised that banks would have to show all of their liabilities in the future. In an interview with Sky News, he said that it was 'not acceptable' that banks could hide information in this way.

> @
>
> All public limited companies have to produce a balance sheet and make it available to the public. Often these are available online. Go to the corporate website of a company in which you are interested and look at its balance sheet. See what judgements you can make about the business from the balance sheet. What else do you need to know to support your judgements?

Balance sheet

The **balance sheet** shows what the business has in the way of possessions and how these have been financed. It therefore shows the business how much it *owns* as against how much it *owes*.

Assets

The balance sheet may be divided into three parts – **assets, liabilities** and how **capital** has been raised. The first part measures the assets of the business – all the things that the business owns. They are either fixed – things like buildings and machinery used in production – or current – items like stocks of finished product or money owed that could be easily turned into cash. Some assets might be difficult to put a figure on. For example, when a business is sold, a value is often put on its 'goodwill'. This means the reputation of the business and its standing with customers. Assets include everything that a business owns to which a value can be attached, so in some cases items like goodwill will be included. Such assets cannot be physically touched so are called **'intangible' assets**.

In most cases an 'asset' entry also means a 'liability' entry in order to keep the balance. Clearly if a business buys £10,000 worth of stock, this increases its assets. At the same time, however, it has either paid for the stock out of cash reserves or, in most cases, still owes the supplier for the stock. This means that a £10,000 liability would appear as a **creditor**, making sure

Machinery is included in assets

that the stock (asset) and its cost (creditor) both appear.

Liabilities

The second part of the balance sheet shows liabilities – these are all the things that a business owes. These are either current – debts that must be paid back within a year, such as bank overdrafts or creditors – or long-term – debts that the business has more than a year to repay, such as long-term loans and mortgages. These are separated out in the account.

Working capital is calculated as current assets minus current liabilities. This figure is important as it shows the ability of the business to repay its short-term debts. If there is a positive working capital balance, then the business can meet its day-to-day needs. Suppliers, banks and other creditors will be confident that they will not only be paid but be paid on time. If working capital is negative, the business will struggle to pay its bills.

Net assets employed shows fixed assets (in this case £200,000) plus working capital (£40,000). From this figure the business then takes away its long-term liabilities to show its **net assets**. This is what the business is worth at this moment in time.

These assets have been financed in various ways, including loans, retained profit and share issues (see page 235). This is shown on the final part of the balance sheet, the capital account.

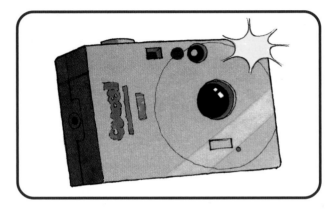

A balance sheet is a snapshot

Using the balance sheet

The balance sheet is of limited use because it can only ever be drawn up to represent the situation at a particular moment in time. It is not therefore looking at flows of finance or changes in such flows. To see what particular trends are, you would need to compare one balance sheet – at one point in time – with another one taken earlier or later. It is therefore often referred to as a 'snapshot', a picture taken at a point in time. Various stakeholder groups will have an interest in using the balance sheet. For example, it is important to:

- investors – to see how well their investment is performing and whether the business looks stable;

- creditors – to see how likely they are to have their debt repaid on time;

- managers – to help measure profitability, the cash situation, and to make comparisons with previous periods and other businesses; also to help them make key decisions;

- competitors – to compare their own performance against that of their rivals.

Summary

- The balance sheet is another important account for a business
- It shows what the business owns (assets) against what it owes (liabilities)
- It also shows how the capital invested in the business has been raised
- The balance sheet is only ever a 'snapshot' – a picture at a single point in time – so is of limited use
- Various stakeholder groups will find the balance sheet useful, but of much more use when combined with other financial information provided by the business

The capital account

BALANCE SHEET		TOTALS
Fixed assets	£	£
Land and buildings	100,000	
Machinery	70,000	
Vehicles	10,000	
Computers	10,000	
Intangible assets (goodwill)	10,000	
		200,000
Current assets	£	£
Debtors	10,000	
Stock	100,000	
Cash	10,000	
		120,000
Current liabilities	£	£
Creditors	60,000	
Overdraft	20,000	
		80,000
Net current assets (working capital)	£	£
Current assets minus current liabilities		40,000
Net assets employed	£	£
Fixed assets plus net current assets		240,000
Long-term liabilities		
Mortgages	40,000	
Long-term loans	10,000	
		50,000
Net assets		190,000
Capital account (shows these assets financed by…)	£	£
Share capital	120,000	
Retained profit	70,000	
Capital employed		190,000

Core knowledge

The balance sheet for a small business will be simple, that for a larger business more complex, but the principles are the same. The law requires limited companies to publish balance sheets with certain details, for example, the amount of finance raised through shareholders (shareholders' funds). Businesses that are not limited companies are not required to publish balance sheets and can keep their affairs private. However, a balance sheet might also be useful to them. The point of the balance sheet, in all cases, is to see what the business is truly worth.

There are three parts to a balance sheet (although often, because of the way in which it is laid out, it might look like more). Each part is linked to the others. They always show what the business owns (assets), what the business owes (liabilities) and how this has been financed. The most common way to set out a balance sheet is called the 'vertical balance sheet'. This shows assets, liabilities and capital in a vertical format so that it is clear where totals came from.

Balance sheets are important in helping investors (and others) to see how a company is developing. To do this, they need more than one balance sheet in order to make comparisons. They can see, for example, if a business is increasing investment, if it has enough to pay current debts or looks overstretched, if it has money to pay dividends or for future investment. The balance sheet also provides information for the managers of the company. They can see the value of capital and how it has been put to work in the business. They can see whether more finance needs to be raised or if debt needs managing better. They can also take into account other possibilities. If it looks, for example, like interest rates will rise or property prices fall, then they can look to adjust debt or mortgages accordingly.

And more

The type of business under consideration will have an effect on the balance sheet and investors need to take this into account when making judgements about a company. Just because a business has millions of pounds worth of assets does not necessarily mean that it is doing well. If it also has millions of pounds worth of debt – and if this debt is due shortly – the company could actually be in a lot of trouble. Companies are also affected by external events over which they have no control. A change in demand, or the introduction of new technology, could reduce the value of assets. Even intangible assets can be affected. If a customer found a foreign body in a chocolate bar, for instance, this could easily cause damage to the chocolate producer's reputation. Sometimes such damage to reputation can be as important as changes in the value of real, tangible assets.

You should always view published company accounts with caution – often they are not meant to reveal the real financial position of the business (internal figures will do this for managers). Window dressing is the practice of presenting accounts in as flattering a light as possible. Sometimes this just tidies up the accounts to make them easier to understand. At other times it hides the true position of the finances. For example, invoices may be issued early so that sales look like they are in the current year when in fact they should be included in the following period. Or extra cash can be injected into the company just before the end of the accounting period in order to make it look a better bet to investors. None of this is illegal unless it strays into actually falsifying accounts, in which case it is fraud.

Have a go!

Group activity

Each person in your group should choose a particular large company which has a website. Look through the website (in particular its marketing pages) and list the tangible and intangible assets of the business. Draw up a master list of possible tangible and intangible assets.

Discussion

Each person in your group should take the role of one stakeholder group and say why the balance sheet of a company might be of particular importance to that group.

Web-based activity

Using the corporate part of the website chosen for the group activity, find the latest balance sheet. Simplify the balance sheet so that a younger pupil could understand it.

Quickfire questions

1   What is meant by an 'asset'?
2   Explain the difference between fixed assets and current assets.
3   A strong brand name would be considered to be what sort of asset?
4   Define 'creditor'.
5   What is meant by a 'liability'?
6   Explain the difference between current liabilities and long-term liabilities.
7   Define 'debtor'.
8   What is meant by 'capital'?
9   Explain what is meant by 'working capital'.
10 Outline what is shown on the capital account.

Hit the spot

➤ Give one reason why the balance sheet may be of limited use.

➤➤ Explain why the balance sheet must always balance.

➤➤➤ Which do you think is most important to a business, tangible or intangible assets? Explain your reasoning.

Cracking the code

Assets **These are all the things that the business owns.**

Balance sheet. **This shows what the business owns as against how much it owes.**

Capital **The amount of investment in the business.**

Creditors **People or organisations to which the business owes money.**

Debtors **People or organisations that owe money to the business.**

Intangible assets **Assets that cannot be physically touched, like a strong brand name or good reputation.**

Liabilities **These are all the things that the business owes.**

Working capital **This is current assets minus current liabilities and shows the ability of the business to repay its short-term debts.**

Chapter 45
Ratios

How does a business manage to lower the price of a product and yet increase its profit ratios? It is all down to keeping costs under control. Apple hit the market with a new product, the iPhone, that was different, fashionable and an immediate 'must-buy'. But it had its drawbacks – not least its lack of 3G capacity – and many criticised it for not doing as much as other phones in this area. It was also tied to a single provider in both the US and the UK. Nevertheless, the hype with which any new Apple product is launched meant that people were prepared to queue up just to own one.

But was it profitable? And is the new 3G phone, launched as a replacement, as profitable? Surprisingly, the 3G version, despite its more modern technology and greater flexibility, has a higher profit margin than the original, 2G phone. iSuppli, a market analyst, says that the manufacturing and component cost of the new phone has been reduced. By taking apart a 3G device and adding together the cost of its components, along with the costs of marketing the device, iSuppli has estimated that Apple has a 55% profit margin. It has estimated the cost of the iPhone (in the US) at $174.33, much lower than the estimated $227 cost of the original iPhone. These totals include materials and manufacturing costs, but do not include research and development, packaging and distribution. The real profit margin, when these are added in, along with the cost of the deal with the phone companies, brings the cost of the 8 gigabyte iPhone to approximately $225. As the price tag of an 8 GB iPhone in the US is $500, this represents a 55%

gross profit margin. Count in research and development and marketing (typically a further 7–9% on the cost) and this falls slightly, but is still impressive.

Some business commentators think that they can now see why Apple launched an 'inferior' version first. Its success meant that it covered most of the development costs and that marketing costs for the new version could also be reduced. As a result, the price of the new iPhone is lower than the original, but profit margins are considerably higher.

 Do a web search for the price of the iPhone in different countries. Use a currency converter (like **www.XE.com**) to put all prices into pounds so that you can compare. Does the iPhone cost the same in every territory? Explain why you think this situation is so.

> ### Did you know…
>
> The nearer an asset is to cash, i.e. how easily it can be turned into cash, the more liquid it is said to be. Cash and money in the bank is therefore completely liquid, a long-term investment much less liquid.

Profitability

When a business is looking at its profitability, it wants to know how much profit it is making on each sale. To do this it can look at its **profit margins**. (The margin is the amount of profit the business is making, expressed as a percentage; it is also called a ratio.)

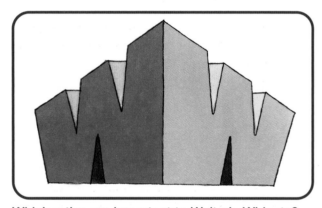

Which ratios are important to Walter's Widgets?

At Walter's Widgets Ltd, Wally is likely to be interested in two ratios – gross profit to sales revenue and net profit to sales revenue. Gross profit to sales revenue calculates the amount of profit the business is making once the cost of sales figure has been subtracted. This can also be called the **gross profit margin**. Net profit to sales revenue calculates the amount of profit the business is making once all costs have been subtracted. This can also be called the **net profit margin**.

Gross profit margin

These figures are taken from the profit and loss account. Below is the trading account for last year for Walter's Widgets Ltd.

Sales revenue	Wally's Widgets Ltd	£825,000
Minus Cost of sales	Opening stock 325,000 plus purchases 200,000 minus closing stock 100,000	£425,000
Gross profit		£400,000

The gross profit margin or gross profit to sales revenue ratio is worked out using the formula:

$$\frac{\text{Gross profit}}{\text{Sales revenue}} \times 100 = \%$$

so in this case is:

$$\frac{400,000}{825,000} \times 100 = 48\%$$

This figure tells Wally that his business is making 48p on each £1 of sales and that 52p goes on the cost of sales. Wally can then look at this year's trading account. He can see that sales revenue is up, but so is the cost of sales and so is his gross profit. To find out if he is more or less profitable, he must compare the percentages.

Sales revenue	Wally's Widgets Ltd	£925,000
Minus Cost of sales	Opening stock 100,000 plus purchases 450,000 minus closing stock 50,000	£500,000
Gross profit		£425,000

$$\frac{425,000}{925,000} \times 100 = 46\%$$

Wally knows that his business is actually now slightly less profitable, so can see that he needs to cut costs if possible.

Net profit margin

The net profit to sales revenue, or net profit margin, is worked out in a similar way. The formula for this is:

$$\frac{\text{Net profit}}{\text{Sales revenue}} \times 100 = \%$$

From the profit and loss account, the figures show:

Sales revenue	Wally's Widgets Ltd	£925,000
Gross profit		£425,000
Minus Expenses	Rent 75,000 Wages 100,000 Transport 25,000 Power 50,000 Fuel 50,000 Computers 35,000	£335,000
Net profit		£90,000

$$\frac{90,000}{925,000} \times 100 = 9.7\%$$

This means Walter's Widgets is making just 9.7p for each £1 sold. Whether this is good or not may depend on the product. Some products (like crisps) rely on high-volume sales with low margins. Other products (designer clothes, for instance) have few sales but high margins. Wally can also, as with the gross profit figure, compare this with both previous time periods and other businesses in the same industry.

Current ratios

Businesses (and their stakeholders) also want to know whether the business can pay its debts. The **current ratio** shows whether the business can meet its liabilities (debts) easily by turning assets into cash. These figures are taken from the balance sheet. This extract is from the balance sheet you looked at on page 251.

Current assets	£	£
Debtors	10,000	
Stock	100,000	
Cash	10,000	
		120,000
Current liabilities	£	£
Creditors	60,000	
Overdraft	20,000	
		20,000

The formula for working out the current ratio is:

$$\frac{\text{Current assets}}{\text{Current liabilities}}$$

This is usually expressed as a ratio rather than a percentage. It always helps if you can reduce one side to '1'. In this case it is:

$$\frac{120,000}{80,000} \text{ or } \frac{12}{8} \text{ or } \frac{3}{2} \text{ or } 1.5{:}1$$

This shows that Walter's Widgets can meet its short-term debts one and a half times over – a healthy position for a business. A ratio less than this would be a worry, more than this (say 3:1) probably means that too many assets are being held as cash.

Acid test ratios

The current ratio, as you can see, assumes that stock can be sold. This may not always be the case, particularly in the short run. The **acid test ratio** takes stocks out of the calculation and is a much sterner measure of a business's ability to meet liabilities. The formula is:

$$\frac{\text{Current assets} - \text{stocks}}{\text{Current liabilities}}$$

In this case, this would be:

$$\frac{120,000 - 100,000}{80,000} \text{ or } \frac{20,000}{80,000} \text{ or } 0.25{:}1$$

This shows that the business could have trouble paying off its debts. A healthy acid test ratio is seen as 0.5:1 to 1:1.

Summary

- Profit margins show the amount a business is making on each sale
- These are also called profitability ratios, as they compare sales revenue totals with profits
- Profitability ratios can be found by using the published profit and loss account of a business
- Comparisons between profitability ratios are often clearer if percentages are used
- Current ratios show the ability of the business to pay its debts
- Current ratios can be found by using the published balance sheet of a business
- The acid test ratio does not assume stocks can be sold, so is a more accurate indicator of the ability of the business to pay its debts

What is the **ratio** of teachers to pupils in your school or college?

Did you know...

When you are using financial ratios, the examination board will always provide you with the formulae that you need, so you don't have to worry about getting figures the right way round. Just make sure that you have a calculator.

Core knowledge

Businesses need to use the accounts that they prepare in order to see how well they are doing. They need to be able to use figures from the accounts to judge whether they are performing well or badly. Comparisons may be made to other businesses, to the performance in previous years, or between different products within a business. In the case of the iPhone, for example, Apple can compare the impact of the new model on the business to that of the old model. Using the figures on profit and loss accounts and balance sheets, businesses can find the answers to vital questions such as:

- Are they profitable and if so, how profitable?
- Have they improved profit?
- Are their finances sound, i.e. are they capable of paying their debts, not borrowing too much, not holding too much money in cash?

This is information that is vital to the various stakeholders in a business. Owners and managers want to see efficiency and profitability; creditors such as suppliers and lenders want to know that the business can pay its debts; customers want to know that the business can continue to provide quality products. The answers to these questions often lie in the use of financial ratios.

A ratio is simply one thing measured in terms of another. If there are 16 boys in your class and 8 girls, then the ratio of boys to girls is 16 to 8 or 2 to 1. In other words (as is obvious), there are two boys to each girl. This can also be shown as a percentage.

$$\frac{\text{Number of boys}}{\text{Number of girls}} \times 100 = \frac{16}{8} = 200\% \text{ i.e. twice as many boys as girls.}$$

You can see that you have to be careful with ratios as this can also be expressed as the ratio of girls to boys. In this case:

$$\frac{\text{Number of girls}}{\text{Number of boys}} \times 100 = \frac{8}{16} = 50\% \text{ i.e. half as many girls as boys.}$$

The reason for using a percentage is clear when the business tries to make comparisons as figures are not often as clear-cut as 2 to 1. For example, is a ratio of 89:98 better than 90:99? A percentage calculation shows us that the answer is:

$$\frac{89}{98} \times 100 = 90.8\%$$

$$\frac{90}{99} \times 100 = 90.9\%$$

You will see in the example of Walter's Widgets that this is important for a business when both sides of the equation (e.g. sales revenue and profit) increase.

And more

Although these are the key ratios for profitability and liquidity (current and acid test ratios are called 'liquidity ratios'), there are other ratios that are equally important to a business. Perhaps the other most important ratio is ROCE or Return on Capital Employed. This measures how efficiently the business is using the capital invested in it, so is a key ratio for investors. The formula is:

$$\frac{\text{Net profit}}{\text{Total capital employed}} \times 100 = \%$$

Investors can then compare efficiency with previous years, other similar businesses and other investments. Clearly if this percentage fell below bank interest rates, then it would be a better bet for an investor to open a bank account than invest in the business!

It is also important to know how managers and owners can make use of ratios when judging in which direction to take a business. To choose the most appropriate action, owners and managers need to weigh up the advantages and disadvantages. For example, cutting costs might look like a good bet, but this might also lead to less efficiency or lower quality if inferior raw materials are used. It is not always easy to increase revenue – a price increase might lead to less of the product being bought, sales and offers could sell more products, but at reduced margins. Ratios and accounts can be used to help predict what might happen and thus to make the business more efficient or more profitable, or both.

Did you know...

Always compare like with like – it would be pointless comparing a power station with a corner shop!

Have a go!

Group activity

Work out the ratios for a number of groups chosen at random to familiarise yourselves with how ratios work. For example, you could do the number of boys to girls in your class, the number of fair-haired people to dark-haired, the ratio of teachers to pupils, of cars to lorries on the road. Each person should then present one ratio to the rest of the group and explain who might find it useful and why.

Discussion

Which do you think is the most important ratio to a business, profitability or liquidity? Do you all agree? Is it the same for every business?

Web-based activity

Visit the corporate part of the website of a well-known company and, from its profit and loss account and balance sheet, work out its gross and net profit margins and its liquidity ratios. Would you recommend that someone invest in the company? Why?

Quickfire questions

1 Define what is meant by gross profit margin?
2 Define what is meant by net profit margin.
3 What is a ratio?
4 From which published account would you take the figures for profitability ratios?
5 How would you work out a profitability ratio?
6 Why do we use percentages to compare ratios?
7 What is a liquidity ratio?
8 From which published account would you take the figures for liquidity ratios?
9 How would you work out an acid test ratio?
10 Why is the acid test ratio important?

Hit the spot

➤ Describe how a business would work out its profit margins and give an example.

➤➤ Explain why a business would need to know its liquidity ratios.

➤➤➤ Identify three other groups which may need to know about the ratios of a business. Which of these do you think is the most important and why?

Cracking the code

Acid test ratio **This compares assets (not including stock) and liabilities to show if the business can meet its debts. The formula is: current assets – stock/current liabilities.**

Current ratio **This compares assets and liabilities to show if the business can meet its debts. The formula is: current assets/current liabilities.**

Gross profit margin **This calculates the amount of profit the business is making once the cost of sales figure has been subtracted from total sales revenue.**

Net profit margin **This calculates the amount of profit the business is making once all costs have been subtracted.**

Profit margins **The amount of profit the business is making on sales, expressed as a percentage.**

ADVANCED PEOPLE IN BUSINESSES

Chapter 46
Introduction to advanced people in businesses

In this section of chapters you will be studying how larger companies deal with the people they encounter in business. Clearly, the people who work for the business, its employees, are an important group. Many large companies go as far as to state publicly that they recognise the importance of employees in making their business successful. A search of the internet using 'valuing our employees', or similar phrases, will result in many examples of such businesses.

So, why does a business feel the need to let everyone know that it believes its employees are so crucial? It could be that it hopes that the message gets out and the public views the business in a positive light. This might persuade some consumers that the business is a decent organisation and worth their custom. Alternatively, it might encourage those looking for employment to consider working for that particular business. Or it could be it just wants the world to know that it genuinely is a caring organisation.

Motivation

Whatever the reason, a large business needs to ensure it recruits the best people to work for it, trains them properly so they can do their work competently and treats them well so they are motivated and loyal to the company. Without motivation, a business will never get the best from its workers. Without loyalty, employees will leave on a regular basis, making it hard for teams to develop, besides pushing up recruitment and training costs.

There is no single answer to the question 'How do you motivate employees?' Each person is different, with differing needs and personal circumstances. For some it will be the wage that is the driving force, for others it will be other factors. The owner of a small business is likely to know his or her employees sufficiently well to have a good idea what needs to be done to keep them working efficiently. Close personal relationships are less likely to operate between manager and employee in larger businesses. However, many large businesses are encouraging managers to get to know their employees better. The 'them and us' way of thinking, where managers and workers distrust each other, is slowly breaking down in favour of more co-operative working.

Communication

Providing good communication is a theme that cuts through many of the chapters in this section. A large business can seem impersonal to an individual employee. Unlike small businesses, where it is likely that all the employees know each other, communications can be an issue. There is a sense of pulling together in a small business that cannot always be reproduced in larger companies. Businesses do, nevertheless, try to ensure that employees are kept informed, or at least they feel that they are. Businesses will spend time, effort and money producing company magazines or newsletters, purely to make employees feel they know what is going on.

Training for the workplace

Training

Many students might view training as giving each employee the necessary skills to be able to do his or her job properly. Training is that, but more besides. Training is used by business to motivate employees. Broadening a person's skill levels can make that person feel appreciated, even if there is no immediate prospect of putting the new skills into practice. What it does instead is raise that employee's interest levels in the work he or she does, increasing that person's efficiency. While it might not be thought of as training, changing employees' attitudes is an aspect of training. If a business wants its employees to take more responsibility for the quality of the work that they produce, it will have to train them. This training would not just be in the techniques they would use to check their own work, but would also be in getting them to realise how important this new way of doing things is.

People other than employees

Of course, employees are not the only people within a business, there are many others, shareholders for example. These people effectively own the business and, for most, their main consideration is how profitable the business is. Shareholders get money in two ways: from their annual or twice-yearly dividend and when they sell their shares for more than they paid for them. Most shareholders take the view that as long as the company in which they own shares is performing as well as other similar businesses, they are happy. Company directors represent shareholders' interests within the business.

Suppliers are important to a business, particularly when they provide raw materials or components that cannot easily be obtained elsewhere. Forging good working relationships with suppliers is important if a business is to be assured of continued supplies. We will read in Chapter 53 how a Japanese company takes it upon itself to ensure that its suppliers receive support if they are having difficulties. The principle of thinking about the long-term success of a business is central to this company.

Without customers, a business would fail to sell any goods. This might sound a ridiculous statement to make, but it does illustrate the importance of a business providing goods or services that its customers want to buy, at a price that they are happy with. Clever marketing can influence consumers' preferences. Establishing a successful brand name can convince consumers to buy one product rather than a competitor's, even if the price paid is higher and the quality no different. No business would be advised, though, to assume that its customers will continue to be loyal and buy its goods indefinitely.

Chapter 47
Organising a growing business

IN THE NEWS

Southern Demolition Company Ltd

Southern Demolition Company Ltd is a private limited company with headquarters at Byfleet in Surrey. The business was started in 1953 by Sidney Hunt Senior and it has expanded considerably since those early years. Southern Demolition is involved, as its name suggests, in the dismantling of buildings and other structures. If developers are to improve or change the use of an industrial area, they might need the services of a company like Southern Demolition. Buildings may need to be demolished to make room for other, more modern constructions to be put up in their place.

Demolition is sometimes seen as the poor relative of the construction industry. Some people view it as destructive and not really requiring any skill beyond brute force. This is far from the case. Many old buildings, for instance, contain dangerous materials such as asbestos. Employees who are used to remove this hazardous waste must be fully trained to keep themselves and others safe. By law, workers who remove toxic materials must have followed recognised courses and be fully qualified to do so. Demolition sites are also very dangerous places, so proper training is required to avoid injuries.

As managing director, Sidney Hunt, the son of the founder, has chosen to create a clear organisational structure, which is represented in its organisation chart (see next page). This diagram shows the breakdown of the business into its different departments or functions. The chart is published on the company's website, so anyone who deals with the business knows who is in charge of each function and what the different functions are. A customer making enquiries about a contract would, for instance, know whom to contact within the organisation. The chart might also be useful for those who work at Southern Demolition. Employees can see how the different functions work together and how their contribution fits into the whole organisation.

The chart also conveys a hidden message about Southern Demolition. It says: we are organised and have well-qualified staff. So, it could also be seen as a form of marketing. Potential customers who go on to the website might be influenced by the organisation chart. They may be more willing to use Southern Demolition because the chart makes it appear professional and organised.

Take a look at the
Southern Demolition website at
www.southerndemolition.co.uk

Span of control

The number of people which a manager directly supervises is called the **span of control**. We can see on Southern Demolition's organisation chart that the managing director, Sidney Hunt, has a span of control of many people. We cannot tell exactly how many are under Mr Hunt's direct control, as we don't know how many supervisors and subcontractors there are. It is clear, however, that Mr Hunt appears to have control of much of the business. The two other directors do not seem to have any **subordinates**, or at least the chart would suggest this.

It is unlikely that a managing director would be able to supervise every single employee within a business, unless the organisation was very small. A manager will often delegate responsibility to a subordinate, who will take control of a particular area of the business. In the case of Southern Demolition, we can see that the office manager has delegated responsibility for the office administration staff. Delegated responsibility means that the manager has the authority of the managing director to supervise the employees in that section. Sometimes the power of delegation allows the supervisor to make important decisions without referring to his or her **line manager** for permission. In other cases, there might be a limit on how much authority the supervisor has. But whichever system is used, the overall responsibility for the business lies with the managing director.

What is the ideal number of people that a manager should supervise? This can depend upon several things.

- *Physical location*. If a business is spread over a wide area, possibly having several sites, it may

not be easy for one manager to supervise many people. This would also apply to a business whose employees worked from home, or whose work took them away from their managers, such as engineers who service people's central heating boilers.

- *Complexity of tasks*. A manager might also find it difficult to supervise several employees who were highly skilled. They would probably be involved in complex work and need more detailed support and attention.

- *Ease of communication*. Generally speaking, the easier it is to communicate with employees, the wider the span of control can be. A manager dealing with employees who do not speak English, for instance, would not be able to have a wide span of control.

Layers of management

An organisation chart also shows how many layers of management there are. In the Southern Demolition chart, there are three distinct layers: the managing director, the other managers,

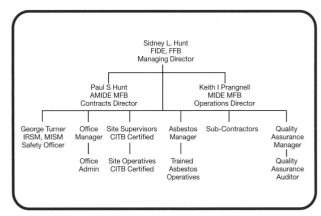

The Southern Demolition organisation chart

including the two directors, and finally the people on the bottom layer who work in the offices or at the building sites.

This three-layer system probably means that communications in this organisation are quite good. A decision made by the managing director could, in theory, be passed quickly on to everyone in the organisation. If a business has too many layers, communications can suffer and the organisation could become inefficient.

Summary

- Larger businesses often produce an organisation chart to show the different functions of a business
- Organisation charts make it easy for outside people to understand how the business is split up into different areas or functions
- The chart makes it easier for employees to know who is in charge of the different parts, or functions, of the business
- An organisation chart can also give the impression that a business is well organised and professional

Core knowledge

An organisation chart shows which subordinates are accountable to each of the line managers. The chart demonstrates how important each person is within the organisation. We call this a hierarchy and use terms like 'those at the top' and 'people at the bottom'. Usually those further up the hierarchy have more status and earn more than those lower down. With most hierarchies decisions tend to be made at the top and are communicated with those below. Some businesses do not like this structure as it does not encourage people lower down the chart to show initiative. Many layers of management can also mean it takes a long time for messages and ideas to travel to everyone in the business.

Some businesses have tried to reduce the number of layers within an organisation chart. This process is often called delayering. This can be achieved by looking carefully at which layers of management are not really required and removing them. Some managers may have assistants when there is no real need for this additional help. A manager might have insisted on having assistants to make him or her appear more important within the business. Delayering is a good opportunity to streamline the business as well as improve communications.

Some managers prefer to operate a flat hierarchy. This means removing some, or even all, of the layers of management. With this system, there is less distinction between managers and workers. Employees are allowed to take more responsibility for what they do and to show initiative. They are not supervised closely and are trusted to work well. Many employees prefer this method and respond positively to the trust the business has placed in them. Others workers can be reluctant to accept this new responsibility. They prefer to be told what to do by a line manager and not have to worry if anything goes wrong. Rather than thriving on problem solving in the workplace as others do, this type of employee would rather leave it to someone else to sort out. So, in order for a flat hierarchy to work successfully, it is important that employees have the right attitude towards working unsupervised.

Did you know...

The word hierarchy is Greek and was originally used to show who the important people in the Greek Church were.

And more

Matrix hierarchies. Some businesses have experimented with different kinds of management hierarchies. One such type is a matrix hierarchy. With this system, employees have more than one manager to check on them. If a group of employees is working on a project, they might have a specialist manager who monitors the skills they use and a project manager who checks on the progress of the assignment. For instance, a construction company might be building several hundred new houses on a site. The bricklayers might be responsible to a manager who knows how to deal with bricklaying issues as they arise. They might also be accountable to the project manager who will be concerned that the houses are finished on time and within budget.

Centralisation/decentralisation. As they develop and grow, many businesses realise that the decision-making power of the organisation has been centralised. This means that the key decisions on what the company does and what it plans to do in the future are made by a small group of people in one location. Quite often the people who are dealing with customers have a much better idea of what needs to be done to sell products for the best price. Some supermarket chains are starting to decentralise and allow individual store managers to make policy decisions. Rather than having to accept the 'official' price that the goods are sold for, managers can alter them if appropriate. If the weather is cold and rainy in an area, the manager of the local supermarket might decide to lower the prices of salads and barbecue food so they do not remain unsold.

Outsourcing. An increasing number of larger businesses are subcontracting work out to other organisations rather than doing the work themselves. This is known as outsourcing. A business may, for example, decide to pay a contractor to be responsible for cleaning its offices or use a human resource contractor to look after its recruitment. This allows the company to concentrate on its core business, the thing it is probably best at doing. In the example at the start of this chapter, we can see that the managing director of Southern Demolition is responsible for overseeing the work of the subcontractors that his business uses.

Inverted hierarchy. Some management experts argue that the organisation chart should be shown upside down, something called an inverted hierarchy. The idea of this is to get across the message that those lower down are, in fact, most likely to recognise when changes need to be made and how these changes should be implemented. These experts argue that the workers now at the top of the chart should be empowered to make their own decisions for the good of the business. While this is accepted in theory, many managers are reluctant to give up their status and power, so it is unusual to see an inverted hierarchy in practice.

Did you know...

Laurence Peter wrote a humorous book about business hierarchies. He suggested that employees keep on being promoted until they can no longer cope with the new level of responsibility they face and they remain in that job. The Peter Principle says that the posts in an organisation are held by managers who cannot really do their jobs properly!

Have a go!

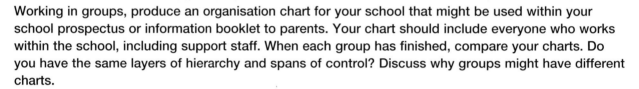

Group activity

Working in groups, produce an organisation chart for your school that might be used within your school prospectus or information booklet to parents. Your chart should include everyone who works within the school, including support staff. When each group has finished, compare your charts. Do you have the same layers of hierarchy and spans of control? Discuss why groups might have different charts.

Discuss how you might rearrange the management hierarchy for your school. Give your ideas in a presentation to the rest of the class, or invite the head teacher or deputy to listen to your ideas.

Discussion

Discuss whether a flat hierarchy would work better than one with more layers in it.

Web-based activity

Search the web to find more examples of organisation charts. Comment on those you find in terms of the number of layers and the spans of control.

Quickfire questions

1   Describe the type of work that Southern Demolition undertakes.
2   Why is training important for Southern Demolition employees?
3   Describe two reasons why Southern Demolition's employees need to be well trained.
4   Explain, using Southern Demolition as an example, what is meant by a span of control.
5   What is decentralisation?
6   What is meant by delayering?
7   Give a reason why delayering might not work.
8   Give a reason why a business might outsource some of its jobs.
9   Give two reasons why a business might choose to decentralise.
10 Explain what a matrix hierarchy is.

Hit the spot

> Describe what is meant by an organisation chart.

> Explain how an organisation chart with several layers can result in poor communications.

> Discuss whether employees work better when they have less supervision.

Cracking the code

Span of control The number of people for which a manager is responsible.

Subordinates Those people who are below someone on an organisation chart.

Line manager The person to whom a subordinate is directly responsible.

Chapter 48
Recruiting staff

Tesco

The supermarket chain, Tesco, employs over 300,000 staff in its stores, its distribution centres and head office in central London. The company sells food, clothing and household items. Tesco has recently started to offer other services, such as insurance.

Tesco believes that its employees should reflect the different cultures of the people who are its customers. The company is always trying out new ideas to attract employees from a wide range of backgrounds and religions. It is also keen to take on older workers who are past the traditional retirement age, and those who have disabilities. Tesco even has a panel of people who monitor the workforce to see how well the company is doing at achieving a mixed group of staff.

Tesco also tries to make sure everyone can work in a way that suits their circumstances. Employees are offered flexible working patterns, such as part-time roles. Job sharing and shift swapping are also

encouraged to make employees' **work–life balance** more acceptable. Tesco believes by providing flexibility employees will be loyal and remain with the company.

The method that Tesco uses to recruit and select new employees will depend upon the type of job vacancy. The business uses the internet as the main way to advertise for staff. Application forms can be downloaded from the internet, where applicants can also discover more about the benefits of working for the company.

Customer assistants

These are the people who help customers in supermarkets or who are pickers at one of Tesco's distribution centres. Pickers gather together the goods in a warehouse that need to be sent to stock Tesco stores around the country. The company website will have details of any vacancies, but local stores might also advertise the job where it can be seen by customers. Applicants wanting to become customer assistants are encouraged to visit the store or centre and talk to the people there.

If Tesco believes that the applicant appears to be suitable, he or she will be invited to an interview. The interview will be friendly and low pressured. Tesco managers will ask the applicant many questions. They will want to find out the applicant's background and work experience. The interviewers will also be interested to discover whether the person applying has the right attitude and skills to deal with people. The applicant will be able to ask questions about the job, working conditions and about Tesco too.

Managers

Applicants for managers' and head office workers' jobs are also advertised on the internet. Applicants for these posts are more likely to be drawn from a wider geographical area than those who are applying for assistant jobs. Unlike applications for assistant jobs, those applying for managers' jobs must do so online. Interviews for managers take place in central London. Tesco will pay the applicant's travelling expenses. As part of the process, applicants will be asked to complete a questionnaire on their attitudes to certain situations. Tesco uses this questionnaire to find out whether the person has the right approach to dealing with people and the other skills that they will need to do the job properly.

 Take a look at the Tesco careers website at **www.tesco-careers.com**

Did you know...

Chief Executive Sir Terry Leahy joined Tesco as a trainee manager in 1979 and rose through the ranks to the company's top position.

A large business like Tesco will have many vacancies to fill each year. Staff will leave for a variety of reasons and their posts will probably have to be filled. Recruiting applicants, and then selecting the most suitable of them, can be both time consuming and expensive. When a manager is showing somebody around the store, reading applications or interviewing, his or her time could be spent doing other things. Training a new employee is also expensive. The person will not work effectively until he or she has been trained. Training will often involve another employee showing the newcomer what to do, which means that person is also not working effectively.

Businesses want to attract the best staff, but they also want their employees to remain with them. The rate at which employees leave a business is known as **labour turnover**. A high turnover means a large number of employees are leaving each year. Large businesses like to see some turnover of staff. Having new people come with fresh ideas and enthusiasm can be good for a company, but large numbers of employees leaving is usually a sign that people are not motivated.

When somebody resigns, the business needs to decide whether that person should be replaced. It is possible that circumstances have changed

Did you know...

The name Tesco was made up from the initials of T E Stockwell, a tea supplier, and the first two letters of founder Jack Cohen's surname.

since the person leaving was recruited and the job is no longer needed. Technological advances might mean that much of the work the person did might be able to be done more efficiently using computer technology. If the managers do decide to replace the employee, they will want to get the best recruit for the job. They do not necessarily want an exact clone of the person who has left. It is an ideal time to stand back and think carefully about how the job has changed and where they want to see the business going in the future.

Large businesses are likely to produce two documents before they even think about advertising for a vacancy: a job description and a person specification. To save time, Tesco will probably have standard documents for jobs for which it recruits regularly, such as customer assistants. These documents will usually be sent out with the application form, or published online.

- *Job description*. This outlines the duties and responsibilities of a job. It will contain such information as the job title, the wage or salary, the day-to-day tasks, who the person's manager will be and whether the successful applicant will be supervising anybody else.

- *Person specification*. This document lists what skills, qualifications and experience are required for the job. It will often state whether each of these things is essential or desirable. Tesco managers might think it is essential that customer assistants have good communication skills, but experience of shop working might be just as desirable.

Advertising

Once these documents have been produced, the business will need to let potential applicants know about the vacancy. Tesco relies on the internet to advertise any vacancies it has. Other businesses prefer to place advertisements in the media. The medium through which a job is advertised will usually depend upon the nature of the post being filled. If the job is low skilled and there are many people who could do the work, the advertisement will probably appear locally. This could be in a local newspaper or on a company notice board, inviting staff to pass on the details to anyone looking for work. If a more specialist job needs to be filled, it might be more appropriate to advertise more widely. Many industries have specialist newspapers or journals that employers might use to place their advertisement.

ASSISTANT CHEF, ANGLIA HOTEL

Cambridge   Full-time   Competitive salary

In this role you will assist the kitchen staff with the day-to-day running of the kitchen, and prepare food to a high standard. At the Anglia Hotel Restaurant, we offer an à la carte menu with daily specials to showcase the best local, organic food.

We are looking for someone who is passionate about food and about hospitality. Previous experience is not essential, but commitment and enthusiasm are.

We offer an excellent package of benefits, and you will receive a share of the service charge earned. We also run a training and development programme and encourage all staff to work towards further qualifications. The Anglia Hotel offers many opportunities for a rewarding career.

Did you know...

Four out of five Tesco employees shopped at the supermarket chain before getting a job there.

Summary

- The internet is becoming an increasingly important way for large businesses to attract job applicants
- Recruiting staff is expensive, in terms of both money and managers' time
- Businesses use application forms, interviews and different tests to help them determine the best person to fill a vacancy
- The way an employee is recruited will often depend upon the type of vacancy being filled

Core knowledge

Many businesses choose to recruit managers and supervisors internally. This means rather than advertise the job outside the organisation, they offer the post to someone who already works for the business. The attraction of recruiting managers this way is the company knows the applicant and his or her strengths. It avoids the situation of being taken in by someone who performs well at interview but then fails to live up to expectations when appointed to the job. There are ways of avoiding this situation, however, and these can be found in the section 'And more', below.

There are benefits of bringing in somebody new to the business rather than recruiting internally. Fresh ideas and new ways of doing things can be introduced into the organisation. Also, if someone was promoted internally, the person might not find it easy to command the respect of the co-workers with whom he or she has worked before.

Businesses rely on application forms to determine which of the applicants would be suitable to interview. This is known as the short list. The form will contain questions asking for details of the topics that the employer sees as being important. By doing this applicants must provide essential information, which they might not if they applied by writing a letter.

It is usual to ask for personal details from the applicants, such as their name, address and contact telephone numbers. Some items of information are considered too sensitive to ask as the business does not want to be accused of discrimination. For this reason, it is unlikely that age or date of birth will be requested, or whether the person is married. Sometimes businesses include a separate form asking for details of ethnicity, race and disabilities, so they can monitor if they are recruiting a good mix of people. This second form is kept apart from the main form and does not influence who is taken on.

Interviews vary according to the nature of the job to be filled. For a low-paid job, it may be little more than a short conversation with a manager. The applicant might be asked about his or her work experience and why he or she wants to work for the organisation. More skilled jobs might require a full day, or even two days, of tests and group interviews. The applicants will be placed in difficult situations to see how they perform. They might have to perform role-play exercises and other professional tests to see how competent they are. Sometimes the employer just wants to see how people respond under pressure.

Did you know...

It might be helpful to go back to Chapter 21 to remind yourself about how small businesses recruit staff.

And more

Psychometric tests. Some businesses are starting to use psychometric tests to find out more about the people who apply for jobs. Applicants are usually given a questionnaire to complete as part of the selection process. The answers the applicant gives to these questions can allow the employer to discover a great deal about those applying for the job. The test could determine what motivates the applicants, how they react to authority, how creative and imaginative they are and how open they are to learning new skills. Critics of psychometric testing say that those being tested can often work out which of the answers the employer is looking for and not answer the questions honestly.

Probationary period. When an applicant is appointed to a job, the business might decide to take them on for a probationary period. This means the employee's contract is not made permanent until the applicant has proved that he or she is capable of doing the job properly. If the business finds that the person is not shaping up, the managers are able to terminate the contract at the end of the probationary period. This is really an insurance policy for the business; it will not be left with someone whose application form, references and interview are all good but who fails to live up to expectations when appointed, Probationary periods are usually used only for senior jobs within a business. The problem with probationary periods is that they can discourage people from applying for the job. Accepting the job and working a probationary period does have a risk. The successful applicant would have to resign from his or her current job and if they failed the probationary period they would end up jobless.

Recruitment agencies. These are businesses that specialise in finding employees, which saves managers the task of having to do it themselves. In return for recruiting a suitable person, the agency will receive a fee from the employer. This, in a way, is a form of outsourcing which was covered earlier in the book. By using a recruitment agency, a business can concentrate on more important jobs, while the agency spends time searching through application forms and interviewing potential candidates. A recruitment agency can save a business time and effort.

Have a go!

Group activities

Produce a suitable application form to use to recruit teachers to your school.

Imagine Tesco has asked you to come up with a way of finding out how well applicants for customer assistants' posts are able to deal with people. In a group, come up with as many tests and activities that you think would be suitable. Choose the best two and produce all the paperwork you would need to run both of them.

Produce a person specification for a Tesco customer assistant. Show which of the items should be essential and which desirable.

Discussion

Discuss how useful formal interviews are in determining who is the best person for the job. Are there better ways that could be used?

Web-based activity

Compare the recruitment process used by Tesco with the other major supermarkets. Produce a list of similarities and differences.

Quickfire questions

1 Where is Tesco's head office?
2 How does Tesco advertise for its staff?
3 What job does a Tesco picker do?
4 What is a job description?
5 What is a probationary period?
6 What does a recruitment agency do?
7 Give two items of information that might be asked for on an application form.
8 Explain why a firm might be worried about a high labour turnover.
9 Explain why an applicant's date of birth is not usually included on an application form.
10 Give two disadvantages of recruiting managers internally.

Hit the spot

> What is meant by labour turnover?

> Explain two ways a business might reduce the amount of labour turnover.

> Discuss whether advertising vacancies on the internet is the best way of attracting applicants for a job.

Cracking the code

Work–life balance Ensuring a reasonable split between the time a person spends working and other family and leisure activities.

Labour turnover The rate at which employees leave a business. If a business had 80 employees and 20 left during the course of a year, the turnover would be 20/80, or 25%.

Chapter 49
Appraisal and training

IN THE NEWS

British Gas Services

British Gas Services (BGS) is part of British Gas, which is owned by the Centrica Group of Companies. British Gas supplies gas and electricity to households and businesses around the UK and Europe. It is the UK's largest supplier of fuel. BGS is not directly involved in supplying gas, but is responsible for installing and maintaining gas appliances, such as boilers and cookers.

BGS needs to have the right staff in order to deliver these services effectively. Because of the hazardous nature of gas and electricity, BGS employees need to be fully trained and motivated. As the BGS employees deal directly with British Gas's customers, it is important that they create the right impression. If customers feel that the service they receive from BGS staff is poor, this could have a serious impact on British Gas. Consumers are always looking for the best deal from their fuel suppliers and will switch to another if they are unhappy with the service they are receiving. So it is important that BGS employees not only have good technical knowledge but also good people skills. It is for this reason that the British Gas Academy was created, where BGS employees are trained.

The British Gas Academy trains both new recruits and established employees who need to be updated.

New recruits are taught the relevant skills they will need to do their jobs and learn about British Gas and the gas industry. The training also covers communication and problem-solving skills. Trainees are taught how to listen to people and to deal with them politely. BGS also has an apprentice system, where recruits work alongside an experienced employee to learn 'on the job'. All employees regularly attend refresher courses or training to update their skills. The need for these courses is identified at the regular review meetings that each employee holds with his or her manager.

 Take a look at the British Gas Academy website at
www.britishgasacademy.co.uk

BGS recognises that it costs more to recruit and train a new employee than it costs to retain an established one. So it makes financial sense not only to attract the best people as employees but also to ensure they are happy and satisfied in their work so that they are not tempted to go elsewhere. Providing employees with good quality training so they can do their work confidently is a good way of both making staff happy and keeping the company in business. This is especially true in a **competitive market** like gas services.

BGS has an established training programme for new recruits to the industry. They need to be taught the basics of their jobs at the training academy. Dealing with existing employees is another matter though. BGS needs to check on established employees to make sure that they are fully trained to be able to undertake everything that is expected of them. This is usually done at the employee's performance review, or appraisal, meeting.

Performance management

Managers use performance management meetings to try to get the best out of each employee. The employee might be asked a series of questions about his or her work since the last review. The manager is trying to find out if there are any gaps in the employee's skills that need to be addressed. Evidence could be looked at where the employee's performance falls short of the required standard. In the case of BGS, this might be an engineer who has not been as friendly to a customer as the company would have liked. Or a job that the engineer undertook needed to be redone because it was below standard. When this is the case, training needs will be identified. This is particularly true in an industry, such as gas servicing, where technology is changing all the time and skills need to be updated.

It is normal at these performance review meetings for objectives or targets to be agreed between the reviewer and the person being reviewed. These targets give a focus to the employee and should be achieved before the next meeting. The target might be to undertake some form of training, or possibly to increase the speed at which jobs are completed. Some businesses use the performance management meetings to decide whether an employee's wages should increase. If targets are achieved or exceeded, the employee is paid more. The increase may be permanent or in the form of a one-off bonus.

Summary

- Employees need to be trained not just in the work they do but also in how to deal with customers
- It is not just new employees who need to be trained; all workers need to have their skills updated on a regular basis
- Performance management meetings allow a business to check on how well the employee is doing his or her work and what additional training is needed
- Objectives are often set for the employee to reach before the next performance management meeting. Wage increases might depend upon reaching these objectives

Core knowledge

When a business trains an employee, it must decide upon the best way to do this. Traditionally, training was undertaken using the apprentice system. This involved a recruit working alongside an experienced worker, who would pass on their skills. This approach is known as on-the-job training. It was recognised, however, that apprentices might not be getting the best form of training. Older employees might not be fully up to date with modern techniques and they would sometimes pass on bad habits to the apprentice. For these reasons, many apprentice schemes included the trainee working at college, sometimes called day release, to learn modern practices.

Training while working is known as on-the-job training, while training in a classroom or similar place is called off-the-job training. In the case study, BGS uses its own training facilities to train not only new recruits but established staff. Because the workers are not actually undertaking real work, they are receiving off-the-job training. BGS probably finds it can ensure that the quality of training is better at the British Gas Academy than relying wholly on the apprentice system.

When a new recruit joins a business, he or she will probably be given induction training. This is the training a person first receives to make sure they are as informed about the business as established employees. The new recruits might be shown a video about what the company does, so that they are familiar with the things that are important. Health and safety issues will be explained. Recruits will be given safety information, such as what they should do if the fire alarm sounds. The company might also use this training to explain company rules on phoning in sick or what to do if employees need to take time off work for family or other reasons.

Businesses want their employees to be efficient, which means they want them to be able to undertake their work quickly and accurately. If an employee is not skilled enough to do the work, or

The apprentice system

lacks motivation, this can have a negative impact on the business. Employees are more likely to make mistakes that result in wastage of materials and time spent re-doing the work. It is also more difficult to introduce changes to the business when employees do not feel that they are properly qualified. Spending money training and motivating employees can mean that they will be less likely to resist change and will support the company.

Performance management, or appraisal as it is sometimes called, is frequently used by managers to try to get the best out of their employees. At appraisal meetings, the manager and employee have the opportunity to talk about what has gone well and not so well over the last year. The employee's training needs will be considered. It may be that the employee did not do well last year because he or she was not competent in some aspects of the job. The interview will probably come up with objectives that need to be achieved in order to improve. The manager may also set a target that the employee has to reach by the time of the next interview. A shop assistant in a computer store may be set the target of increasing the sales he makes by 10% or getting to know more about some of the products. This way he can be more helpful to customers.

And more

Types of performance management. How a business conducts its performance management meetings will vary between organisations. In one business a manager might simply have an annual meeting with each employee. This meeting could take the form of a brief conversation with one or two objectives, or targets, set at the end. The whole process might then be forgotten until the next meeting in a year's time. Other businesses will take the process a lot more seriously. The manager, or reviewer, will have a structured questionnaire to work from in the interview. The manager and employee will have to decide how well the last year's objectives were achieved. This would be particularly important if the employee's salary was linked to reaching these objectives, which is often called performance-related pay. When new objectives are set for the forthcoming year, a development plan will be created. This will outline what needs to be done so the objectives can be achieved, which will probably include some form of training. It will also set out a time scale for achieving these things and a date when progress can be checked.

One difficulty that can arise with performance-related pay is that it is not always possible to determine just how much of a contribution an individual employee has made. Many employees work as a group or team and it is not easy sometimes to work out just who has done what to make the team successful. Reviewers have to be careful that an individual is not singled out for reward.

Workforce planning. A business that is forward looking cannot afford to be caught out by not having enough skilled employees when it needs them. For this reason, many larger businesses choose to undertake workforce planning. It can take several months to recruit a suitable person and to train him or her so that they are in a position to start work. So, if the company is expecting to see an increase in demand for its products or services, it is important that there are enough trained people when they are needed. If a business was planning a big promotional campaign to increase the sales of its product, the campaign would need to ensure that there were enough products available, which would probably mean enough staff to produce the goods.

Have a go!

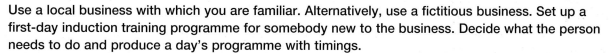

Activity

Use a local business with which you are familiar. Alternatively, use a fictitious business. Set up a first-day induction training programme for somebody new to the business. Decide what the person needs to do and produce a day's programme with timings.

Discussion

Discuss which type of training is better: on-the-job or off-the-job.

Web-based activity

Research on the web how companies conduct their performance management, or appraisal. Produce an information sheet or booklet giving practical advice to businesses new to performance management.

Quickfire questions

1 Which company owns British Gas?
2 What type of work is undertaken by BGS?
3 Give two reasons why BGS employees receive training in how to deal with people.
4 What is the name of the centre where BGS employees are trained?
5 Why do experienced employees also have to receive training?
6 Give an example of off-the-job training.
7 How does the apprentice system of training work?
8 What is performance-related pay?
9 Explain how training can help motivate staff at BGS.
10 Give two reasons why businesses hold performance management meetings.

Hit the spot

> What is meant by on-the-job training?

> Explain two ways in which off-the-job training might be delivered.

> Discuss whether having a system of performance management helps motivate employees.

Cracking the code

Competitive market An industry where there are many companies, each trying to attract customers.

Chapter 50
Motivation

Egg Banking – the 10:10 approach

Egg Banking plc is the largest internet-only bank in the world, employing 2500 people in three UK locations. The bank makes its money by encouraging savers to deposit money in one of its internet accounts and then issuing loans to customers. Egg is owned by the pension and financial services giant Prudential, or The Pru as it is often called. Banking is a very competitive business, with customers becoming increasingly willing to deal with foreign banks to get the best deals.

About half of Egg's employees deal directly with customers. If customers have any queries about their accounts, they will phone or e-mail one of the contact centres to have their questions answered. Another quarter of the employees are involved in IT work within the business. It is very important for an internet bank that the computer systems are functioning properly and safely. Egg has to be sure that criminals do not attempt to withdraw funds from other people's accounts and that there are secure records of all transactions. The remaining staff members are finance specialists. Banks will need employees who deal with such matters as risk assessment, which means calculating if a borrower is likely to pay the money back. They will need marketing and human resource specialists and professional managers, who have a good knowledge of the financial services business.

Egg recognises that it can be successful in a competitive market only if its employees are prepared to deal effectively with its customers. Egg believes that the only way you get the best from your employees is to allow them to develop within the business. The management at Egg realises that if the employees are not motivated, the business will suffer. Poorly motivated employees are less likely to be **loyal** to the company. This would probably result in employees regularly leaving the business and having to be replaced.

10:10 is how Egg describes the way in which employees and the company all benefit from working together. Each employee, and Egg itself, aims to achieve 10 out of 10. By enabling its employees to become motivated so they can reach their personal goals, Egg reaps the rewards of increased profits. So how does Egg manage to motivate its employees?

The company tries to create a working environment for employees so that they can get satisfaction from the challenges of their work. The line managers are crucial in helping the employees reach their potential. The managers are expected to have a good relationship with employees so that they get to know them well. Managers must understand what makes each of their subordinates tick and what drives them. In schools, students learn in different ways – some like to watch how things are done, then copy it themselves, others prefer to read about it and learn that way. It is the same with adults: they have different learning preferences. Egg managers are expected to find out the best way to train and motivate each individual so that each can then focus on high performance at work.

Take a look at the Egg website at
www.egg.com

Did you know...

The first online banking service was set up in New York in 1981. The Nottingham Building Society offered the first UK internet banking facilities in 1983.

Egg believes that its business will be successful only if its employees are well motivated. This is why it calls its programme to motivate staff 10:10. If the employees enjoy their work and are committed to the business, they feel good about themselves and Egg benefits too. Both their employees and Egg get 10 out of 10.

This might sound like commonsense, but not all businesses operate this way. Some take the view that time and money spent on keeping employees happy and content cause a reduction in profits. If you provide good facilities for employees such as a restroom or staffroom, they will be more inclined to enjoy these than get to work. Similarly, training in team building is seen by some as just a waste of the business's money.

Motivation is about getting people to work effectively because they want to. To help motivate its people, Egg makes sure that employees operate in an environment where they are able to:

● plan for themselves;

● work well with managers;

● enjoy their work;

● be rewarded for their efforts;

● feel they have the power to create change.

Egg refers to this as 'unleashing the power of people'. This power of people is achieved through good leadership and empowering employees to make changes they feel would improve their own performance and that of Egg. This means being willing to trust employees to work in the business's interests. Employees are given work to do that interests them and which they do well. This way the employee is likely to do a better job and to be more efficient. But, of course, this relies on the manager knowing each employee well.

Did you know...

The Prudential Mutual Assurance Investment and Loan Association, now known as The Pru, was set up in 1848 in London to lend money to both professional and working people.

What is motivation?

Motivation is the skill, or some say the art, of getting people to do things because they want to, rather than having to be told to do them. Employees who are motivated can see the benefit to themselves of working at their highest level of performance. At its most basic level, motivation in the workplace is linked to pay, or **remuneration**. It is the attraction of the weekly or monthly wage that drives some employees. They enjoy the things their wages can bring, such as holidays and consumer goods. These people work well because they do not want to give up their lifestyles which would happen if they lost their jobs.

Much research has been carried out on what factors drive employees to become motivated. There is no clear single method by which a business might guarantee being able to motivate its staff. We're all different, after all. What is clear, though, is that wages might motivate some people, but most others are driven by other factors. For some people, the amount you get paid is far down on the list of priorities. People who work for charities or undertake voluntary work probably do not value their job in terms of how much income they receive for doing it, if they get paid at all. Certain jobs are renowned for not being well paid, but still they attract motivated, qualified professionals. Nursing is a good example of this. Clearly, there must be something about the work that compensates nurses for the shortfall in their salaries.

In the Egg case study, we see that the company recognises that the working environment is important. The environment would include not only suitable heating and lighting in the workplace but factors such as feeling valued by the management, which make people feel comfortable. These features are often called **hygiene factors**. It is argued that without hygiene factors being satisfied, you will not be able to motivate staff. Being paid on time at the agreed rate is another example of a hygiene factor. If you were unsure you would receive your pay cheque at the end of the week, would you give your boss your best?

A cold, unpleasant work environment does not motivate employees

Summary

- Employees work best when they are motivated
- Poorly motivated staff are more likely to leave a business, resulting in having to spend time and money recruiting and training new staff
- Some businesses believe that spending money on motivating employees increases costs and reduces profits

Core knowledge

The way employees feel about their job and their workplace determines how motivated they are. There is a clear link between job satisfaction and productivity. Job satisfaction depends partly on tangible rewards – for example, how much a person is paid and what benefits they receive. However, job satisfaction also depends on the culture of an organisation. This means the things that make the business distinctive and make the people who work there proud to do so. People can be motivated by many factors. These are just a few examples.

- *The style of management*. At Egg, managers are encouraged to get to know their subordinates well. Employees are consulted about changes and they play a role in making key decisions in the business. They are made to feel that their contributions are valued within the business. This approach to management is often called a **democratic** style. Not all managers, however, operate this way. Some believe that consulting employees is both time consuming and unnecessary. Such managers would probably argue that they are paid to manage, so this is what they should do. This **autocratic** management style usually involves issuing instructions and expecting employees to follow them without question. Most employees are better motivated by the democratic style – they are more likely to accept change if they feel that they have had a say in the process. Nevertheless, some employees prefer not to have the responsibility that decision making brings.
- *Training and development*. Most employees like to feel that they are developing in their work. They want to become more competent at doing what they do so they are more expert in their job. We saw in Chapter 49 that BGS believes that all employees need to be trained throughout their careers if they are to keep their skills up to date. Training an employee shows the person that the business values him or her, and can lead to improved motivation.
- *Good communications*. As businesses grow, communications can become a problem. This is particularly true when there are many layers in the organisation chart. It can take time for messages and ideas to trickle down the hierarchy until they reach those at the bottom. If employees feel that they are out of the loop they can get the impression they are undervalued and their motivation levels fall. Businesses can overcome this problem in many ways. Many large businesses issue newsletters or even newspapers, while notice boards can keep people up to date. An intranet is another option, or operating a system of managers to brief employees regularly about what is happening in the business.
- *Regular feedback and appraisals*. If performance management is undertaken properly, rather than being seen as a threat, it can actually motivate employees. The regular meetings are opportunities for the manager to recognise the importance of the employee's contribution. Everyone likes to be told that they are doing a good job and people will be motivated by this.
- *Opportunities for employees to socialise*. This can take the form of team working or even having places at work where people can meet during their breaks. Some businesses go as far as having social clubs, often with sporting or gym facilities, where employees can socialise.

A pleasant break room can increase job satisfaction

And more

Many businesses believe that teambuilding is a good way to motivate individuals. If you can get everyone in your business to feel part of a team, the theory is you will get more out of them. Teams build motivation in people for several reasons.

- There is a social aspect to working in a team. People often find it more rewarding to work with others than alone.
- Teams stimulate fresh thinking and ideas. Working with others will often throw up different ways of looking at problems and how they might be solved.
- People will feel loyalty to the team and not want to let others down. This helps improve things like absenteeism, as well as increasing motivation levels.
- Team working brings out the competitive element in individual members. If this is managed properly the competition can help drive performance.
- Working in a team brings a sense of belonging and makes people feel valued.

Working as a team can be valuable

Have a go!

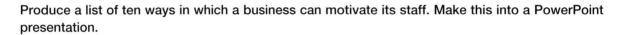

Activity

Produce a list of ten ways in which a business can motivate its staff. Make this into a PowerPoint presentation.

Discussion

'Teambuilding exercises are just an opportunity for employees to have a good time and they offer no real advantages to businesses.' Discuss how true you feel this statement is.

Web-based activity

@

Many companies use newsletters or magazines to keep their employees informed about what is happening in the business. Look on the internet for examples of these communications. Produce a report on what can be found in these newsletters and magazines.

Quickfire questions

1 What type of bank is Egg?
2 What type of work takes place at Egg's contact centres?
3 What is meant by employee motivation?
4 What is meant by hygiene factors?
5 What is phishing?
6 How can regular appraisals raise an employee's motivation?
7 Give an example of how the style of management can motivate an employee.
8 Give two reasons why businesses want to keep employees from leaving.
9 Give two reasons why people can work better in a team than individually.
10 Explain how Egg's 10:10 system works.

Hit the spot

> Describe what is meant by employee motivation.

>> Explain two ways a business might motivate an employee.

>>> Discuss whether increasing the rate of pay is the best way to motivate employees.

Cracking the code

Loyal Being willing to remain with a business and support it.

Remuneration Another term for wages, salaries and other benefits employees receive.

Hygiene factors The things that make people comfortable in their work so they can get on with their jobs.

Democratic A management style where employees are consulted and asked for their views on the business.

Autocratic A style of management where employees are told what to do and are not involved in any decision making.

ADVANCED OPERATIONS MANAGEMENT

Chapter 51
Introduction to advanced operations management

In this section

Introduction to advanced operations management
Production methods
Efficiency and lean production
Benefits and challenges of growth
Maintaining quality assurance in growing businesses

We have already seen that the manufacturing industries in the UK are becoming less important. The amount of money earned by the service, or tertiary, industries, however, is increasing steadily. You might remember that this process is called deindustrialisation. Manufacturing still takes place and has a role to play in Britain, but it has experienced many changes since it was the key industrial sector.

In this section of chapters we will be looking at manufacturing businesses and discovering the changes that have taken place. Much of this change has to do with the way in which products are made. Technology has revolutionised manufacturing. Routine tasks can be performed by computer-controlled machinery or robots. This has resulted in employees becoming less important in the production process than they were a generation ago. There has also been a change in the relationship between managers and employees. These two groups of people are more likely to co-operate than would have been the case 20 years ago. Many of the ideas and ways of doing things have evolved from the way that Japanese manufacturers are organised. It should be noted, though, that the principles that are covered in this section can often apply equally well to service industries.

A common business objective is to achieve growth. This is often the case for one or more of these three reasons:

- to sell a larger number of goods and, thereby, make more profit;
- to gain a larger market share, so the business has some control over the market;
- to reduce the cost involved in making each item.

Small businesses, therefore, have an incentive to grow bigger, even if it is done purely to make the owner feel that he or she has been successful in creating such a large company. But the very act of growing brings with it the types of problem for a manufacturing business that it would not have encountered when it was small.

Standardisation

Standardisation is a theme that cuts across much of the material covered in the next few chapters. In a way it is the complete opposite of job production, which we studied in Unit 1, Starting a Business. You may remember that job production involved making a single item to suit a customer. We used the example of builders re-fitting a kitchen. The units and tops would have to be adjusted to suit the shape of the room, as would the water and gas pipes and electricity sockets. With standardisation, the same-size components are used as much as possible to avoid having to make adjustments. A manufacturer of flat-pack furniture, for instance, would attempt to use the same parts in the wardrobes that it manufactures as it does for chests of drawers it sells. By reducing the number of types of components it uses, it can save money and simplify the production process. Standardisation can also be applied to labour, in other words, the employees. If jobs are kept the same as much as possible, the worker can become competent very quickly at doing that job. This saves on training and also allows employees to swap between jobs without it being a problem.

Mass production

Producing very large amounts of a single product, or mass producing, allows manufacturers to make the goods cheaply and quickly. This is usually achieved by having each employee concentrating on a small part of the production process. The product then moves from one work station to the next until it is completed, often on a conveyor belt. This system of manufacturing has enabled the price of products to be reduced for the consumer. A car might still be an expensive item to buy, but if the old ways of making cars had been maintained, only the extremely rich would have been able to afford to buy a car these days.

Mass production is not without problems, however. Assembly lines, once set up, are notoriously difficult to change if the demand for the good falls and another product must be made. So the managers of the business must be confident that there is sufficient demand for the product before considering mass production. Working on a mass production assembly line can be very repetitive too. Workers are expected to perform a small task over and over, which can be extremely boring. Employees might believe that

they are not really making a useful contribution and feel alienated from their work. It is not unknown for the quality of products to suffer when this form of production is used.

Mass production

Lean production methods

Lean production methods were introduced by Japanese manufacturers to overcome the problems they discovered when they studied American and UK businesses. Companies, such as Toyota, wanted to produce goods with the lowest possible costs, but recognised that if the company was not careful it could create a production process where the work was so dull and repetitive that employees would lack the motivation to work well.

Lean production is really about keeping costs as low as possible by continually looking for ways in which small cost savings could be made. No change is dismissed as being too small and insignificant. If a cost saving can be made then, it is argued, there must be waste, even if this waste is simply someone's time that could be better used.

It is not just the managers who are told to look for ways to save costs by reducing waste. It is felt that those who operate the machines and produce the goods are more likely to be aware of how improvements can be made. Indeed, employees who work for a lean production company are empowered to accept responsibility. This means they have far more authority than an employee in a conventional business. Empowering employees is also a way of making their work more interesting and increasing their loyalty to the business.

Chapter 52
Production methods

Ben & Jerry's Ice Cream

Ben & Jerry's is an ice-cream manufacturer, based at the luxury end of the market. The business was started in 1978 by two friends, Ben Cohen and Jerry Greenfield, and it grew quickly. Within ten years of starting, the business had a turnover of nearly $50 million. The business is now owned by the **conglomerate** Unilever.

Ben & Jerry's ice cream has always been presented as a fun product. The business regularly develops new flavours and ditches those which have lost their appeal. The names given to the ice cream are jokey and reflect the fun image of the business. Names include Fossil Fuel, Cherry Garcia, Chunky Monkey and Phish Food. The ice cream is made in batches of about 5000 litres, enough for around 8000 pint cartons. The basic ice cream base is produced in large containers, or vats, using good-quality ingredients. The milk used in Ben & Jerry's ice cream comes from selected farms close to the factory. Later in the process, flavours, chunks and swirls are added to give the ice cream its distinctive look and taste. Ben & Jerry's ice cream uses large chunks of chocolate, cookie dough and similar ingredients to give the product an unusual texture when it is eaten. Members of the public are encouraged to experiment with the flavours when the company's factories have visitors' days.

The production processes

The processes the ingredients go through to become Ben & Jerry's ice cream are as follows:
1 Milk is collected from farms and stored in refrigerated 25,000 litre storage units.
2 Milk is blended with other ingredients, including sugar and egg yolks.
3 Mix is heated to remove any bacteria that might be present.
4 Blend is then homogenised to break up fat particles.
5 At this stage the flavours are added to the ice-cream mix.
6 Mix is then frozen and ice cream produced.
7 Chunks of chocolate, fudge and other ingredients are added to the ice cream.
8 If the ice cream has swirls, these are produced in the variegator.
9 Pint cartons are filled and lids fitted.
10 Ice-cream cartons are deep frozen to allow them to be transported.
11 Before they are dispatched, sample cartons are opened and tasted to check the quality is right. Pint cartons are bundled into eight packs and dispatched.

Take a look at the Ben & Jerry's website at
www.benjerry.co.uk

As a manufacturing business grows and needs to produce more, it will probably look at the methods it uses to make the goods. Most likely it would not make commercial sense simply to buy larger quantities of equipment and continue to make products the same way it did when it was a much smaller operation. One advantage of growing large is that businesses can achieve **economies of scale**. This means it can be cheaper to make each product when larger amounts are made. You will be able to find out more about economies of scale in Chapter 54.

Machinery and automation

A growing business will look for ways in which production can become more efficient. Ben & Jerry's makes ice cream differently now than it did when it started in 1978. One thing that has changed is the greater use of equipment and **automation**. Machinery is used whenever possible as it is quicker and therefore more economical than using more labour-intensive methods. It is also much easier to maintain quality using machinery. In the case of ice cream and other food manufacturing, using machinery extensively can avoid contamination of the product.

Quality

Ben & Jerry's has a reputation for producing top-quality ice cream and this reputation must be protected. Quality control is important to the company, but so is its reputation for being an ethical business. The ingredients that it uses have to be of good quality. It only uses milk from controlled herds of cows from local farms. The eggs it uses are free range and it uses fair-trade goods for some of its other ingredients.

Batch production

The advantage of making batches of ice cream is that a wide range of flavours can be made using the same equipment. There does not have to be a separate production run for each flavour. Also, as flavours become more or less popular, different quantities can be made to suit the demand for each type of ice cream.

- Ben & Jerry's ice cream is marketed as a fun product at the luxury end of the market
- Production methods for large businesses can be more efficient than those of smaller businesses
- Batch production allows machinery and equipment to produce a variety of products without having to have separate production runs for each product

Core knowledge

Ben & Jerry's produces ice cream in large batches. Not all mass producers make their products this way; some find it better to use flow production methods.

This is the method used by most car manufacturers, as well as companies that produce many household appliances, such as washing machines. While some minor changes can be made to the product as it is being made, **flow production** is more suited to items that are standardised. This means the products are identical.

The term flow gives a big clue to how this system operates. Products are made continuously along an assembly line, moving or flowing from one stage of production to the next. This is usually in the form of a conveyor belt carrying the partly made product from one worker to the next. If the product being made is heavy, an overhead monorail might be used instead for all or part of the journey around the factory.

So, in the case of a car, the chassis will start the process and as it moves around the factory, a different part will be added. Suspension, steering, brakes, wheels and hundreds of other parts will be assembled as each vehicle passes through different areas of the factory. Some of the components for the car might be assembled using flow production elsewhere and brought to this assembly line. This would include items such as engines and metal panels. Alternatively, parts might be brought in from other manufacturers rather than being made by the company.

The advantage of flow production is that **division of labour** can be used. When each worker concentrates on one particular job and becomes expert at doing it, we say this is an example of division of labour. Workers can be organised so that they are responsible for adding a single item on the product as it moves around the factory. An employee's job might be to fit the windscreen on the car. This person would have the necessary tools to hand and because the job is repeated many times each shift, the worker soon becomes very competent at completing the task.

There are disadvantages to flow production, however. It requires large amounts of capital equipment in order to work. This equipment is set up to make a particular product, such as a model of car. If the business decides to change the product, it can be very difficult, if not impossible, to make the changes. This, and the fact that very large numbers of products need to be made to keep costs down, keep it out of the reach of small businesses. Another issue is that working on a flow production line can become repetitive. Workers can get bored doing the same thing many times a day. Mistakes can result, meaning the business must keep a careful watch on quality at each stage of production.

Flow production

And more

Mass production was made popular by Henry Ford more than 100 years ago. Ford moved car making away from craft production, when a small number of cars were made at the same time, to mass production. The idea was not new even then. The benefits of having workers specialise in one part of the production process had been known for years. Adam Smith, an early economist, had written about the advantages of division of labour and specialisation in 1776.

Mass production is far more capital intensive than **labour intensive**. By capital, we mean buildings, machinery and equipment. With craft production it is the skill of the worker that is most valued, but mass production values capital more. The whole assembly line is designed to make it as simple as possible for workers to make their contribution to the process. Jobs have been deskilled, so anyone could perform the tasks with the minimum of training. It is said that it is the skill of the engineers who set up the mass production system that matters, rather than the workers who operate it.

Automation helps keep down labour costs. Many mass production processes use robots, which are able to perform repetitive jobs without a break. Robots are expensive to buy and install, but once they are set up they only have energy and maintenance costs. Robots also have the advantage of being able to undertake jobs that would be regarded as having a health and safety concern for human operators. Spray painting cars would be an example of this.

Mass production has enabled standardised products to be manufactured much faster than using traditional craft methods. The amount having to be spent on capital and energy is far higher, but with output being so much greater, the cost of making each item falls. This effect of unit costs falling as output increases is known as an economy of scale.

Not all products are suitable for mass production, even if they are able to be standardised. It would be no good going to the expense of setting up an expensive assembly line if it was felt that the item being manufactured would have only a short product life cycle. Assembly lines are difficult to convert to making a different product, so the manufacturer needs to be confident that demand will be strong enough to justify the expenditure. The risk of the product not succeeding in the marketplace, therefore, needs to be minimised if this method of production is to be used.

Even with reduced labour and other costs, UK businesses might find it difficult to compete with foreign manufacturers, such as China. Competition from emerging countries often have untapped sources of raw materials. There are also fewer restrictions on manufacturing. The laws on health and safety and the environmental impact of business are far less regulated in these countries.

Mass production

Did you know...

Adam Smith's portrait appears on the back of £20 notes. There is also an illustration of division of labour on the banknote.

Have a go!

Group activities

Design a building, or something similar, that could be made using children's Lego bricks. Break down the construction into a series of tasks needed to produce the item. Draw a flow chart to show these different stages. Use this flow chart to lay out your classroom to become a Lego building factory. You will need to make sure you have enough of the right-sized bricks at each production stage. Now start production, with one person at each stage. Time how long it takes to produce each item when production gets started. Compare this time with how long it takes for one person to make the item from start to finish.

Discussion

Discuss what issues a business faces if it decides to move from labour-intensive to capital-intensive methods of production.

Web-based activity

Produce a series of information sheets on the stages involved in making Ben & Jerry's ice cream. Use the Ben & Jerry's website to help you with this assignment. Display the information sheets in the classroom to show the processes involved in making ice cream in large quantities.

Quickfire questions

1. In which year was Ben & Jerry's set up?
2. Why is the ice-cream mix heated in the production process?
3. What is the function of a variegator in ice-cream production?
4. Most of Ben & Jerry's ice cream is sold in what size carton?
5. What is flow production?
6. Give an example of deskilling.
7. What is meant by capital-intensive production?
8. Explain two disadvantages of flow production from the employee's point of view.
9. Explain two advantages of using robots in the production process over human labour.
10. Explain why emerging economies, such as China, are able to produce products cheaper than UK companies.

Hit the spot

⟩ Describe what is meant by flow production.

⟩⟩ Explain two advantages of using flow production to manufacture goods.

⟩⟩⟩ Discuss whether flow production is the best way to manufacture products.

Cracking the code

Conglomerate A large business that operates in a number of markets with a wide range of products.

Economies of scale The reasons why costs per item fall as more output is made.

Automation Machinery that can control itself when running without human intervention.

Flow production Products made continuously along an assembly line, with something being added at each stage.

Division of labour Having workers become specialists at one part of the production process.

Labour intensive Requiring a large number of workers compared with the amount of capital used. The opposite of capital intensive.

Chapter 53
Efficiency and lean production

IN THE NEWS

Toyota

Toyota Motor Corporation is a Japanese multinational manufacturer that has been operating since the 1930s. The company has manufacturing bases in several countries spread throughout the world. It is the world's largest car maker in terms of the number of cars made. The company has shares in other car makers, for instance, it owns half of Daihatsu, and has many subsidiary businesses. Toyota produces a range of products in addition to cars. It makes weaving looms, electric sewing machines and robots used in assembly lines, among many other items.

Toyota has been a key company in developing a completely different way of looking at manufacturing. The company calls this system the Toyota Way. One aspect of the Toyota Way is building a culture of stopping to fix problems before they develop. At one time, if an employee stopped the assembly line in a traditional UK factory, he or she would be disciplined. The view then was that by stopping production, output was lost and, therefore, revenue. Only senior managers were given the authority to halt production in this way. Toyota takes a different view. It believes that it is the duty of any employee to stop production if he or she feels that there is a problem with the quality of the product. By recognising the problem early, it avoids inferior-quality goods being made and having to be scrapped. Toyota believes that empowering employees to make important decisions like this motivates them and keeps them loyal to the business.

Toyota treats problem solving as an important skill for all employees to have. When errors are discovered, they are made clear to all who are affected by them. Identifying and being open about production problems allows the organisation to learn from its mistakes. The company's view is that a problem that is hidden can easily be ignored and repeated.

Having a well-trained workforce is important for Toyota. Only by investing time and money in employees, the company says, can the business grow. Toyota also tries to standardise tasks as much as possible so that employees become good at doing these jobs. By having many tasks the same, it builds familiarity and avoids mistakes being made.

Toyota also believes in working alongside its suppliers to allow them to improve. By forming close relationship with suppliers, they are more likely to support Toyota in its quest to maintain high standards. They do this by ensuring that supplies are themselves of good quality and are delivered on time.

 Take a look at the Toyota website at
www.toyota.co.uk

Standardisation

Toyota, along with other car manufacturers, makes cars in a far different way than when car manufacturing started. In the early days, cars were effectively hand built, using highly skilled workers, a process known as craft production. A result of this was that each product was unique. But while the cars were of high quality and designed to last the owner's lifetime, spare parts often had to be hand built, which made them expensive and hard to come by. Later car manufacturers recognised the problems associated with this and set about standardising spare parts. By doing this, the parts could be used on a range of car models and were far more economical to produce.

Cell production

Cell production

Many manufacturers choose to use flow production to manufacture their products. This is mainly as a result of the benefits identified in the last chapter. You may remember, though, that flow production can have disadvantages. Much of the work has been deskilled and made repetitive and can be completed without too much thought by the worker. Employees also might find themselves working in isolation from everyone else in the factory. As a result of these issues, employees can become bored and there is a temptation to not do as good a job as they should. To overcome the problem of employee motivation, some companies have turned to another system of manufacturing, cell production.

With cell production, products are manufactured in separate areas within the factory. Each of these areas will have a responsibility for a different part of the manufacturing process. So, in the case of cars, one section, or cell, would produce the bodywork, another would be responsible for the electrical wiring, another would add the engine and so on. Each cell would have its own group of workers, with a job that was big enough for them to have to use a range of skills. Once a job had been completed, the vehicle is moved to the next cell for another job to be done.

Cell production can lead to efficiency improvements due to increased motivation. Employees often find the experience of working in a team and being given responsibility to complete a large job rewarding.

The production method used to make a product will depend upon several factors. If the demand for a product is very high and the item is standardised, it will probably be cost effective to use flow production. This method allows for the greatest division of labour and economies of scale to be obtained.

Many UK businesses have been influenced by Japanese production processes. Japanese manufacturing developed rapidly during and after the 1950s, long after the UK and the US had industrialised. Japanese businesses studied UK and US companies to see how they could improve on the methods that these countries used. Many of these techniques are known as lean production.

Manufacturing in Japan

Summary

- Toyota has been a key business in changing the way that manufacturing is undertaken
- Employees are empowered under the Toyota method to take more responsibility for improving the production process
- Cell production is a way of eliminating some of the problems caused by flow production

Core knowledge

Lean production

Lean production techniques share an objective – to get as much output (or products) as possible from a fixed amount of inputs (or raw materials and labour). This involves looking at ways to increase the amount that each employee produces, called **labour productivity**, and at methods to reduce the amount of waste produced.

Lean production came about because of the problems associated with mass production. There are good reasons for producing items in bulk:

- cost savings can be made, called economies of scale;
- division of labour allows workers to specialise and become expert and more efficient at their particular jobs;
- there are opportunities to use machinery and automation that reduce the need for labour-intensive methods of production.

Of course, mass production requires a high demand for the product. Many of the products will need to be sold overseas as local markets can become saturated. But we have seen that there are problems with producing in bulk. Work can become limited and repetitive for employees, who can feel that their contribution is small and not valued. As a result, employees become less conscientious in what they do and efficiency falls.

One of the first attempts to create lean production was used by Henry Ford when producing his Model T car. Ford recognised that production costs could be minimised by standardising components as much as possible. Different versions of the Model T were made. Some had different styles of bodywork, some were convertibles and others were more like trucks to be used as delivery vans. But Ford used as many standardised components as possible on these different versions to keep costs down. This even went as far as the range of colours available. Ford once joked: a customer can have a car painted any colour that he wants so long as it is black. Setting up paint shops to use only one colour helped to reduce production costs. Equipment would not have to be cleaned when a new colour was introduced, which saved the company time and money. Black paint was chosen because it dried quicker than other colours, which was another cost saving.

And more

There are many aspects to lean production. Here are just three of them. While each is different, they share the same approach of attempting to improve efficiency and by so doing bringing down production costs.

- *Just in time (JIT).* JIT involves not having large amounts of raw materials in stock but having only enough for a company's immediate needs. This saves money for the business in several ways. There is no need for a warehouse where materials are held or the staff to look after it. When stock arrives at the factory, it is delivered straight to where it will be used. There is a risk involved with JIT, however. JIT relies on sophisticated computer systems to ensure that the quantities of stock ordered and delivered are correct. Stock is ordered only as and when it is needed; there is no scope for having stockpiles. This process needs to be carried out very accurately or production could come to a standstill.

- *Quality circles.* With quality circles, employees are encouraged to meet and discuss ways in which production could improve. It is assumed that those who are actually making the products are in the best position to see how improvements could be made. There is another benefit of these meetings: employees get a wider view of what is happening within the business. The workers are more likely to understand how their own actions affect other parts of the factory, so they will be more inclined to have a wider view of production.

- *Kaizen.* Kaizen is a Japanese expression that translates into continuous improvement. When a kaizen approach to work is followed, employees are empowered to look for ways in which the production process can be improved upon. Kaizen assumes that production is never perfect; there is always something which can be performed better. Even the smallest improvement, it is argued, can cause huge cost savings in the long run. Many small changes can lead to overall increases in productivity. For example, an employee might suggest that rather than reaching down for a spanner to tighten a nut, it is placed in a holder near his or her hand. This might save just two seconds each time the spanner is used. But if the tool is used 100 times a shift, then the saving is more than three minutes. If there are nine other employees using similar tools, the time saving is 30 minutes. For three shifts a day, the saving becomes about 475 hours a year, which is about 12 weeks' work for one person.

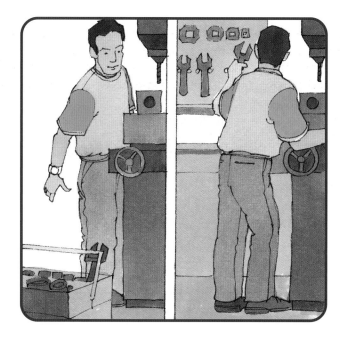

Taking a kaizen approach: moving the spanner

Did you know...

The first type of car to be made using mass-production methods was the Ford Model T, which sold 15 million vehicles.

Have a go!

Group activity

Visit a fast-food restaurant or draw on your memory of previous visits. These places often use very efficient ways to produce and then serve you with the food that you buy. Give some examples of where you think lean production techniques have been used. Suggest ways in which the efficiency of these restaurants can be improved even further.

Discussion

Some people believe that lean production will work only if employees have the right attitude to joining in. Discuss ways in which businesses could convince employees that lean production is the way forward in a business.

Web-based activity

Find examples of ways in which real businesses use lean production techniques.

Quickfire questions

1 Besides cars, what else does Toyota make?
2 When would a Toyota employee stop the production line from running?
3 Why did Toyoda become Toyota?
4 Kaizen is a Japanese term: what does it mean?
5 How did Ford save money by making only black Model T cars?
6 What is meant by standardisation?
7 What do the initials JIT stand for?
8 Outline two disadvantages of flow production to employees.
9 Give two ways in which cell production differs from flow production.
10 Give two advantages to a business of operating quality circles.

Hit the spot

> Describe what is meant by lean production.

>> Explain two ways in which just in time can result in lower costs for a business.

>>> Discuss which production method has the lowest costs: cell production or flow production.

Cracking the code

Subsidiary businesses **Businesses often known by their own names but which are owned by a parent company.**

Standardisation **A system of using identical parts or ways of making products, in order to reduce production costs.**

Labour productivity **A measure of how much each worker produces. If 10 employees produce 150 items a day, their productivity is 150 ÷ 10 = 15 items per worker. The higher the productivity, the more on average each person produces.**

Chapter 54
Benefits and challenges of growth

Alliance Boots plc

Chemist business Boots can trace its history back to 1849 when John Boot opened a herbal remedy shop in Nottingham. The business expanded, not just by opening more high-street stores but also by manufacturing pharmaceutical products at its Nottingham factory. After some unsuccessful attempts to diversify into non-healthcare industries, the shareholders agreed to a merger with rival Alliance UniChem in 2006. Alliance UniChem was a European healthcare distribution company that supplied pharmacies and hospitals. The company itself was formed by the merger of UniChem with Alliance Sante in 1997. When Alliance Unichem merged with Boots to create Alliance Boots, the business owned more than 1000 of its own pharmacies.

The creation of Alliance Boots allowed both merging companies to save on their costs. It was estimated that by merging, the cost savings would be more than £100 million each year. When cost savings occur as the size of a business increases, it is known as benefiting from economies of scale.

Two large companies cannot just decide to go ahead and merge. They may need to seek permission from the government. There may be reasons why the government is unhappy about the merger and can decide to stop it from happening, or impose restrictions on the arrangement. In the case of Alliance Boots, the government was worried that the two businesses both had pharmacies and that there could be a reduction in the amount of competition.

The government was not concerned too much about the amount of competition nationally in the pharmacy business but it did express concerns about local competition. It would not make commercial sense for the new merged company to operate two pharmacies that were close together. The government identified 38 places where the merger would result in one pharmacy closing because another Alliance Boots chemist existed within a mile. There were another 61 locations where there were three competing pharmacies, which would be reduced to two. Yet despite these reservations, the government allowed the merger to go ahead.

Take a look at the Alliance Boots website at **www.allianceboots.com**

The same amount of milk: which is cheaper?

Economies of scale

The main reason why businesses merge is to help them reduce their costs. When a business doubles in size but costs go up by less than double, we say there are economies of scale. These economies of scale come about for several reasons.

Bulk-buying economies

These are sometimes called purchasing economies. You are probably aware that, if you buy large quantities of a product, you tend to get a better deal than by buying in smaller volumes. A large packet of cornflakes is cheaper per serving than the same-size portion from a small packet. It is the same in business. Suppliers will usually give a discount if large amounts are bought. They do this because the suppliers themselves find it relatively cheaper to deal in large amounts. It will probably cost the supplier the same for the paperwork and delivery van to supply an office with 500 reams of stationery as it does for an order of 50 reams. This cost saving can be passed on to the customer. Also suppliers offer reductions on big orders to encourage these customers to remain with them.

Financial economies

Small businesses can find it hard to obtain finance and when they do obtain it, the cost of the finance is often quite high. This is because small businesses are seen as being riskier than larger businesses that have developed a good track record. Banks and other financial institutions feel more confident about lending funds to larger businesses, as the risk of the loan not being repaid is lower. As a result, the banks are often willing to lend at a lower rate of interest.

Technical economies

Larger businesses will make more efficient use of existing machinery. A machine that is used for only a few hours a day might be running far longer when the business expands. If the machine costs £200 a week to lease, it is far more cost effective to have it running for longer. Large businesses can justify using more advanced machinery, possibly that which is automated and lowers labour costs. As the business grows, it may be worth considering mass production techniques, which are a more efficient form of production. A larger business can also afford to invest more in research and development.

Managerial economies

As a business grows, there is greater potential for the managers to specialise in particular tasks. Rather than having a general manager who takes on all roles, specialists can be hired. There may be a human resource manager, a sales and marketing manager and a finance manager. Specialist managers are likely to be more efficient as they are more experienced and qualified at performing these particular roles compared with a general manager in a smaller firm trying to perform all of the jobs.

Summary

- A merger occurs when two businesses agree to join together to become a single organisation
- Many businesses merge to save costs and to become more profitable
- Economies of scale is the term used to describe the ways in which the cost per item produced falls as a business gets bigger

Did you know...

Merger negotiations are often conducted with great secrecy because the two businesses do not want their share prices to be affected by the talks. Share prices can be used to work out how much each business is worth.

Core knowledge

Mergers are a good way for a business to expand rapidly and achieve cost savings that can help it improve its profitability. There is another advantage too: if the two companies are in the same business, the merger takes out a competitor. A merger between two similar businesses is known as horizontal integration.

Governments are particularly concerned about horizontal mergers. The reduction in competition can have an effect on consumers. Less competition tends to reduce the quality of the service and to raise prices. If the government feels that a potential merger is not in the public interest, it has the power to block it. This is not something that a government will do without careful research. Sometimes a merger might be the only way that two businesses can remain profitable. Without it, they may both go under, with many job losses, something the government would not want to happen.

It is also possible that the cost savings made by merging businesses might be passed on to customers as lower prices. Because it has made cost savings, the new business can afford to lower its prices yet maintain its former profit levels. It is never entirely clear whether a merger will result in lower or higher prices – both are possibilities.

Did you know...

When two businesses merge, it is usual for both companies to keep their separate identities. This is because they often have strong brands that could suffer with a name change.

And more

When businesses become larger, it doesn't necessarily mean that there will be cost savings. Growing businesses bring with them several challenges that could actually cause costs to rise rather than fall. We call these factors diseconomies of scale. If output doubles and costs rise by more than twice, then diseconomies of scale have taken place. Possible reasons for diseconomies include the following:

- *The divorce of ownership from control*. In a small organisation, the owners of the business will probably be the people who manage it. So the owners and controllers are the same people and there will be no conflict of interests. The owners will direct or manage the business so their own personal objectives are achieved. As businesses grow, we have already seen that specialist managers are recruited. These managers may not have the same objectives as the owners, the shareholders. Managers might be more concerned with making themselves look important by employing more staff than are really needed or by having an expensive company car. Such things would reduce the business's profitability, which could be what the shareholders expect from the business.

- *Communications and co-ordinating activities*. Large businesses can bring with them communication problems. Businesses that have become large and complex will very likely have an organisation chart that contains several layers. We read in a previous chapter about difficulties that can arise from having a top-down approach where messages and ideas need to move from layer to layer until they reach the people at the bottom of the hierarchy. This can be a particular issue if the business is based in more than one location. Businesses can tackle this problem by decentralising and delegating authority to each site. However, this could result in losing the benefits of some economies of scale. Having to duplicate managers and other resources at each location, for instance, could undo the potential cost savings. The same is true when it comes to managers co-ordinating business activities. It is much easier for managers to keep an eye on projects, making adjustments as required, when everyone involved is in a single location. Overseeing activities over a range of locations and employees can be far more difficult to co-ordinate. As a result, costs could rise once again.

- *Demotivation and alienation of staff*. Many large businesses undertake some aspect of mass production. We have already seen that specialisation, or the division of labour, can make work dull and repetitive. This can, in turn, lead to employees being switched off and demotivated, leading to sloppy work and increased wastage of materials. Working in a large business where you are responsible for only a small part of the process can make employees wonder whether their contribution really matters. Consequently they can lose heart, resulting in an increased number of mistakes.

- *The optimal size of a business*. Some economists and business experts believe that there is actually an ideal size for a business, which they call the optimum level of output. This is the point at which a business's economies and diseconomies of scale balance each other out. This would be the output where the cost of making each item is at its lowest. If businesses increase output beyond this point, costs rise. If output is below the optimum, then costs could be cut by raising the amount produced. This theory assumes that everything remains the same, which is unlikely in reality. We saw earlier in the book that companies that use Japanese-style lean production methods could overcome some of the problems encountered by growing businesses.

Have a go!

Group activity

Produce a PowerPoint presentation or a podcast, explaining how businesses can reduce costs for each of the economies of scale mentioned in this book.

Web-based activity

Purchasing economies of scale are the discounts that businesses get by buying large quantities. Research the price of sports clothing or footwear on the internet to discover how big a discount can be achieved by buying in bulk. You will need to search for a wholesaler for the product that interests you.

Discussion

Managers of large companies are sometimes accused of not worrying too much about what the owners, the shareholders, want from the business. Very likely shareholders are looking for high profits so that they receive a good dividend and the value of their shares will rise. Discuss ways in which managers of large businesses could be held more accountable to what the shareholders want.

Quickfire questions

1 In which city did Boots first open a shop?
2 In which year did Boots merge with Alliance UniChem?
3 What is the most important reason why businesses merge?
4 Give another name for bulk-buying economies of scale.
5 What is the name of the economy of scale gained by using machinery for more hours each week?
6 What is a horizontal merger?
7 Outline what is meant by the optimum size of a business.
8 Explain why many merged businesses keep their own separate identities.
9 Explain how flow production can result in diseconomies of scale.
10 Explain what is meant by the divorce of ownership from control.

Hit the spot

➤ Describe what is meant by an economy of scale.

➤➤ Explain two reasons why the government might not allow two businesses to merge.

➤➤➤ Discuss whether businesses will always benefit from growing bigger.

Cracking the code

Pharmaceutical **To do with the medicine and drugs industry.**

Merger **Two or more businesses joining together and operating as a single organisation.**

IN THE NEWS

British Standards Institution (BSI)

The BSI Group was founded as the Engineering Standards Committee in London in 1901 and became known as the British Standards Institution in 1921. The organisation produces and publishes standards which are sold on to other businesses. What this means is BSI, along with a committee of volunteers, looks at the way products should perform and sets the standard for the quality of the finished product. BSI and the technical committee decide what the minimum standard should be for a product or service, which BSI then publishes. These standards are sold to other businesses to cover the costs involved. When a business makes a product that meets the minimum standards and has been independently tested by BSI, it is allowed to place the Kitemark on the item. This shows potential buyers that the product meets the published standard, and also the Kitemark scheme rules. Many businesses choose to make their products to BSI and Kitemark standards as customers want reassurance that the products they buy are up to scratch.

So, what exactly is a standard? A standard is an agreed set of requirements for a product or a repeatable way of producing a product or providing a service. It is a description of the quality of a product and how this quality is achieved in practice. This detailed information is then produced in a document that is called the standard.

Standards are created by drawing on the experience and expertise of producers, sellers, buyers and users. A group of experts will meet and decide what standard is needed for a particular product. For example, BSI would talk to the manufacturers and users of industrial safety boots. Between them they would agree what the minimum standards should be for this type of footwear. They would agree how high and heavy a weight could be dropped on to the boot without damaging the wearer's feet. They would also agree how long it would take acid and other dangerous materials to seep into the boot. Having set this standard, manufacturers of safety boots would have to make sure their boots passed the tests in order to be compliant with the standard.

Standards help to make life simpler for consumers and for businesses as the requirements for and quality of the product are established by an independent organisation. This saves companies having to spend large amounts of money on research and product marketing. Marking the product with the number of the standard, e.g. BS 1234, also sends a message to consumers: this product reaches a recognised standard, which increases their confidence in the item.

 Take a look at the BSI website at
www.bsigroup.com
or visit **www.Kitemark.com**

By law, some products have to conform to national or European standards before they can legally be sold in this country. Motorcycle helmets are an example of this. Those businesses not required to possess a standard may still choose to use one. There are several reasons for doing this.

Standards are not just about the quality of the final product. They are also used to ensure that working practices are efficient and improve productivity. If a business looks at the way it makes goods or provides a service, it could gain a competitive advantage over other businesses by improving its efficiency and effectiveness. Improved efficiency mean that costs are lowered, which can result in extra profits and becoming the key player in an industry. Increases in market leadership can allow a business to take a leading role in shaping the industry in which it operates.

Standards can be used to improve the quality of communications within an organisation. If a business can demonstrate good links with its suppliers, it can be given an award for this. This would also apply to the system of communications within the business, whereby all employees are kept informed about what is happening in the company.

Standards allow a company to attract customers by assuring them that the product it sells is of good quality. Operating to a recognisable and trusted standard makes the product stand out from competitors. This is particularly important as consumers become increasingly informed about the choices available to them. An example

of this is consumers' growing concern for environmental matters. There are standards available to businesses to reassure customers that they are conforming to recognised procedures when it comes to acting responsibly towards the environment. This would include attempting to reduce the business's carbon footprint and ensuring that all waste material is recycled rather than being sent to landfill sites.

There is often a mistaken belief that all businesses should produce goods to the highest possible standards. If this was to happen, the manufacturing costs would be far higher and, as a result, prices would more than likely have to increase. Consumers would clearly not be happy with rising prices. Most are willing to accept 'good enough' quality within the products that they buy. This means the quality of the product must be at least as good as the consumer expects. A customer will not expect a coat to last half a lifetime, as people did 100 years ago. Fashion changes mean people want to change the style they wear regularly. Therefore, there is little point in manufacturers spending a lot making clothes durable when consumers do not really want this. The opposite will be true as well. Even if people buy low-priced goods from budget stores, they expect that certain standards are maintained.

At one time it was considered the responsibility of the purchaser to check that the quality was good enough before the item was bought. This requirement was known by the Latin legal expression **caveat emptor**, which translates to 'let the buyer beware'.

Summary

- BSI is an organisation that sets agreed standards for the quality of a range of products and services
- By law some safety equipment must conform to a British or European standard before it can legally be sold in the UK
- Businesses can gain a competitive edge by being able to state to customers that their product reaches a BSI standard and has a Kitemark
- Conforming to production standards can improve a business's efficiency

Did you know...

BSI has produced over 30,000 standards and publications that businesses and government bodies can access and use.

Core knowledge

Quality is much easier to maintain in a small business than it is in larger organisations. The owners of small businesses are more likely to know first hand what is happening in their organisation and can respond quickly when sales suffer because quality is falling. As a business grows, however, communications within the organisation can become more difficult, resulting in deterioration in quality. There are also effects of mass production that we looked at in an earlier chapter. Repetitive, low-skilled work can make the work boring, which can lead to errors being made.

Quality assurance

Larger businesses often adopt a system of quality assurance (QA) to maintain quality within the business. A set of activities or procedures is created to ensure that products satisfy customer requirements. No system of quality assurance can guarantee that the quality will always reach minimum standards, but by having procedures in place it makes it less likely that faulty goods will get through to the customer.

Two principles that many businesses use when creating a QA system are:

- fit for purpose – the product should be up to its intended use;
- right first time – avoids having to re-do things, causing waste, by making sure no errors happen.

Both of these principles try to avoid discovering mistakes after the product has been made, as this can be very costly. Even worse are customers discovering the mistakes, which can lead to the business getting a poor reputation. To avoid these errors, a business will probably have QA procedures for checking that production systems are operating as they should be and that areas such as communications both within the company and with suppliers and customers function properly.

Under TQM (see below), everyone on the production line is responsible for quality

Testing product quality

And more

Total Quality Management (TQM) is a quality assurance method. What is different about this method is that rather than leave quality in the hands of company inspectors, everyone within the organisation is meant to have responsibility for quality. This system is used by Toyota, which was studied in an earlier chapter.

The principle of TQM lies in making the maintenance of quality second nature to those who work in the company. It is not seen as something that needs to be looked at occasionally as production takes place, but should be at the forefront of everyone's thinking. An office worker would not walk past a machine that was malfunctioning – he or she would be expected to stop the machine or sort the problem out if possible, even if that was not his or her job.

An argument in favour of TQM, besides the improvement in quality, is that it motivates staff. Many people respond well to being given responsibility and they become more enthusiastic as a result. Others might argue that not everyone is looking for this level of responsibility and many prefer to get on with doing their job, letting others worry about the quality.

Have a go!

Group activity

Produce a set of standards tests for a portion of fries from a fast-food outlet, or another product. Meet as a group and agree upon what you regard as the basic standards for this product. You might want to decide upon the weight of the portion, the width of the individual fries, their length and how crispy they are. You will need to devise tests to see whether your sample passes. This could include a bending test to see how far the fry bends before breaking. When you have agreed the standard, buy some fries and test them. Produce a league table of which outlets' fries pass the test. Write a report on your findings.

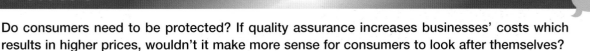

Discussion

Do consumers need to be protected? If quality assurance increases businesses' costs which results in higher prices, wouldn't it make more sense for consumers to look after themselves?

Web-based activity

Research the standards that apply to cycle helmets. You should be able to access this information at sites such as www.cyclehelmets.org. Produce a poster to summarise your findings.

Quickfire questions

1 What do the initials BSI stand for?
2 What does the organisation BSI do?
3 What is a Kitemark?
4 Describe what is meant by a standard.
5 Give an example of a good that is fit for purpose.
6 What do the initials TQM stand for?
7 What is another expression for 'let the buyer beware'?
8 Explain why some products by law must have passed a standard.
9 Explain possible reasons why businesses do not always produce products at the highest quality.
10 Explain why a business that has been awarded a Kitemark would have an advantage over a competitor that has not.

Hit the spot

> What is meant by quality assurance?

>> Explain why it might be more difficult to maintain quality in large businesses than in smaller ones.

>>> Discuss whether the system of TQM would work in all businesses.

Cracking the code

Research and development Often a department within a large business, which is responsible for finding ways of improving products and production, and for putting these ideas into practice.

Caveat emptor The name of an old law that makes the buyer responsible for checking the quality of the product.

Preparing for the controlled assessment

What is a controlled assessment?

Controlled assessments have replaced coursework across all awarding bodies, including AQA. Unlike coursework, there are some restrictions (or controls) which your teacher has to ensure are in place while you do the work.

Your hard work on this GCSE course will be assessed by a combination of exams and controlled assessments.

Why is the controlled assessment needed?

The one-hour exam paper that you sit for each unit of study cannot assess all of the assessment objectives thoroughly.

The controlled assessment gives you the time to show the examiner just how good you are at using business ideas, when you have more time to think carefully about the issues. In the past this was done using coursework, but schools found that coursework took too long to produce, taking away valuable learning time. The controlled assessment was designed to take less time.

Which assessments do I need to do?

The assessments you do will depend on the course you are taking.

- A **short GCSE** business studies course (your school may call this a **half-GCSE**): you have to take a controlled assessment and one exam.
- The **full GCSE** course: two exam papers and a controlled assessment.

- The **double award GCSE** in Applied Business: you do not need to take a controlled assessment for this part of the award, so count your blessings, but remember you will have other assessments to do later.

The controlled assessment is a significant part of your GCSE. Your final GCSE grade will be greatly influenced by how well you do in this assessment:

- The Unit 14 controlled assessment makes up 40% of the final grade for the short course GCSE.
- The Unit 3 controlled assessment makes up 25% of the final grade for the full course GCSE.

The Unit 14 controlled assessment

The controlled assessment for the **short course GCSE** is called Unit 14: Investigating small businesses. (Remember that, if you are taking the full course or the double award, you will take a different assessment, not this one.)

'Investigating small businesses' is a very general title. Before you start your course, the awarding body, AQA, will set a more specific task that you will need to complete under controlled conditions – the controlled assessment. It will include some background information relating to the topics you learn about during the course.

The task changes each year. This means if you need to re-sit the controlled assessment, you will be tackling a different task the second time.

AQA publish details of the latest controlled assessment each year: they send the details to teachers and publish them on the web notice board for Business Studies.

Table of assessments for the different courses: who does what
Note: Each exam mentioned here lasts one hour.

	Exam: Setting up a business (Unit 13)*	Exam: Setting up a business (Unit 1)	Controlled assessment: Investigating small businesses (Unit 14)	Exam: Growing as a business (Unit 2)	Controlled assessment: Investigating businesses (Unit 3)	Other assessments
Short course GCSE	✓		✓			
Full course GCSE		✓		✓	✓	
Double-award GCSE		✓				✓

* Unit 13 covers the same material as Unit 1, and everything you need to know is covered in this book. However, the Unit 13 exam paper will have different questions to the Unit 1 paper.

The Unit 3 controlled assessment

This assignment is called Unit 3: Investigating businesses. You will take it if you are following the full GCSE course.

It is very similar to the Unit 14 controlled assessment, described above: it assesses the same skills, but on different topics.

Carrying out the assessment

Your teacher will give you information about the controlled assessment task when he or she feels the time is right.

If you would like to research more about this assessment, then you will find plenty of information on the AQA website, www.aqa.org.uk. The fastest way to find the information is to do a search on the site for 'GCSE business studies controlled assessment 2012' (if you are taking your exams and controlled assessment in 2012).

There are two stages to the controlled assessment:

- Planning and researching the topics covered in the assignment.
- Writing up the assignment.

Planning and research

You teacher should only set you off on the assignment once you have been taught the material that it covers. For example, if the assignment scenario deals with marketing, then you need to be familiar with the marketing section of this book before you start to work. Your assignment research should relate to the particular details of the assignment, not the basic terms.

During the planning stage, you will be allowed to work with other students, if your teacher thinks that this is suitable for you and your class. (The next stage, writing up, is done under test conditions.)

You are advised by AQA to spend between five and eight hours preparing for the task. During this time you are expected to be able to:

- Select relevant information from a variety of sources.
- Explain what you have discovered in your research, and **why** you chose to do the

research in the way that you did. For instance, if the scenario is about an entrepreneur thinking about starting a small service sector business, you may be required to conduct some market research into the service to be provided.

- Consider the methods that would be suitable for that type of business, and conduct the market research yourself.

- Support your choice of method when you write up the assessment, as well as outlining your actual findings.

- Explore any issues that have been raised in your research. For example, if a business has a choice between two options, such as lowering its prices to attract customers, or advertising more instead, you will have to put forward clear points for and against both options in order to score well.

Keep careful notes of all your findings during this stage of the assessment, as these notes can be used when you write up.

You are allowed to ask for help from your teacher at this stage in the assessment. He or she may, for instance, get you to look at alternative ways of thinking about the topic or solving the problem. Your teacher may also advise you on sources of information, maybe by suggesting a website to visit. Your teacher, however, has to let AQA know exactly what type of assistance has been given to you.

Writing up the assignment

You will have about three hours to write up your assignment. This time is not fixed; it is just a recommendation from AQA. You are allowed more time, but it shouldn't be necessary. Extra

time is available if you have special educational needs, and this will be explained to you by your school.

AQA is not looking for very long and rambling answers. It is possible to score high marks with brief pieces of work that get straight to the point and show your skills of application, analysis and evaluation.

Your teacher will probably run the writing-up time in more than one session, probably during normal timetabled lessons. If there is more than one session, you will not be allowed to take any of your notes or your written work out of the room between sessions. This material must be collected by your teacher and kept safe until the next session.

During the writing time, you will need to complete the task that has been set by AQA. This may take the form of a report, or some other style of presenting your findings. You may be able to produce your account on a computer, but hand-written responses are just as good.

You will need to sign a declaration when you hand in your assignment to say that your assessment is your own work

How is the assessment marked?

Your teacher will give your work a mark out of 40. Teachers will be looking for three skills, called Assessment Objectives (see table).

The teacher will also assess your ability to write good quality English and present clear arguments. This is known as the quality of

Assessment objective (AO)	Maximum marks
AO1: having knowledge and understanding of business ideas and terms	12 marks
AO2: being able to apply, or use, these business ideas and terms to explain the issues in your assignment	14 marks
AO3: showing evidence that you have brought in business ideas to explore the information that you have collected. You also need to make judgements on how useful this evidence is.	14 marks

written communication (QWC). Writing with few spelling or other mistakes will be rewarded. You will also score well on QWC if you are able to use business terms as you write.

Once your work has been marked by your teacher, AQA will ask for a sample of the work or, in some cases, all the students' work to be sent away. This is simply to check that everyone's work has been marked to the same standard, whichever school they are at.

Appendix: International Financial Reporting Standards

A European Union regulation of 2005 says that financial statements must use International Financial Reporting Standards (IFRS). You may therefore come across different names for the same things: the old name and the new IFRS name.

Balance sheets

The structure of the balance sheet has not changed.

Old term	IFRS term
Fixed assets	Non-current assets
Stocks	Inventories
Debtors	Trade and other receivables
Creditors	Trade and other payables
Long-term liabilities	Non-current liabilities
Shareholders' funds	Total equity or total shareholders' equity

Reserves now include 'retained earnings', which used to be called 'retained or undistributed profits'.

Profit and loss accounts

The appropriation account is now dealt with separately from income.

Old term	IFRS term
Turnover	Revenue
Stocks	Inventories
Gross profit less expenses	Operating profit

Index

Note: page numbers in **bold** refer to key word definitions.